MW01131013

LEARNING
AMERICAN SIGN LANGUAGE
TO EXPERIENCE THE ESSENCE OF
DEAF CULTURE

Newly Revised First Edition

Edited by Lisa Koch
Ohio University

cognella®
academic publishing

Bassim Hamadeh, CEO and Publisher
Michael Simpson, Vice President of Acquisitions
Jamie Giganti, Senior Managing Editor
Jess Busch, Graphic Design Supervisor
Amy Stone, Acquisitions Editor
Mirasol Enriquez, Senior Project Editor
Alexa Lucido, Licensing Coordinator
Sarah Wheeler, Interior Designer

Copyright © 2016 by Cognella, Inc. All rights reserved. No part of this publication may be reprinted, reproduced, transmitted, or utilized in any form or by any electronic, mechanical, or other means, now known or hereafter invented, including photocopying, microfilming, and recording, or in any information retrieval system without the written permission of Cognella, Inc.

First published in the United States of America in 2016 by Cognella, Inc.

Trademark Notice: Product or corporate names may be trademarks or registered trademarks, and are used only for identification and explanation without intent to infringe.

Cover image copyright © 2011 Depositphotos/BasheeraDesigns.

Interior Images copyright © 2013 Depositphotos Inc./ptnphoto.
          copyright © 2012 Depositphotos Inc./mhatzapa.

Printed in the United States of America

ISBN: 978-1-63487-692-6 (pbk)/ 978-1-63487-694-0 (br) / 978-1-63487-693-3 (sb)

www.cognella.com   800-200-3908

Contents

SECTION THREE

SECTION
ONE

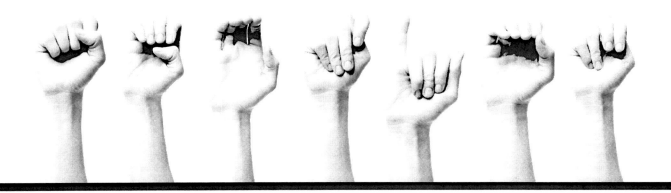

Interacting with Deaf People

WRITTEN BY

GRETCHEN WAECH

Keep in mind that no two deaf or Deaf people are alike; these are all general points to remember, and may or may not apply to every person you meet.

A—Ask a Deaf person how they wish to communicate. Not all Deaf people communicate in the same way. American Sign Language (ASL), Signed English (SEE), lipreading/speechreading, writing, gesturing, and speaking are all methods of communication which may be utilized by different Deaf people.

B—Behind—Never approach a Deaf person from behind! Instead, walk around the person so he or she can see you are there, or otherwise signal your presence. If the deaf person is startled, don't feel bad... ask the best way to get his or her attention the next time.

Bluntness—Deaf people often seem blunt to a hearing person. While there is some debate about whether this is truly a Deaf culture issue or simply due to the lack of incidental education regarding socially appropriate use of language, the fact remains that hearing people who are used to the delicacy of social interaction are often shocked by the directness displayed by Deaf persons.

C—Culture—Culture is defined as a set of learned behaviors of a group of people who have their own language, values, rules of behavior, and traditions (Padden, 1988). Deaf people have a culture which centers around ASL, valuation of their community and history, behavioral expectations, and traditional Deaf events and activities.

D—Deaf vs. deaf—Be aware that if you see a capital "D" in the word "deaf," this is a reference to a person who values her cultural identity within the Deaf community. As with any minority community, maintaining respect for self-identity is critical. Use of the small "d" is in reference to the state of having a profound to severe hearing loss, and is in no way indicative of a cultural state.

E—Eye Contact - In many social circles in America, in particular, eye contact has a specific meaning. This may range from aggression to romantic interest. In the Deaf community, however, eye contact is a critical part of communication, and should not be interpreted as anything more or less than paying attention and engaging in conversation.

F—Facial Expressions—As with bluntness, hearing people are often taken aback by the facial expressions exhibited by Deaf people. Facial expressions are an important part of communication in Sign. Additionally, deaf people learn to read facial expressions when communicating with hearing people. Be aware that your body language and face are communicating a great deal to a Deaf person, intentionally or not.

G—Goodbyes—The "Deaf Goodbye" is both a humorous label and a fact of life within the Deaf community. Open social interaction was, for generations, limited to those occasions when Deaf people were physically together and could communicate freely, as opposed to the constant social interaction that hearing people had. Taking full advantage of the opportunity often meant that leaving was a protracted affair characterized by saying goodbye to nearly everyone in the room! Thus, the "goodbye" phase of an event may actually take (or at least seem to take) longer than the event itself.

H—Hand Waving, Light Flashing, Foot Stomping—These are all appropriate ways to get a Deaf person's attention.

Hugging—Deaf people tend to hug each other on arrival and leaving, even if it is the first time they have met! This is sometimes jarring to an observer, but is an example of the instant camaraderie that often appears between two Deaf people even if they are from completely different backgrounds and areas of the country.

I—Intelligence—American society, in particular, takes stock of a person's intelligence based on their skill or expertise with English. This is, of course, a grave mistake, and is often made with regards to Deaf people. Intelligence in the Deaf community, as with any group of people, varies... but is not at all dependent on the Deaf person's grasp of English.

Incidental Learning—Learning which takes place outside of a formal educational setting. Hearing people have access to a wealth of (primarily auditory) environmental information that is soaked up and processed from casual conversations, TV, radio, etc. Some research has shown that up to 80% of what we know about interaction with the world around us is due to incidental learning. Deaf people often do not have access to this information on the same level as hearing people, and there may thus be pieces missing from their general knowledge base that most hearing people would consider to be obvious.

J—Jargon—When using an interpreter, try to either supply the interpreter and the Deaf person with vocabulary ahead of time, or explain any jargon used in practical terms to the interpreter. This will ease the interpretation and ensure the Deaf person understands the concept you are attempting to convey.

K—Kmart interpreters—Kmart interpreters – a somewhat humorous, but unfortunately accurate label. As the story goes, a hearing mother and her deaf son were at Kmart stocking up at the beginning of the school year. The cashier noticed the mother signing to her son, and began to laboriously sign to the child. The mother perked right up and said to the cashier, "We haven't been able to find an interpreter for him for school... would you be willing to interpret for him?" This illustrates the common and shocking level of ignorance regarding what, exactly, makes someone qualified to interpret. Standards are now becoming more established nationwide; however, Kmart interpreters are still out there.

L—Labels—The term "hearing impaired," which implies that Deaf people are broken in some way, is not an appropriate label. Nor is "deaf and dumb," "deaf-mute," or any mutation thereof. "Deaf" and "hard of hearing" are the preferred terms. "Person with a hearing loss," while better than other labels, is still unwieldy and not generally preferred.

Lipreading—Lipreading (or speechreading) is difficult at best for many deaf people. Only about 30% of the individual phonemes of English are actually visible on the lips; a skilled lipreader may enhance her comprehension level with cues and knowledge of the subject matter. This comprehension level is almost entirely dependent on circumstance, and can range from 0-100%. However, the near-mythical abilities of deaf people to lipread from afar are, by and large, mythical. Do not assume that all deaf people can read lips. This would be akin to assuming all hearing people can sing (which I'm sure you realize IS a myth!).

M—Muscles—When you listen, you are using no muscles. While you may become bored or tired of listening to a speaker, there are no muscles to become physically exhausted. Eyes, by contrast, have many muscles, and become physically tired. Deaf people must use their eyes constantly; for lipreading, watching an interpreter, identifying visual cues in their environment, etc. Interpreters often team up and interpret in short shifts so they get needed breaks; a deaf person does not get those breaks, and indeed is often seen to be rude if he closes his eyes briefly or leaves the room.

N—Noises—Deaf people are deaf, and generally not mute. They make noises while signing, may be oblivious to how loud they are when doing various things (i.e. closing doors, etc), and in general are just not as quiet as most people think they would be.

O—Obstructions—Obstructions – Obstructions to communication for Deaf people are not always apparent to hearing people. Pens in the mouth, flowers on the table, a glass held at just the wrong angle... all can interfere with communication. Don't be surprised if a Deaf person moves the condiments off the table at dinner!

P—Paper and Pen Many deaf people carry paper and pen to communicate with those poor hearing people who don't understand sign language. They may also ask to borrow a pen to communicate with you.

Pointing—Pointing is acceptable in the Deaf community, and is indeed often used as a means of establishing a reference point in ASL. This disconcerts many hearing people who were taught "it's not polite to point!"

Q—Qualified Interpreter—An interpreter may be certified, but not qualified. And a qualified interpreter may or may not be certified. An example: Someone who is certified to interpret for and works as an interpreter with a five-year-old in his kindergarten class would generally not be qualified to interpret for that same child in a medical setting. Your best bet: ask the Deaf person if he or she is comfortable with this interpreter for this setting.

R—Restating—Oftentimes, when communicating via speech and lipreading, people tend to repeat themselves if a deaf person doesn't understand what is said. This is fine... once. After repeating once, if a deaf person still doesn't understand, RESTATE rather than repeat. Find a different way to say the same thing, whether it's a different word or explanation of the concept. This will often give the deaf person enough cues to figure out what was said.

Referrals—Make sure that any referrals you make for a Deaf person are appropriate. For example: in referring a Deaf person to a therapist, make certain that therapist is prepared and willing to provide an interpreter for the Deaf person. If a referral is made to an inappropriate professional, the Deaf person will often simply give up in frustration. See "X" for further clarification.

Relay—Relay is a method of communication via phone which utilizes either an operator (traditional text-based relay) or an interpreter (video relay) for hearing people to communicate with deaf people and vice versa.

S—Speech—Do not assume that Deaf people cannot speak. Some can, but choose not to; some cannot. Compare this with hearing people and their ability or inability to sing... some can and choose not to, some cannot. Those Deaf people who do choose to speak will often have an accent which is sometimes difficult to understand; don't give up! Use additional means of communication for clarification if necessary.

T—Touch—Deaf people tend to touch during conversations, when greeting or taking their leave of each other. Additionally, it is perfectly permissible to touch a Deaf person to get their attention; this is in contrast with hearing social norms, which prohibit unsolicited touch.

Topics—During conversation (and particularly in group situations) it is helpful to "feed" the deaf person the topic, in particular if he or she is attempting to lipread. This holds true even if an interpreter is present.

U—Use concepts—When communicating with a deaf person, if a word is unfamiliar to him, try to explain the concept behind the word. Use small words as opposed to big words; an example would be to use the words "gun, knife, baseball bat, big pot" in place of the term "weapon," or explaining the idea of "taxation" as "you pay the government a bunch of your money to provide you with services you may or may not want or need."

V—Visual Noise/ Environment—Visual noise is just as disruptive to a deaf person as auditory noise can be to a hearing person. Visual noise is found in an environment that is visually distracting and chaotic; think flowered wallpaper or a restaurant decorated with very bright patterns. If you must be in an environment with this sort of visual noise, try to position the Deaf person with his or her back to the chaos. Also, be aware of lighting; make sure there is adequate lighting for the Deaf person, but not shining in his or her eyes. This includes natural light from windows, which can be very overwhelming and blinding.

Visual Aids—The value of visual aids and alerts cannot be overstated. This applies not only to communication (i.e. using handouts, overheads, powerpoint presentations, flip charts, paper and pen) but also to things such as weather alerts, fire alarms, and the like. Keep in mind that many people (not only deaf, but hearing as well) learn best with the aid of visuals; in an educational setting, try to accommodate different learning styles, and you will also be accommodating a Deaf person's needs.

Vibration—Deaf people are often very sensitive to vibration. They may feel someone coming down the hall before a hearing person hears the approach, or a sound that a hearing person can ignore creates so much vibration that a deaf person cannot ignore it. Also, do not assume that a deaf person can work in a noisy environment; many have residual hearing on top of their sensitivity to vibration, and noisy environments are often just as difficult for them as for someone who can hear.

W—Walking through a conversation—When walking through a conversation between two signers, it is not necessary to crawl on the floor or stand and wait for a lull in the conversation. Simply walk quickly and politely between the signers.

X—eXtreme frustration of being deaf in a hearing world—(Hey, you come up with a better example for "X!") There are two layers to this: the world and the personal. At the world level, there is what I call Hearing Privilege. The world is set up for people who can hear; for examples, look at drive through windows, phone menu trees, buzzers on shelter doors, intercoms on planes. When a deaf person asks for modification of these things, hearing people often act as if this is a huge imposition... thus making the deaf person feel of less value as a human being. At the personal level is something I call Hearism... the assumption that everyone can hear. Thus, when a deaf person does not respond to something which is said or announced, the assumption is that the deaf person is rude, stupid, or obstinate... instead of just deaf. Being confronted by these attitudes and behaviors on a daily basis is demeaning and frustrating for a Deaf person.

Y—Yelling—People tend to speak very loudly, and even yell, at deaf people, believing this will make it easier for the deaf person to understand them. News flash: a deaf person is DEAF... this means they cannot hear, and yelling won't help! The person will still be deaf!

Z—last handshape in an ASL ABC story—ABC stories are an example of one of the cherished traditions in Deaf culture. ABC stories use the handshapes of the American Sign Language alphabet, in alphabetical order, of course, to tell a story. Excellent examples can be found online (on YouTube, or by using a search engine and typing in "ASL ABC Stories").

DEAF CULTURE

WRITTEN BY

WILLIAM VICARS, ED.D.

Deaf Culture consists of the norms, beliefs, values, and "mores"* shared by members of the Deaf Community.

Note: the term "*mores*" means: "The accepted traditional customs, moral attitudes, manners and ways of a particular social group." — dictionary.com

Culturally Deaf people in America use American Sign Language. We love to swap stories about Gallaudet University, and the various state residential schools for the Deaf. We value deaf children and our Deaf heritage. We hate the thought of anything that would destroy our Deaf world. We believe that it is fine to be Deaf. If given the chance to become hearing, most of us would choose to remain Deaf. We tend to congregate around the kitchen table rather than the living room sofa because the lighting is better in the kitchen. Our good-byes take nearly forever, and our hello's often consist of *serious* hugs. When two of us meet for the first time we tend to exchange detailed biographies and describe our social circles in considerable depth.

In general, the global "Deaf Community" consists of those Deaf and hard of hearing people throughout the world who use sign language and share in Deaf culture. Hearing family members, friends, interpreters, and others are also part of this community to the extent that they use sign language and share in the culture.

As used here in America, the term "Deaf Community" refers to Deaf and hard-of-hearing people, (along with our families, friends, and others), who use ASL and who are culturally Deaf. Being *culturally* Deaf means sharing the beliefs, values, traditions, moral attitudes, manners, and ways of the Deaf community.

The Deaf *World* refers to *all* "d"eaf-(physically) and hard-of-hearing people and the people with whom we regularly interact. For example: teachers of the Deaf, interpreters, audiologists, social workers, religious workers, parents, siblings, etc. They are all part of the Deaf *World* but not necessarily members of the Deaf *Community*.

Note: Even though I make a distinction here between the Deaf World and the Deaf Community you can be sure that there are many writers / bloggers who consider those two terms to be interchangeable. Such individuals use the term "Deaf World" to refer to Deaf Community. It is a non-issue really. I'm simply striving to point out that a "community" involves a degree of sharing and interactivity that is more intimate than a "world." Some people also use the term "Deaf World" to refer to "all things experienced by a person who is Deaf" or "the world as experienced by a Deaf person."

Members of the Deaf *Community* do not consider themselves to be disabled. They see themselves as **a cultural group bonded together by common experiences and a common language**. Members of this community don't want be be Hearing! If given a choice the vast majority would choose to remain Deaf!

That doesn't mean that there aren't "d"eaf (physically not-able to hear) people in the U.S. who consider themselves disabled. There are indeed many such individuals, but they are generally not fluent in ASL and are not *culturally* Deaf, therefore they are not members of the "*cultural* Deaf Community."

> *People who feel that being Deaf is about language and culture subscribe to the "cultural view" of deafness (or Deafhood).*

> *People who feel that deafness is problem to be solved subscribe to the "pathological model" or the "medical model" of deafness.*

QUESTIONS

1. Name two models or ways of thinking about deafness:
2. True or false, "In general, a member of the *cultural* Deaf Community would rather remain deaf than receive the ability to hear."

History of Deaf Education in America

EDITED BY

LISA KOCH

The founding of the first public school for the Deaf (The Connecticut Asylum at Hartford for the Education and Instruction of Deaf and Dumb Persons in Hartford, Conn., in 1817 was a crucial milestone in the way society related to people with disabilities in the US. The Connecticut Asylum at Hartford was incorporated as the "American Asylum for Deaf-mutes" in May 1816. The school is now the American School for the Deaf.

Many threads in developing U.S. society coalesced in Hartford in the early nineteenth century. The importance attached to universal literacy (by no means common in the world at the time) and the particular missionary religious doctrines of the prevalent Protestant sects provided both means and motive for the attempt to educate deaf people. The concept of self-reliance and the belief that religious salvation is possible through understanding the Bible determined the methods and purposes of the founders. Literacy, salvation and the skills needed to earn a living were the goals. Achieving these required clarity and fluidity of communication. This is why the school was based on sign language from the start.

The experiment aroused great interest. In 1818 the public was asked to assist Deaf people who have been considered as incapable of mental improvement. Deaf people were found to be capable of not only instruction but understanding moral and religious truth. This was a great change in attitude toward deaf people which had only just occurred.[1]

The first half century of the school's existence was a time of flowering and growth for deaf education in America. Numerous schools for the deaf which opened during this period. Instruction was in sign language, with the goals of imparting literacy, training for productive labor, and religious salvation.

An important feature of manual communication as a teaching language is that it allows deaf people to be teachers. Many alumni did go on to become teachers and principals at schools for the deaf throughout the United States, which spread sign language throughout the country. A deaf culture developed during this period, with periodicals, organizations, social relations and all the other features to be expected of a minority culture dispersed through the general population. So rapid and positive was the spread of this language and culture that the period is today referred to as a golden age.

The culminating achievement of that time was the establishment of the Columbia Institute for the Deaf at Washington, D.C. in 1864. Now called Gallaudet University, it is still the only liberal arts college for the deaf in the world, although there are now many other institutions offering college and post graduate degrees to the deaf.

The later half of the nineteenth century witnessed the rise of oral theories of deaf education. Although there are a variety of these theories, they have in common an emphasis on the importance of oral skills (speech-reading and speech) in the education of deaf children. A leading proponent of oral methods was Alexander Graham Bell, whose mother and wife were both hard of hearing. The first major oral school in the U.S., Clark School for the Deaf in Northampton, Massachusetts, opened in 1867.

This difference in philosophy between the proponents of traditional sign language and supporters of the oral method was a crucial division throughout the second half of the nineteenth and well into the twentieth century. The dispute was often bitter, leading to deep divisions within the deaf education community. It is beyond the scope of this history to go into the merits of the argument, but a few points are worth noting.

The ability to learn oral skills depends in large part on the degree of hearing loss, the age at which the student became deaf (especially whether it was before or after acquiring spoken language), and other factors. There is therefore a wide range of success and failure dependent, not on intelligence, but on these factors. Oral skills are not usually very useful for communication among deaf persons, and the use of the oral method practically bars the deaf from careers as teachers. The American School for the Deaf, during this period, tried out students in oral classes first, and if they did not succeed, put them in manual classes instead, under a philosophy called the Combined System. Many other schools for the deaf embraced the oral method to a greater extent.

The twentieth century has seen a loosening of the grip of the oral method, as sign language has regained legitimacy. The school's current educational and communication philosophy, Total Communication, is described in the last paragraph.

As the oral/manual dispute has waned, a new philosophical division has appeared; the mainstreaming debate. Public Act 94-142 mandates that each child be taught in the "east restrictive environment" possible, and this has been widely interpreted to mean the local public school. The mainstreaming, or "inclusionist", movement has led to a decline in the proportion of deaf and hard of hearing students attending center schools such as the American School for the Deaf.

This debate shares some features with the oral/manual debate of 100 years ago. Success in a mainstream setting is very dependent upon degree of hearing loss and degree of oral skill. Deafness is a very low-incidence condition, and very few public schools have more than one or two deaf students within their districts. Since it is uneconomic to hire a teacher exclusively for the education of those few children, once again, deaf people are prevented from obtaining teaching positions, and deaf children in the mainstream setting are prevented having deaf adult role models in the school setting.

It can also be very restrictive to be blocked from easily communicating with classmates and teachers, from participating in sports or from normal social interaction without the need for an interpreter. The philosophy of the American School for the Deaf is that there is no one easy answer that applies to all situations, but that each child's education should be based on the specifics of that child's needs. There is a place for mainstreaming and center schools both.[2]

This is a general overview of the main placement options available to deaf children. There are many individual circumstances that influence what, if any, additional services may be provided to the child. Some children who are mainstreamed may or may not need services from speech and language therapists or educational interpreters.

Residential Schools for the deaf are most often state run schools. They are both an educational facility and a housing facility for large numbers of deaf and hard of hearing students. Some students who live in the area of the school may commute to and from the school each day, while others stay during the week and return home on the weekends.

Day schools are located in larger cities and are separate schools for the deaf. They do not enroll hearing students.

Day classes are usually district or county run programs on public school campuses with hearing children. Instruction may range from self-contained classrooms with a teacher of the deaf to varying amounts of mainstreaming with regular classrooms.

Resource rooms are a place for the child to receive additional services from additional instruction in English or other academic subject areas to speech and language therapy. The child spends the majority of their time in a regular classroom.

Itinerant programs are for children who are placed in regular classrooms. They receive "itinerant" services from a teacher of the deaf as additional support. The itinerant teacher often works with a number of students at different school sites. The amount of time and number of days that a child receives services varies according to each student's need and is usually specified on the child's IEP.

Within these educational placements, there are three general approaches/philosophies to the education of a deaf child: oral, bilingual/bicultural, and total communication. Below you will find a basic description of each program and some of the variations, if any, you might find in these programs. I have tried to include websites for each of these methods.

There are many factors that must be considered when looking at different programs. Each factor can play a role in the success of any Deaf child in their education.

- **Hearing Loss**: the amount of hearing that a child has lost or the amount of residual hearing that a child has will influence the amount of information that may be gained auditorily. The amount of loss can but does not always affect the ability to acquire speech. Some hard-of-hearing children have a difficult time learning to speak, while some profoundly deaf children do learn to speak.
- **Identification of Deafness**: the earlier a child is identified to have a hearing loss; the sooner intervention can be given. A child with a hearing loss needs to have access to language whether the choice is oral or sign language.
- **Parental Support**: The amount of parental support and involvement, regardless of program choice, is extremely important to a child's success in school.
-

Oral philosophy programs have an emphasis on spoken language and listening. They are taught through oral/verbal instruction or the use of an oral interpreter. No sign language is used. Oral programs may use one or more of the following strategies/tools for instruction: speech/audiological training, assistive devices, developing listening skills. Many oral programs are private schools; however there are some public oral programs. Three variations of the oral approach are:

- Auditory/Verbal Method utilizes intensive therapy to develop listening skills and to build language through listening. Sign language is not used.
- Aural/Oral Method has some similarities to auditory/verbal method. Students learn to listen and lipread. Natural gestures are accepted as a way of communication.

Bilingual/Bicultural Philosophy recognizes American Sign Language (ASL) as the primary language of the deaf child and uses ASL for instruction and conceptual understanding of material. In addition, they teach English as a second language for reading and writing. The child is considered "bilingual" when they have mastered both languages. The "bicultural" aspect of this philosophy is that they teach both hearing and deaf culture. They teach deaf children to be proud of their deaf heritage. They expose the children to deaf adult role models.

Total Communication Philosophy has many variations. In general, they use a combination of various methods and approaches to meet the individual child's needs. A combination of sign language, fingerspelling and spoken words is often used. Sign language used may vary: Signed Exact English (SEE), Signed English, American Sign Language (ASL), or Pidgin Signed English (PSE). In addition, some programs may include the use of Cued Speech to assist the child in English Access. These programs may use speech and language therapists, audiological training, and assistive devices in the course of instruction for deaf children.

- **Signed Exact English (SEE)**: is a system of signs that code English into a visual form. SEE includes prefixes and suffixes to assist Deaf children in seeing all aspects of the English language. It is not the native language used by the majority of Deaf adults.
- **Signed English**: is a manually coded form of English similar to SEE; however it often borrows vocabulary and uses three-dimensional space which makes Signed English more ASL-like.
- **American Sign Language (ASL)**: is the accepted native language among Deaf adults. It is recognized by linguists to be a true language having its own structure, syntax and other features found in other languages. It is NOT English.
- **Pidgin Signed English (PSE)**: is a form of sign that has evolved as a dialect of sign language that is not English nor is it ASL. Many Deaf adults use this as a form of communication, often when signing to hearing people. It may vary on a continuum from manually coded English on one end to ASL on the other.
- **Cued Speech**: is NOT a form of sign language. It is a tool to make spoken language visible to the Deaf. It is not used as a form of communication among Deaf adults. It uses 8 basic handshapes representing groups of consonant sounds and 4 locations representing groups of vowel sounds. The general rule is what looks similar on the lips looks different on the hands and vice-versa.

NOTES

1. http://www.asd-1817.org/page.cfm?p=10
2. http://www.asd-1817.org/page.cfm?p=430

Medical and Cultural Views of Deafness

WRITTEN BY

F.C. STAMPS

The medical perspective and the cultural perspective of deafness are quite different. Because doctors almost always have a hearing perspective of deafness and look at it as a disability, impairment, or handicap to be treated so that patients can enjoy hearing, almost invariably medical specialists propose treatment, such as implants or speech therapy, in order to help enable deaf individuals to get along in a hearing world.

In contrast, Deaf culture focuses on the strengths rather than the weaknesses of deafness and see deafness not as a disability but as a linguistic minority. Never having experienced deafness themselves, this cultural view often baffles hearing people. Nevertheless, many Deaf people are proud to be Deaf, not just deaf with a lowercase d, meaning unable to hear, but Deaf with a capital D, meaning they are part of the culture.

Thus, in the audiogram below you can see the differences in the labels that the medical view and the cultural view of deafness apply. Notice that the cultural view has gray areas because from a cultural perspective, individuals largely define where they see themselves in the culture. Some people who have profound hearing loss consider themselves to be hard of hearing, while some people who have mild or moderate hearing loss consider themselves to be Deaf.

DECIBELS	COMMON SOUNDS (IN DECIBELS)		MEDICAL PERSPECTIVE	CULTURAL PERSPECTIVE
0			Normal Hearing	Hearing
10	breathing			
20	whisper			
30			Mild Hearing Loss	
40		conversation		
50			Moderate Hearing Loss	Hard of Hearing
60				
70	typewriter		Severe Hearing Loss	
80	rush hour traffic			
90	food blender		Profound Hearing Loss	Deaf
100	train, lawnmover			
110	chain saw			
120	jet airplane			
130				
140	shotgun blast			

Source: Oregon Disabilities Commission and Lectures by Portland Community College ASL instructor Mark Azure.

ASL Continuum

WRITTEN BY

F.C. STAMPS

AMERICAN SIGN LANGUAGE (ASL)

As its name denotes, American Sign Language is an actual language. It is a conceptually based language that uses hand and body position and movement, as well as facial expressions, as opposed to most other languages, which use spoken and written forms of communication. ASL is a different language than English; it is not just hand signals that represent English words that spell sentences in English word order. Rather, ASL has its own vocabulary, grammar rules, common expressions, wordplay, etc.

The Federal Communications Commission (FCC) defines ASL as "A visual language based on hand shape, position, movement, and orientation of the hands in relation to each other and the body" (47 CFR § 64.601). Refer to the parameters of ASL.

ASL and systems of MCE are the predominantly used systems of communication by Deaf people in the United States and Canada. Other regions of the world use their own sign languages, such as the U.K. where deaf people use BSL and Australia where Auslan is used.

MANUALLY CODED ENGLISH (MCE)

Manually Coded English, or MCE, refers to a number of signing systems that are metalanguages, or codes, for English. MCEs are often simply referred to in the Deaf community as "English sign" or a variation of that term. The term "manual" in Manually Coded English can mean that the codes are not true languages but artificially contrived systems of communications, as well as that the codes are expressed manually or by hand as opposed to spoken English. In their book, *A Journey into the Deaf-World*, Harlan Lane and his fellow authors describe MCE systems as "any of several signing systems invented by educators to represent words in English sentences using signs borrowed from ASL combined with signs contrived to serve as translation equivalents for English function words (articles, prepositions, etc.) and prefixes and suffixes" (270).

Although many if not most Deaf people greatly prefer ASL over MCEs because ASL is conceptually based, leaving out the need to sign words such as "is," "the," and "am," and the need to adhere to English grammar, MCEs are useful in instances such as quoting English word for word, clarifying communication with English speakers, and teaching English to the deaf. Not uncommonly, even those who prefer ASL will use a sign from an MCE system to clarify the exact meaning of a word. The continuum between pure ASL and English has a full spectrum of varying levels of use per individual, region, and situation, with the vast majority of Deaf people (with a capital D) in the United States using ASL for most communication.

MCE systems include:

- Signed English
- Seeing Essential English (SEE 1)
- Signing Exact English (SEE 2)
- cued speech
- The Rochester Method
- Conceptually Accurate Signed English (C.A.S.E.)
- Linguistics of Visual English (L.O.V.E.)

PIDGIN SIGN ENGLISH (PSE)

Pidgin Sign English is somewhat in the middle of the continuum between ASL and English. Researchers at The University of New South Wales have noted that a person's signing style changes depending on whom they are conversing with; two Deaf people signing together may use very conceptual sign, whereas when signing to a hearing person, their signing style can tend to become more pidginized towards English. Some hearing people who sign may not know ASL grammar well, but sign great PSE.

Continuum between ASL and MCE:

ASL	PSE	MCE
Conceptual	Mixed	English

PSE is also known as contact sign, or a contact language, referring to contact between people who speak different languages and how they use a pidgin to communicate.

Example Sentence:

ASL: Store, I go.
PSE: I go store.
MCE: I am go-ing to the store.

Communication Technologies

COMMUNICATION TECHNOLOGIES

WRITTEN BY

F.C. STAMPS

TELECOMMUNICATIONS

For many years the TTY ("TeleTypewriter" or "text telephone") has been the main means of telecommunication for Deaf and Hard of Hearing individuals, as well as for mute persons. TTYs are also known as TDDs, which is short for "Telecommunications Device for the Deaf". Of the two terms, TTY is more commonly used in the Deaf community, while the term TDD is used in government legislation.

With advances in technology in recent years, other means of telecommunications that have become popular in the Deaf community include **IP relay** (a.k.a. web-based text relay), **text messaging, video phones** (VP), **email, instant messaging** (IM), and **chatrooms** on the Internet.

A few companies also provide **video relay service** (VRS). VRS allows people who use video phones and hearing people who use a regular telephones to call each other using a relay operator. A relay operator tells the hearing person on the telephone what the video phone user signs and also signs to the video phone user what the hearing person says on the telephone.

As the use of email, video phones, video relay, mobile devices and other technolgies increases in the Deaf community, TTYs are being used less and less. Interestingly enough, some abbreviations used historically by deaf people typing on the TTY are the same as some abbreviations still being used in texting. Here are some commonly used abbreviations used on TTYs. This is not an exhaustive list of abbreviations used on TTYs.

CD: could. Same as CUD.
CUD: could. Same as CD.
CUL: see you later.
CUZ: because.
HD: hold, meaning wait. Same as HLD.
HLD: hold, meaning wait. Same as HD.

21

GA: go ahead (indicating it is your turn to talk or type).
GA to SK: go ahead to stop keying (meaning the person is ready to hang up unless you have anything else to say).
MSG: message.
MTG: meeting.
NBR: number.
OIC: oh, I see.
OPR: operator.
PLS: please.
QQ: question mark. (Often QQ is used instead of the question mark (?) because it is easier to type for many people.)
R: are.
SHD: should.
SK: stop keying (meaning the person is hanging up).
SKSK: stop keying (meaning the person is hanging up).
THX: thanks.
TMR: tomorrow. Same as TMW.
TMW: tomorrow. Same as TMR.
U: you.
UR: your or you're.

Of these abbreviations, some of the most important terms for hearing persons who converse with TTY users via relay to be familiar with are GA, GA to SK, and SK. When the TTY user types GA, the relay operator will tell you, "Go ahead," meaning it is your turn to talk since you need to take turns talking similar to using two-way radios. When you are done speaking, say, "Go ahead," and the relay operator will type GA so that the TTY user knows it is their turn to type.

When the TTY user is ready to hang up, he or she will type, "GA to SK," meaning "go ahead to stop keying," and the relay operator will tell you, "The person is ready to hang up." You can either continue the conversation if you have more to say, or simply say goodbye to end the phone call. To end the conversation yourself, after you are done speaking, tell the relay operator, "Go ahead to stop keying." When the TTY user hangs up the phone, they will type SK or SKSK, and the relay operator will tell you, "The person is hanging up."

See also Using Relay.

FACE-TO-FACE COMMUNICATION

Many if not most Deaf people prefer a live interpreter who translates language spoken by hearing people to sign language (voice-to-sign interpretation) and translates what Deaf people sign into spoken language (sign-to-voice interpretation). However, one alternative to using an interpreter made available through technology is **real-time captioning**, also known as C-print captioning. This is where a person types out what is being spoken, which typed text is then displayed on a screen for the Deaf person(s) to read. The person typing the captions can be on location or listen remotely through a phone connection. This technology has been using for including Deaf people in business meetings and also classes. One limitation to using real-time captions is that it is only one-way voice-to-sign. For the Deaf person to respond, he or she would have to type out or write a reply. Another limitation to real-time captioning is that there is no cultural or linguistic mediation between the spoken English and ASL, which can be a problem if the Deaf person(s) has limited English proficiency.

See also Using an Interpreter.

MOVIES, TELEVISION, AND OTHER VIDEO PRESENTATIONS

All televisions larger than 13 inches sold in the United States are required by the Television Decoder Circuitry Act of 1990 to have built-in closed caption decoders. **Closed captions** (CC) are text on the screen showing spoken language and sound effects that can be turned on and off. The Telecommunications Act of 1996 requires that most television programming in the United States have closed captions.

Unlike closed captions, **subtitles** on videotapes or dvds do not always include information for Deaf people such as sound effects, but instead just the dialogue of the movie on the videotape or dvd. Subtitles can also be turned on and off.

Some movie theaters offer limited showings of movies with **open captions** (OC). Unlike closed captions and subtitles on your television that can be turned on and off, open captions are shown for the duration of the movie. Advertisements and previews shown before movies are not captioned.

See also Regal Cinemas and Captionfish Open Captioned Movie Showtimes

Other video presentations such as those shown at national monuments, museums, and theme parks sometimes offer **reflective captions**, also known as **rear window captioning**, where captions are displayed in mirror image behind the viewing audience. People who wish to view the reflective captions can ask for a clear sheet of plastic on a stand, which they set up at an angle to view the reflection of the captions behind them and the video in front of them at the same time. Reflective captions are also being offered increasingly in movie theaters as an alternative for businesses to open captions. One reason for this may be because only the viewer of reflective captions sees the captions, whereas with open captions, some hearing movie goers complain about the captions, which is why box office attendants almost always ask customers if they understand that the tickets they are buying are for an open captioned showtime, as to reduce complaints.

Avenues Into the Deaf Community

CONSIDERATIONS FOR MEDIATING WITH PEOPLE WHO ARE CULTURALLY DEAF

WRITTEN BY

ANNETTE LEONARD, DEB DUREN, AND JOHN REIMAN

Historically, mediation has not been an effective venue for dispute resolution for Deaf [1] people because of linguistic inaccessibility and cultural non-recognition. Like other linguistic minority groups who experience and resolve conflict in a manner consistent with their social and communicative norms, Deaf people have some unique perspectives. The following article illuminates some of these perspectives and explains how mediators can address these differences when working with Deaf people, in order to make mediation a more linguistically and culturally respectful and responsive endeavor.

THE AMERICAN DEAF COMMUNITY: AN IN-DEPTH LOOK

Bound together by a common language, American Sign Language (ASL), the Deaf community in the United States views itself as a cultural and linguistic minority. Through friendships, marriages, clubs, formal organizations, shared experiences and culture, the Deaf in America have created a community. While most hearing people see deafness as a disability, Deaf people don't view themselves as disabled. As I. King Jordan, the president of Gallaudet University (the only University for the Deaf in the world) put it: "Deaf people can do anything anyone else can—except hear." Affiliation with the Deaf community is based not on a physical location or ethnicity but on a shared language and shared experiences.

In America today, 90% of all deaf children are born to hearing parents.[2] Many hearing people have never met a deaf person unless they have a deaf family member. Because of the obvious barriers that learning English without the benefit of hearing presents, many deaf children have poor communication with their parents and hearing family members. Associating with other Deaf people thus becomes desirable and is the means by which Deaf culture is transmitted. People in the Deaf community believe that ASL is "the most accessible and primary language" for Deaf individuals and typically view English as a second language.[3] For this reason residential schools play a significant role in Deaf culture. At these schools values, traditions, acceptable behavior, and other aspects of Deaf culture are learned through interaction and instruction. These schools have a place of high value and esteem in the culture: when Deaf people meet each other for the first time, it is typical for them to introduce themselves not only by giving their name but also by identifying what residential school they attended.

According to Carol Padden, a Deaf activist and scholar, membership in the Deaf community is based on four points of entry: political involvement, social identity, language use and audiological profile.[4] Taking a leadership role to advance political issues related to deafness and Deaf culture evidences *political involvement*. This includes large and small scale activism such as lobbying state governments to accept ASL for foreign language credit at colleges and universities, or working with the local residential school to adopt a bilingual / bicultural philosophy of education. *Social identity* means that a person identifies herself or himself as culturally Deaf and participates in the life of the Deaf community. Supporting Deaf clubs, attending sporting events at Deaf schools, and providing leadership in Deaf organizations are examples of the social aspects of the Deaf community.

Linguistic access to the Deaf community is limited to the use of American Sign Language. Because language and culture are so tightly linked, this is a central requirement for an individual's involvement in the Deaf community. Baker and Padden explain the importance of ASL by recognizing that "at the heart of every community is its language. This language embodies the thoughts and experiences of its users, and they, in turn, learn about their own culture and share in it together through their language. Thus, Deaf people learn about their own culture and share their experiences with each other through American Sign Language."[5] Finally, some degree of hearing loss is the audiological requirement for full participation in the Deaf community. However, degrees of hearing loss, audio grams, and specifics about frequencies and decibels are not descriptions of value to the Deaf community at large; it is the experience of being Deaf—not the condition of being audiologically deaf that is significant.

While hearing people play important roles in the Deaf world, they can never become "core" members of the Deaf community. Growing up with Deaf parents, having a Deaf sibling, working as an interpreter, or teaching at the Deaf school are some ways that hearing

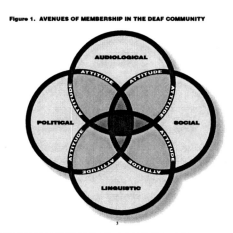

Figure 1. AVENUES OF MEMBERSHIP IN THE DEAF COMMUNITY

Figure 1. AVENUES OF MEMBERSHIP IN THE DEAF COMMUNITY

people gain access to the Deaf community. In general, hearing people's proximity to the Deaf community depends on the degrees to which they (hearing people) are informed and sensitized about Deaf people (see figure 2).

Characteristics of the Deaf community include the high value placed on interpersonal relationships, the prevalence of reciprocity, affiliations with Deaf schools, and clubs and national organizations of / for the Deaf. Because Deaf people spend so much time in the "hearing world"—at work, with family, and in day-to-day living—relationships with other Deaf people are particularly valuable. It is common for calendars to be marked months in advance of upcoming social events in the Deaf community, and time with Deaf friends locally and around the country is cherished. These kinds of gatherings happen in homes, at schools, in Deaf clubs and at larger scale events like the annual World Deaf Timberfest and the World Deaf Games (the Olympics of the Deaf).

As is true for any minority group, the Deaf community has a shared heritage that is the foundation of its literature, culture, traditions, values, and organizations (e.g., Deaf clubs, the National Association of the Deaf, the American Athletic Association of the Deaf, the National Fraternal Society of the Deaf, as well as other local, state, national and international associations and groups). Within the Deaf community there is a sense of pride in affiliating with these organizations, and a high value is placed on ensuring that Deaf people comprise the leadership of these associations. Just as it would be unusual for a white person to preside over the United Negro College Fund, it would be unlikely that a hearing person would lead the National Association of the Deaf.

While some cultural differences between the hearing majority and the Deaf community are obvious, other differences are more subtle. One of the most common and unifying experiences Deaf adults describe (much to the surprise of most hearing people) is the realization of their own deafness. This "breakthrough" experience occurs when one's identity as a Deaf person and a member of the Deaf community becomes clear. So many deaf people are raised by hearing parents or thinking of themselves as "hearing impaired" that they don't become aware of their cultural identity until later in life. When one recognizes the implications of being Deaf, and therefore the importance of ASL and shared experiences with other Deaf people, there is a freedom that comes with this new perspective. "The essence of Deafness is not the lack of hearing, but the community and culture based on ASL. Deaf culture represents not a denial but an affirmation."[6] Part of the collective identity of the Deaf community is a strong commitment to cohesion. Because the use of ASL has been threatened for more than a century by those who would rather see deaf children educated through oralism (the use of spoken English, rather than ASL), the Deaf community has had to band together to create a unified front in the face of those who would invalidate or endanger their language. Unlike the hearing majority in the United States, who seeks autonomy and independence and makes decisions based on what is most useful for the individual, the Deaf community values collectivism—considering community needs more than individual needs, seeking group success rather than personal gain.

When hearing parents of a new baby first learn about their child's deafness, they are typically informed about the baby's condition from a medical perspective, and they see their new child as imperfect and lacking.[7] There is in fact a grieving process associated with a parent learning that their child is deaf.8 However, most of those parents do not seek out Deaf adults and do not know about the existence of the Deaf community. Because parents of deaf children get their information from the medical community and not Deaf adults or organizations, deafness has historically been viewed from a pathological perspective as something to be fixed.

The state of having diminished hearing has been seen as a deficiency, as if a person with a hearing loss were broken. Since deafness in the Deaf community is not seen as an inadequacy, Dolnick explains that "talk of cures and breakthroughs and technological wizardry is both inappropriate and offensive—as if doctors and newspapers joyously announced advances in genetic engineering that might someday make it possible to turn black skin white."[9]

The stigma associated with being deaf combined with external attempts to discontinue the use of ASL and otherwise undermine Deaf people's linguistic and cultural integrity are strongly suggestive of oppression. In his groundbreaking work, *The Pedagogy of the Oppressed*, Freire, a Brazilian sociologist, identified some common characteristics of oppressed people: ambivalence, self-deprecation, distrust of oneself/peers, horizontal violence, passivity/adaptation/fatalism, emotional dependence, and fear of freedom or backlash. These responses and patterns of action, however subtle, will have a direct impact on mediations when a Deaf person is involved in a dispute with a hearing person. Recognizing these characteristics of the oppressed and the oppressor is an important step in balancing the power between Deaf and hearing participants.[10]

MEDIATING WITH DEAF PARTICIPANTS

When mediation involves Deaf participants, their language and culture must be a primary consideration in shaping the process and structure of the mediation. To that end, we suggest five guidelines for mediators:

1. Ensure that the mediation process honors and accommodates Deaf people's linguistic needs and differences.

Recognizing that Deaf people often have limited English comprehension, it is best to be sensitive about using written English in mediation. Whether it's making use of intake forms, mediation agreements, or flip charts, it is important that language is accessible for all clients, not just those with advanced English skills. Additionally, it is helpful to consider and limit the use of euphemisms, idioms, and metaphors. Not only are these phrases more difficult to interpret, but they are also often culturally based and not relevant to the lives and experiences of Deaf people. However, since language ability differs from person to person, no assumption should be made that a linguistic approach that worked well with one Deaf person will be successful for all Deaf people.

If there are materials to be read, participants should be allowed adequate time to read them thoroughly without talking or receiving an explanation until they are finished reading. Hearing people are accustomed to reading and listening at the same time. For example, a hearing person can look at an Agreement to Mediate contract and simultaneously listen to the mediator's description of that contract without difficulty. However, when someone accesses information visually, he or she cannot take in both sets of information (the written contract and its signed description) at the same time.

When working with participants who use a different language, it is also extremely important to define concepts and terms to ensure accurate comprehension. Any opportunity to clarify meaning, check with the participants' perspectives, and restate essential ideas should be utilized.

**2. Recognize the cultural values that will influence both the Deaf and hearing parties'
behavior, response and understanding of the mediation process.**

Mediation is a foreign concept for most Deaf individuals. In fact, mediation is likely to be viewed as an extreme measure, as another method of oppression (the outcome of which will automatically favor the hearing person), or at least as a culturally unfamiliar way to manage a conflict. Therefore the "normalization" of mediation is an important concept. By explaining the process of mediation (addressing any fears of an oppressive procedure), placing mediation within a continuum of dispute resolution alternatives, and validating clients' reasons for being part of a mediation, mediators can ease Deaf participants discomfort and thus heighten the likelihood of an effective and egalitarian process.

Mediators should learn about and be attentive to Deaf cultural norms [see the *Additional Resources* at the end of this paper]. Some of the most significant cultural cues are related to eye contact and body language. Eye contact is a necessary part of visual communication with Deaf participants. When a mediator or hearing participant is addressing a Deaf participant, he or she should consciously maintain eye contact. Likewise, when a Deaf person is talking, it is respectful to watch him or her rather than the interpreter.

As visually oriented people, Deaf individuals have a heightened awareness of body language, and tend to notice inconsistencies in words and actions. Therefore, mediators should be attentive to their physical habits and gestures. If a mediator covers her mouth while thinking or speaking, for example, it may seem to a Deaf person that she is trying to hide something. Mediators should also be aware of their attending habits. A mediator's habit of nodding to show that she is listening to a participant may easily be misconstrued as a sign that the mediator is agreeing.

Because Deaf individuals are typically more group-focused (as opposed to individual-focused) in their behaviors, a Deaf participant is prone to feel isolated during the process of mediation. While many hearing participants are often grateful for the one-on-one nature of mediation and perceive it to be best for the sake of autonomy and anonymity, a Deaf person is more likely to feel disadvantaged as a result of the individual-focused mediation process. For this reason, it is important that the mediator be aware of the group-centered orientation that embeds the Deaf individual in social and interpersonal networks that transcend self-dependence and the Deaf culture's value of interdependence above individualism. The presence of mutually agreed-to third parties in an initial mediation session can be one mechanism for accommodating the group-centered orientation.

Lastly, because the Deaf community is so small and its members are often intimately connected with one another, it is wise to thoroughly review the confidentiality policy with both parties to avoid future disagreements or misunderstandings about the control of information.

3. Collaborate with interpreters to improve communication during the mediation.

Mediators must take steps to ensure that, when necessary or requested, sign language interpreters are present at all stages of the mediation, from intake interviews to closing statements. (This right is guaranteed under the Americans with Disabilities Act.) Mediators who don't have experience working with or locating sign language interpreters can often get resource information (i.e.; names of interpreters or interpreting agencies) from the Disabilities Commission in their state. [See the *Additional Resources* section of this paper.]

It is important that the mediator(s) and interpreter(s) meet together before the first mediated session in order to discuss their roles and to ensure that the interpreter understands the mediation process. Similarly, the mediator will benefit from a clear description of the interpreting process so that she can become more familiar with issues like lag time, simultaneous and consecutive interpretations, and clarification procedures.

The physical setting will also require attention. Because the interpreter needs to be visible to the Deaf participant at all times, he or she will probably be positioned slightly behind the mediator or hearing participant, although the interpreter's position may need to change during the course of the mediation. Other considerations include the size of the room, the lighting, and whether or not there are any visually distracting features, such as people walking past an open door or a flickering light bulb.

Finally, the sign language interpreter and mediator should be sensitive to potential confusion about their roles on the part of the participants. Just as it is possible for the participant who is Deaf to view the hearing mediator as allied with the hearing participant by virtue of the fact that they both communicate verbally, it is also possible that the hearing participant might perceive the sign language interpreter as affiliated with the Deaf participant. The interpreter's role, her neutrality and ethical guidelines, should be explained at the beginning of the mediation. To further reduce possible misunderstandings, it should be clarified that the interpreter is not here *for* the Deaf participant, but to ensure communication access for *all* participants. To emphasize the fact that the interpreter is not biased toward individuals or outcomes, the interpreter should enter and leave the mediation with the mediator; they should carry themselves with a similar demeanor and attempt to model themselves as a cohesive team.

4. Emphasize ground rules and strategies that will lead to a more fair procedure.

A fair process is critically important in mediation. The mediator is primarily responsible for ensuring that ground rules are followed and people are behaving respectfully. One consideration that should be emphasized when working with a Deaf participant (or any party who is using an interpreter) is the need for turn-taking.

While interruptions are not desirable, some amount of interrupting or talking-over is expected in a typical mediation. People jump in to correct each other, ask a question, or emphasize a particular point. However, when the Deaf participant is receiving all of his information through an interpreter, it is impossible for a single interpreter to simultaneously hear and interpret the words of more than one person. Because of this, the protocol for turn taking should be that no one speaks while anyone else is talking.

Caucusing is another procedure that should be carefully evaluated when mediating with Deaf individuals. Some Deaf people's lives are riddled with experiences of being isolated—experiences like eating dinner with their hearing family and being excluded from conversation, or missing a supervisor's informal feedback to a co-worker. Further, as Cripps and Pizzacalla explain, an examination of deaf education shows "*(a)* that most, if not all, of the [educational] decisions were made by hearing people, with little or no input from the Deaf community and *(b)* that there is a strong tendency for the same mistakes to be repeated time and time again."[11] Because of this history of exclusion, Deaf people will be more sensitive to being asked to leave while the hearing person caucuses with the mediator and are likely to feel embarrassed about the need for individual attention if / when asked to meet in private with the mediator. Therefore, it is up to the mediator to thoroughly explain the role of caucusing to the participants at the beginning of the session, to try to minimize the need for caucusing, and to consider meeting with the Deaf person first if caucusing is required.

It is common in mediation to use techniques like paraphrasing, restating, reframing, and reinterpreting. When the participants in mediation are from different cultures or use different languages, it is even more important to use these clarification tools. The opportunity for misunderstanding is amplified by the use of an interpreter and the realities of a bilingual setting. Whenever possible the mediator should take the time to restate and clarify, or have one of the participants paraphrase what they heard so that the participants can be more certain that they fully understand each other.

5. Understand how being a linguistic minority affects the Deaf party's participation in and expectations of mediation.

Regardless of how empowered an individual seems, she is coming to the table as a Deaf person and may experience disadvantage based on her historic experience of and exposure to painful and limiting stereotypes. Mediators must therefore be sensitive to and aware of characteristics of oppressed and oppressor behaviors in order to facilitate a balanced mediation. Understanding theories of oppression in relation to the mediation setting is thus an important requirement for mediators working with culturally Deaf individuals. While the hearing participant may or may not be responsible for directly oppressing the Deaf participant, society enforces the idea that people with disabilities should be discounted.[12] For this reason, it may be necessary for the mediator to assist the hearing participant in recognizing the Deaf participant as a valuable and contributing member of society.

The mediator should actively try to ensure that power differentials are considered and addressed. A model that promotes a high degree of fairness and emphasizes autonomy and choice is recommended. For example, Bush and Folger's model of Transformative Mediation suggests that:

> *... mediation can give people a sense of their power to solve problems for themselves, even with limited resources, and a sense of control over their lives—it can empower people. Another aspect of the reasoning [is] that mediation can "humanize" people to each other, helping them to look beyond their assumptions and see each other as real persons with real human concerns and needs, even in the midst of a disagreement—it can evoke recognition.*[13]

CONCLUSION

By considering the effects of language, culture, and power, the mediator can structure a mediation that is fair, respectful, and inclusive of the needs of Deaf people. But perhaps most important is the attitude of the mediator: "a good mediator must have a very good attitude regardless of whether or not they can sign. Having a good attitude means understanding [and respecting] the cultural values of the Deaf community."[14] A mediator who is working with Deaf individuals for the first time should seek to familiarize herself with the unique experiences, values, and needs of the Deaf community. The mediator, as steward of the process, is charged with structuring a mediation that accommodates Deaf participants. While the task may seem daunting, having an open mind and a commitment to learning will be handsomely rewarded as the mediator is introduced to a new culture and way of experiencing the world.

REFERENCES

[1] In keeping with recent conventions accepted by members of the Deaf community and many professionals in the field of deafness, "Deaf" with a capital "D" is used when discussing individuals who are members of the Deaf community and consider themselves to be culturally Deaf; "deaf" with a lower case "d" is used to describe an audiological condition.

[2] Rainer, J., Altschuler, K., & Kallman, F. (Eds.). (1963). *Family and mental health problems in a deaf population.* New York: Columbia University.

[3] Cripps, J., & Pizzacalla, H. (1995). Conflict resolution program for the culturally deaf. *Proceedings of the 1995 Conflict Resolution Symposium at Carlton University.* Ottawa, ON: Carlton University Press.

[4] Baker, C., & Padden, C. (1978). *American Sign Language: A look at its structure, history, and community.* Silver Spring, MD: Linstok Press. (Figure 1 depicts the avenues of membership.)

[5] Ibid.

[6] Dolnick, E. (1993, September). Deafness as culture. *Atlantic,* 37 (12).

[7] Sloman, L., Springer, S. & Vachon, M.L. (1993). Disordered communication and grieving in deaf member families. *Family Process* 32 (2) 171–183.

[8] Ibid.

[9] Ibid.

[10] Freire, P. (1970). *Pedagogy of the oppressed.* New York: Continuum Publishing Company.

[11] Ibid., #3.

[12] Smart, J. (2001). *Disability, society and the individual.* Gaithersburg, MD: Aspen.

[13] Bush, R. B., & Folger, J. P. (1994). *The promise of mediation: Responding to conflict through empowerment and recognition.* San Francisco: Jossey-Bass Publishers.

[14] Ibid., #3.

Deaf Culture

WHAT IS IT?

WRITTEN BY

MICHELLE JAY

PERHAPS THE MOST IMPORTANT PART OF LEARNING ASL

Deaf Culture was first truly recognized in 1965 (only about 40 years ago!)

The idea that Deaf people had a culture of their own was first written in the *Dictionary of American Sign Language* by William Stokoe, Carl Croneberg, and Dorothy Casterline.

This was a huge step for Deaf people. Before this book was written, the medical industry and those involved in Deaf education only saw Deaf people in terms of their hearing loss. The thought of Deaf people being a part of their own culture was unheard of.

Carol Padden, a scholar of sign languages at the University of California in San Diego, defines "culture" as a set of learned behaviors of a group of people that share a language, values, rules for behavior, and traditions. Deaf culture consists of all of these things—it is a very vibrant and rich culture.

We only share general information about Deaf Culture in this article, so we highly recommend the book *Don't Just "Sign"... Communicate!: A Student's Guide to ASL and the Deaf Community* if you are learning American Sign Language (ASL). The guide includes all of the essential Deaf Culture information you need to know so you will better understand the Deaf community and be fully prepared to talk to Deaf people.

LANGUAGE

Language and culture go hand-in-hand (no pun intended!) The members of Deaf culture definitely share a common language—American Sign Language, of course!

It was not until the *Dictionary of American Sign Language* was published that ASL was regarded as a real language. William Stokoe was the first to break ASL down into its linguistic components and prove that it truly is a language—not merely "English on the hands" or "pictures in the air" like people thought.

American Sign Language is a living, breathing linguistic masterpiece that is specially made for the Deaf.

VALUES

The culture of the Deaf consists of a few important values:

Language

American Sign Language is the most highly regarded asset of Deaf Culture. Spoken English is almost completely useless to the Deaf. Even if they can learn to read lips, the comprehension of English doesn't even come close to the language of ASL—only 20 to 30 percent of the conversation is understood. If the ears don't work, why would you force them to?

ASL is the natural language for the Deaf. To equate the fluency of English to hearing people, ASL is the match for Deaf people. They are not meant to use a language that is not their own, nonetheless be forced to.

Because of this, a strong goal of Deaf culture is to preserve ASL. There are many language systems that have been invented to try to "help" deaf children learn English (Sign Supported Speech, Signed English, and Cued Speech, to name a few). These are not languages and are not supported in Deaf culture. They have, if anything, deprived deaf children of their true language and ability to communicate effectively.

Not Speaking

Not speaking is highly valued in this culture. Like I stated before, speech is commonly forced on deaf children and represents confinement and deprivation to the Deaf adult. When speech education is forced, deaf children are deprived of one of their core needs—language. The only language that is truly possible and effective is ASL.

An example of the negative use of speech is when a hearing friend of a Deaf person turns and continues conversation as usual with another hearing friend. When this happens, the Deaf person is left out. This is seen as incredibly rude when the person could have used ASL or kept the Deaf friend included on what was being said.

Exaggerated mouth movements can also be seen as rude. There are only a limited number of mouth movements that are used while signing. Much-more-than-necessary mouthing can be seen as making fun of Deaf people (and you don't want that!)

Socializing

Socializing is a very important value of Deaf culture. Because there are so few Deaf people in an area, social lives are invaluable. In a society where the Deaf are commonly misunderstood, the support of others is more than necessary.

Back before text messaging and modern technology, Deaf people would only communicate with each other in person or in letters. They would take advantage of the little time they had to mingle with another Deaf person. And nothing much has changed since then!

Deaf people will stay at a gathering very late to get in as much time as possible with their friends. When a hearing gathering generally ends around 10 at night, a Deaf gathering can end at 3 in the morning!

Literature

Deaf people highly value the literature and art of their culture. There is a wealth of Deaf art, poetry, stories, theatre, media, jokes, and books that teach the culture (most of which are not in a tangible form). Deaf children learn how to fit in with Deaf culture from positive and negative feedback about their behavior and from the stories and literature that are passed down through the generations.

Hearing loss can stir up very strong feelings. The arts offer an outlet for those feelings and always show and support the way Deaf people live their lives—being Deaf and proud!

Deaf art expresses both the positive and negative experiences of the Deaf. I have truly learned a lot about the feelings of Deaf people and their views by studying their artwork.

An example is *Ameslan Prohibited* by Betty G. Miller. The image shows two hands handcuffed together with the fingers cut off. It portrays how Deaf people felt when Ameslan (another name for American Sign Language) was forbidden.

Reading or watching Deaf poetry is also a wonderful learning experience. I recommend watching a video of ASL poetry (such as *Poetry in Motion* by Patrick Graybill, Debbie Rennie and Clayton Valli)—you really can't understand how beautiful ASL poetry is until you see it.

Deaf cultural stories are how Deaf people share their experiences and pass on their knowledge to the next generations. These stories are usually about what it was like growing up deaf, experiencing misunderstandings, etc. Cultural stories are another great way for Deaf people to express themselves.

Deaf theatre is another way for Deaf people to share their experiences. You can find Deaf theatres in the U.S. that perform only Deaf plays that are interpreted for hearing people. If you live near a Deaf theatre, I highly encourage you to see a performance.

Deaf people are also present in the media. My favorite artistic documentary about Deaf culture is the film *Through Deaf Eyes*. If you have not seen this movie, you need to. Two more movies you should see are *Children of a Lesser God* starring Marlee Matlin, a famous Deaf actress, and *Sound and Fury*, which is a documentary about how the deaf community responds to cochlear implants. These movies can teach you a lot about Deaf culture that is difficult to explain in books alone.

There are many famous Deaf stars who have brought the Deaf Community and ASL into people's homes. Linda Bove played Linda the Librarian on *Sesame Street*, Marlee Matlin won an Academy Award for her debut performance in *Children of a Lesser God*, Deanne Bray played Sue Thomas on *Sue Thomas: F.B.Eye*, and Shoshannah Stern is the only deaf actor to ever have a role on two prime-time TV shows at the same time, to name a few.

And let's not forget *Switched at Birth*—a popular television show featured on ABC Family that has truly brought American Sign Language and Deaf Culture into the living rooms of today's generation. It is the first television show to feature several deaf actors/characters and entire scenes shot using only ASL.

Deaf jokes are also an essential part of Deaf literature and are usually passed down "orally". There are two main types of jokes in Deaf culture. The first type is a joke in which the Deaf person wins. These jokes don't necessarily make fun of hearing people, but they favor Deaf culture and the Deaf way of life. The second type is a joke related to the linguistics of ASL. For example, the production or misproduction of a sign can be humorous in certain situations.

ASL not only shares its expressiveness with stories and poetry, it also greatly enhances music. ASL is popularly used in the interpretation of songs. Songs interpreted into ASL aren't used very often in the Deaf community—they are more popular with the hearing and hard-of-hearing ASL crowd—but it is still a common and beautiful Deaf culture art form. And I do know that some members of the Deaf community appreciate song interpretations.

RULES FOR BEHAVIOR

Deaf people are not only part of a like-minded group—they are part of a culture that has a set of learned behaviors that you need to know to be able to "fit in."

Eye Contact

Eye contact is a very important part of signing etiquette. If you break eye contact while a person is signing to you, it is seen as rude. It would be like plugging your ears when someone is speaking to you. It is also important to learn attentive behaviors to use during signed conversations, such as nodding and signing things like "yes," "really," or "wow." If a phone ringing or a knock at the door interrupts you, you need to inform the deaf person why you are looking away.

Don't worry about looking at the signer's hands. You need to learn to see both the signer's hands and the signer's face simultaneously. When you are the one signing, you also need to keep eye contact. Maintaining eye contact communicates interest and respect to the person you are signing with. This behavior is very important in Deaf culture.

Facial Expression

In hearing culture, facial expression is very limited. However, in Deaf culture, facial expression and body movement is required for ASL. Not only does facial expression have a very important role in ASL grammar, but if you do not use facial expressions, you are considered to be a boring signer. In English, this would be like speaking in a monotone voice.

Introducing Yourself

In hearing culture, you normally introduce yourself by your first name only.

Deaf people, however, introduce themselves by their full names, and sometimes even what city they're from or what school they went to. The Deaf community is very small, and Deaf people like to find those specific commonalities with each other.

When you meet a Deaf person for the first time, they will usually ask you a common set of questions. They will most likely ask if you are deaf or hearing, where you went to school (if you are deaf), where you learned American Sign Language (if you are hearing), if your instructor is deaf, etc.

These questions are strongly rooted in Deaf culture. They tell the person how you are connected to the Deaf community and what you have in common.

Labels

The appropriate terms used to refer to Deaf people are very important to know. Some older terms are very offensive and should not be used—like "deaf and dumb" and "deaf mute."

The term "hearing impaired" is often used by political groups and public institutions to refer to anyone with any degree of hearing loss. This term, however, can be offensive and does not distinguish between people with hearing loss and deaf people. Instead, use the phrase "deaf and hard of hearing" to be politically correct.

In hearing culture, the terms used to describe deaf people have to do with their hearing loss. The term "hard of hearing" is better than "deaf." Hard of Hearing people are generally regarded as being easier to communicate with and fit in better with hearing people (this term technically means someone who has a hearing loss who may be able to use the phone with amplification and can understand most speech). Deaf people, on the other hand, are seen as being difficult to communicate with and that they may not even speak.

In Deaf culture, though, the terms are quite the opposite. There is one label for people who are part of Deaf culture...

Deaf.

This label has nothing to do with hearing loss. Regardless of how much better your hearing is than the next guy, you're still all "deaf." Using the term "hard of hearing" can be seen negatively...like you're saying you're better than everyone else (because that's the one-up in hearing culture).

You will also see both the terms "deaf" and "Deaf" used. They are referred to as "little d" and "big D." "Little d" deaf refers to people who have lost their hearing. "Big D" Deaf refers to people who are involved in Deaf culture and share the values, behaviors, and language of that culture. Just because you are deaf, doesn't mean you are Deaf. And in some cases, just because you are Deaf doesn't mean you are deaf (as is the case for some hearing children of Deaf parents—also known as CODAs).

The term "hearing impaired" is seen even more negatively because that term implies that there is something wrong with being deaf (which is the complete opposite of what Deaf people believe!) Most hearing people believe that deafness is a handicap. However, it is not. Deaf people can do everything except hear. Everything! Deafness is not a handicap. The only real handicap of deafness is when deaf children are deprived of true communication—American Sign Language. And that is the true essence of Deaf culture.

THE BEST DEAF CULTURE BOOKS

- Michelle Jay, Don't Just "Sign"... Communicate! A Student's Guide to ASL and the Deaf Community. Judea Media, LLC, 2011.
- Nora Ellen Groce, Everyone Here Spoke Sign Language: Hereditary Deafness on Martha's Vineyard. Harvard University Press, 1985.
- Carol A. Padden and Tom L. Humphries, Inside Deaf Culture. Harvard University Press, 2006.
- Leo Jacobs, A Deaf Adult Speaks Out. Gallaudet University Press, 1974.
- Arden Neisser, The Other Side of Silence: Sign Language and the Deaf Community in America. Knopf, 1983.
- Carol A. Padden and Tom L. Humphries, Deaf in America: Voices from a Culture. Harvard University Press, 1990.
- Sherman Wilcox, American Deaf Culture: An Anthology. Linstock Press, 1989.
- Harlan Lane, Robert Hoffmeister, Ben Bahan, A Journey Into the Deaf-World. DawnSignPress, 1996.
- Harlan Lane, The Mask of Benevolence: Disabling the Deaf Community. DawnSignPress, 1999.
- Paddy Ladd, Understanding Deaf Culture: In Search of Deafhood. Multilingual Matters, 2003.
- John Vickrey Van Cleve and Barry A. Crouch, A Place of Their Own: Creating the Deaf Community in America. Gallaudet University Press, 1989.
- Lois Bragg, Deaf World: A Historical Reader and Primary Sourcebook. NYU Press, 2001.
- H-Dirksen L. Bauman, Open Your Eyes: Deaf Studies Talking. University of Minnesota Press, 2008.

ASL Numbering Systems

WRITTEN BY

LISA KOCH

NUMBERS IN ASL

English has two numbering systems: cardinal and ordinal. Cardinal numbers are 1, 2, 3, 4, 5, and so on. Ordinal numbers are first, second, third, fourth, fifth, and so on. ASL has 14 different numbering systems.

COUNTING NUMBERS

The signs for numbers 1–5 are made with the palm toward the signer. The signs for numbers 6–10 are made with the palm facing away from the signer. The signs for numbers 6–9 are made with the tip of the finger touching the tip of the thumb with a slight bounce.

The signs for numbers 11–15 are made with the palm facing the signer with a repetitive motion where the finger literally "pops out" from the thumb. Numbers 13–15 are made with the extended fingers together.

Numbers 16–19 are made in one of three ways. The first way is to "scratch" the thumb on the inside of the finger. The second way is to sign 16 as 10-6, 17 as 10-7, 18 as 10-8, and 19 as 10-9, with a twist on each one. A third way to produce these numbers is to twist the 6, 7, 8, or 9 repeatedly back and forth.

Numbers 20–29 are produced with the L handshape for 20, and then tapping the index and thumb repeatedly. The number 21 is made with the L and the thumb while the thumb "wiggles." The number 22 is made with the index and middle fingers in a "stamping motion," with the palm facing downward. All multiples of the number 11 are made in this way, with a palm-down stamping motion. For the number 23, the middle finger wiggles while holding the L handshape steady. The number 24 is made with the L handshape and then the 4. The number 25 is produced with the L handshape, palm outward, and then the 5 or the L handshape with all the other fingers wiggling up and down. The number 26 is made with the L and then 6; 27 is made with the L and then 7; 28 is L and then 8; and 29 is L and then 9.

The rest of the counting numbers are fairly easy. The palm faces away from the signer. The number 30 is made with the 3 handshape with the index and middle fingers tapping the thumb repeatedly. Numbers 31–39 are made with the 3 handshape and then the 1, 2, 3, 4, 5, 6, 7, 8, or 9 handshapes, not 30 then 1, 30 then 2, and so on.

Numbers 40, 50, 60, 70, 80, and 90 are made with the fingers tapping the thumb in the same repetitive motion as with the number 30. The number 70 is made with the pinky extended for clarity while the other fingers tap the thumb. Numbers 41–49, 51–59, and 61–66 are performed in a similar way to numbers 31–39.

Numbers 67, 68, 69, 76, 78, 79, 86, 87, 89, 96, 97, and 98 are produced differently. If the first number is smaller than the second number, then there is a small rocking motion inward toward the center of the signer's body, regardless of hand dominance. If the first number is larger than the second number, then there is a small rocking motion outward away from the signer's body.

Multiples of 100 are produced in one of two ways. They can be formed by signing 1, 2, 3, 4, 5, 6, 7, 8, or 9 and then the C handshape. Multiples of 100 can also be produced by wiggling the 1, 2, 3, 4, 5, 6, 7, 8, or 9 repeatedly.

Numbers such as 150 would be 100 and then 50; 210 would be 200 and then 10; 330 would be 300 and then 30; 467 would be 40 then 67; 5076 would be 500 and then 576; 615 would be 600 and then 15; 722 would be 70 and then 22; 880 would be 800 and then 80; and 979 would be 900 and then 79.

Multiples of 1000 are produced with the number 1, 2, 3, 4, 5, 6, 7, 8, or 9 and then tapping the four fingers in the nondominant palm.

Multiples of 1,000,000 are produced with the number 1, 2, 3, 4, 5, 6, 7, 8, or 9 and then tapping the four fingers in the nondominant palm two times.

I've lived here **17** years.

I have **three** children, **one** dog, and **two** cats.

Last week I went fishing. I caught **35** fish.

I decided this Friday that I would have a party: a fish fry. I think **22** people will come.

INFORMATIONAL NUMBERS

Informational (or arbitrary) numbers are always made with the palm facing outward. Informational numbers are used to denote things such as addresses, Social Security numbers, Bible verses, and phone numbers.

ORDINAL NUMBERS

Ordinal numbers are made with the palm facing inward toward the signer when signing first through ninth. For tenth and up, follow the palm orientation for the counting numbers and then add "th," even though in English you might say "rd" or "st," as in first or third.

I live in the **fourth** house.

I like the **seventh** girl.
Call the man up there, the **twelfth** one in line.

RANKING NUMBERS

Numbers denoting a rank order for first through ninth are made with the palm in with the hand moving sideways. For tenth and above, add the "th."
I placed **third**.
He placed **ninth**.
Our team placed **thirteenth**.

AGE

When signing a person's age, counting numbers are used with the index finger of the dominant hand starting on the chin, palm facing outward, for one to five years of age. Move the number outward to the "center" space. Touch the index finger on the chin. Have the number on the hand before you contact the chin. Do not move the hand into the number. For ages 10 years and older, the palm orientation is also the same as the counting numbers. If it is a two-digit number, have the first digit in place on the hand before you touch the chin. Bring the hand out and pause slightly before forming to the second number, not while the hand is in motion.

When using formal register, age numbers are formed with the sign AGE and then the number with the palm facing outward. When using informal register during casual conversations, use the numbers mentioned above. Older Deaf people will use the more formal signs in all situations. For approximate ages, wiggle the number back and forth to mean "approximately." For 30 years of age, wiggle the 3 back and forth. For 60, wiggle the 6 back and forth.
I am **42**.
I have 2 sons: the oldest is **22** and the youngest is **18**.
My mother is **68**, and my dad is in his **70s**.

MONEY

It is not necessary to sign DOLLAR for amounts between $1 and $9. You simply twist the number 1–9 so that the palm turns inward toward the signer. For amounts above $9, add the sign DO LLAR after the number.

The palm orientation for cents is the same as for counting numbers. The contact point, however, is above the dominant eyebrow. The number is already on the hand when the index finger makes contact above the eyebrow.

When dollar amounts are combined with cents, cents are signed differently. For example, $1.45 would be signed 1 DOLLAR (twisting the number 1) and then 45. We already know the first number is a DOLLAR figure, so the following numbers must be cents.

$3.98

$4.72

For dollar amounts over $9, you need to add the DOLLAR sign. If you know that the topic is money, however, you do not need to sign DOLLAR. For example, if you sign SHIRT COST 12 98 (or $12.98), then the topic is obviously about money because you are discussing the cost of the shirt. If you have not specified that the topic is money, however, use the DOLLAR sign. For example, I FIND 12 98 would be unclear. 12 98 what? Be sure to clarify that the topic is money by signing 12 DOLLAR 98. Topic is important.

For dollar amounts through $10 that include 50 cents you can sign 50 cents with the palm facing the signer. Twist the number for 1–9 DOLLAR and then 50 cents with the palm facing inward. For dollar amounts of $11.50 and above, sign 50 cents with the palm facing outward. This only applies to dollar amounts that include 50 cents.

For formal financial reporting situations, use the formal number and include the DOLLAR sign and the decimal point; for example, 125 THOUSAND 589 DOLLAR POINT 52.

Two days ago I went shopping. I bought two pairs of pants and two shirts. The pants cost **$24.95** each. The shirts each cost **$17.98**.

My brother bought an expensive pen for **$5.45**. I was broke so I bought one for **$1.50**.

Last year we set up a Deaf club. We have collected a lot of revenue. We now have **$4800** in the treasury.

Last month I bought a new car. It cost **$9745**. The tax came to **$385**. I put down **$2000**. The monthly payments are **$219.98**.

CLOCK TIME

The contact point for clock time numbers is the back of the nondominant wrist. Remember that age numbers contact with the chin, and cents numbers contact with the area above the dominant eyebrow. Tap the back of the nondominant wrist with the index finger, shaking the number slightly back and forth for 1:00, 2:00, 3:00, 4:00, and 5:00. The number is already on the hand when the index finger makes contact with the back of the wrist. The index finger does not contact the back of the nondominant wrist for 6:00 through 9:00. The contact finger does change to the finger that is used for 6:00, 7:00, 8:00, and 9:00. For 10:00, 11:00, and 12:00, touch the back of the nondominant wrist with the index finger and then sign the number. The signs for 1:00 through 9:00 are made with a slight shake back and forth; 11:00 and 12:00 have a repeated motion.

Hours plus minutes are signed without shaking the hour number. Touch the nondominant wrist with the index finger, form the hour, and then the minutes. Thus, 1:12 would be made without shaking the number 1.

4:18   5:19   2:45   6:22   7:35   8:30   9:54   10:45   12:48

Yesterday I went to the doctor. My appointment was at **4:00**. I arrived at **3:45** and waited until **5:20** until I finally saw the doctor. The doctor finished with me at **6:15**. I arrived home at **7:30**. I made dinner at **8:00**.

To specify am or pm, arm placement will indicate morning, afternoon, or evening. For example, 1 am would be signed with the arm placed downward. Midnight is indicated by the arm placed straight downward.

Two days ago my sister called and said she was coming over to see me at **11:00 am**. She finally showed up at **1:50 pm**.

CALENDAR TIME

Months are indicated by spelling the abbreviations for January, February, August, September, October, November, and December. Spell out the names of March, April, May, June, and July.

Year numbers do require the 10-6, 10-7, 10-8, and 10-9 formation for 16, 17, 18, and 19. To show the first year of a century, sign the century number and then 00. For example, 16 and 00, or 19 and 04. Make sure to indicate the 0.

You should incorporate the numbers 1–9 with the sign for DAY (numerical incorporation). For more than nine days, sign the number and then DAY. Today is signed by repeating the sign for NOW. No movement means NOW PRESENT or CURRENT. The sign for TOMORROW is modified for TWO DAY FUTURE (move the number 2 forward from the chin as you would sign TOMORROW) and THREE DAY FUTURE (move the number 3 forward from the chin.

In the same way, YESTERDAY is modified for TWO DAY PAST and THREE DAY PAST. Move the 2 or 3 backward from the chin as you would for the sign YESTERDAY. Only two and three days in the future or past are modified in this way.

Numbers 1–9 are incorporated into the sign for WEEK. The dominant palm faces downward and the nondominant palm faces upward. For more than nine weeks, sign the number and then WEEK. For one to five weeks in the past, the dominant palm faces the signer and moves backward. For more than nine weeks ago, sign the number, WEEK, and then PAST.

One to nine months is signed by incorporating the number with the sign for MONTH. One to nine months in the future is signed by incorporating the number with the sign for MONTH FUTURE. There is a very slight forward motion of the body with signing future months. One to nine months in the past is signed by incorporating the number with the sign for MONTH PAST. The nondominant hand is held with the palm facing outward. For more than nine months, sign the number and then MONTH. For more than nine months in the future, sign the number and then MONTH FUTURE. For more than nine months in the past, sign the number and then MONTH past.

For years, simply sign the number then YEAR without incorporating the number. Numbers 1–5 are incorporated, though, for past years: 1 YEAR PAST, 2 YEAR PAST, and so on.

My wife's birthday is **February 7. Every year** I try to surprise her. I planned **this year** to order a new car for her. I was waiting for it to come in. She was dying of curiosity wondering what I would give to her. When I was informed by the dealer that the order would arrive late, I told her, "**This year** I'm sorry but I can't give you anything because money is tight." She didn't say anything. **Three weeks** after her birthday the car finally arrived. I took her out and showed her. She asked "what's that?" I told her "it's your birthday gift, even though your birthday was **three weeks** ago!" She was so excited. She has driven the car **every day.** She said "You must check the oil **every month. Every week** you must check the water level." Then something happened to the car: the motor froze up. We had to send it back to the shop. We waited **three months** for them to fix it and get it back.

PRONOUNS

Pronouns such as WE and THEY are not number specific. ME, HE, SHE, IT are singular pronouns.

US –TWO		YOU-THREE	TWO-of-US
THOSE-TWO	YOU-FOUR	THREE-of-US	
YOU- TWO	YOU-FIVE	FOUR-of-US	

The **four** of them, my son and his **three** friends, went out to eat.
The **three** of us, my siblings and I, were born in Texas.
My cousins, the **three** of them, were born in Minnesota.
My neighbor, his wife and I, the **three** of us are very good friends.

HEIGHT OF PEOPLE

To tell a person's height, produce the "foot" number and then raise the hand slightly upward for inches. For babies, sign the number and then INCHES.
  6'2"
  4"0'
I am 5'11" and my wife is 5'4". My son is 5'10". My other son is 6'2".
My oldest son's wife just gave birth to a baby that was **21 inches.**

WEIGHT OF PEOPLE

The WEIGHT and POUNDS signs can be used. However, if you know that the topic of the conversation is weight, just sign the weight number. For a baby, sign LB for pounds and OZ for ounces.
  I weigh **210** but my wife weighs **118.**
  My 10-year old daughter weighs **75 pounds.** When she was born she weighed **4 pounds, 7 ounces.**

My neighbor is enormous. He weighs **472 pounds.** His wife is skinny and weighs **99 pounds**.

MEASUREMENT

Follow the palm orientation used for counting numbers.

1 quart

8 pints

When signing measurements that include fractions, if the whole number palm orientation faces outward, sign the fraction with the palm facing outward. For whole numbers that use palm orientation facing inward, fractions also are made palm facing inward. The fraction, therefore, maintains the same palm orientation as the whole number.

8 ½

4 ¾

Inches are signed as IN and yard as YD. If you have two numbers, such as with 2 × 4, the palm faces outward, as with informational numbers.

Three years ago I built a shed. The shed measures **16 × 24.** I had to go get all the lumber together. I bought 210 **2 × 4**'s. I bought 48 **2 × 6**'s. I bought 16 pieces of **4/8** plywood for the floor. I had to get decking for the roof in **4 × 8** sheets. I bought 20 of them. My friend and I built the shed in 2 days.

My friend and I went bass fishing in a tournament. We fished all day and my friend won the championship. He caught a bass that weighed **8 pounds, 9 ounces.** It was **25 3/4 inches** long and **17 inches** in diameter. The prize was a **17-foot** boat. I'm jealous!

SPORTS SCORES

There are many variations in sports scores. When giving scores when you do not support either team, first set up referent locations for the teams that are playing. Give the score of the winner first and the score of the loser second.

If you support one team over another, sign the score of the team that you support first. Sign the winning score close to the chest and move the hand outward to give the score of the other team.

Football games have quarters. You can use the 4 handshape to represent each quarter. Deaf people refer to the players by their jersey numbers. The number of the player is signed in front of the chest area.

For stopwatch times, sign seconds by dropping the first number down to indicate there is a decimal point. For minutes and seconds, sign the first number point then second number.

When I was in school, a schoolmate of mine ran the 100-yard dash in **9.4 seconds.** I ran the 100-yard dash in **11.1 seconds.** Darn.

MATHEMATICAL NUMBERS

The signs MULTIPLY, DIVIDE, ADD, and SUBTRACT can be used for mathematical operations. It is common for Deaf people to sign one number on each hand along with the operation to be performed. The numbers can be oriented horizontally or vertically.

ASL Name Signs

WRITTEN BY

BARBARA A. DIMOPOULOS

WHAT IS "GLOSSING"?

- "Glossing" is a fancy word for written ASL.
- Yet, ASL does not have a written form, so this is a way to **keep note** of ASL.

WHAT DOES ASL GLOSSING LOOK LIKE?

- Each sentence is written on a different line.

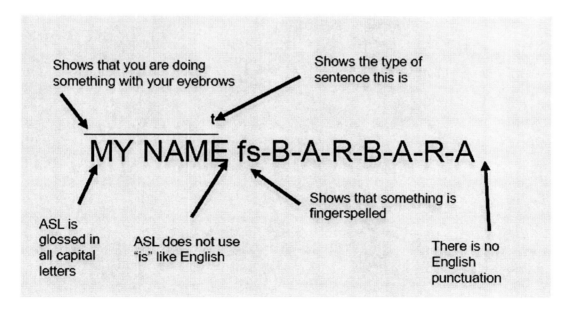

Diagram with "MY NAME fs-B-A-R-B-A-R-A" labeled with annotations:
Shows that you are doing something with your eyebrows
Shows the type of sentence this is
ASL is glossed in all capital letters
ASL does not use "is" like English
Shows that something is fingerspelled
There is no English punctuation

YOUR TURN!

Gloss these sentences:
1. I live in Sacramento.
2. Where do you live?
3. Are you attending CSUS?
4. What's your name?

ANSWERS

1. ME LIVE SAC
2. WHERE YOU LIVE

YOU LIVE WHERE
WHERE YOU LIVE WHERE

3. CSUS YOU GO-TO
4. YOU CALLED WHAT

WHAT YOU CALLED
NAME WHAT
NAME

NAME SIGNS

WRITTEN BY

LISA KOCH

One aspect of Deaf culture is the use of personal "name signs." Name signs are used to identify persons instead of fingerspelling names, which can be tedious. Unlike names in spoken languages, where most people share many of the same conventional, common names, such as John in English, Maria in Spanish, or Makoto in Japanese, name signs in ASL are unique to each individual. ASL does not have specific name signs for common English names. Instead, name signs are individualized for each person.

Within the Deaf community, a name sign is used in place of spelling out the whole name. These signs are used to identify a person, similar to a nickname. Sign names are used for introductions and references to that person, but in conversation references to people present are made by indexing or gesturing. The Deaf will sometimes assign you a name. A typical method is to take the first letter of your name and put it in the location of a sign that means something that you do. A person cannot give himself or herself a name sign. Someone needs to come up with a name sign for that person.

There are two basic types of name signs: arbitrary and descriptive. Arbitrary, or random, name signs do not describe anything about the person but instead just follow linguistic conventions for name signs. Descriptive name signs are based on something about the individual's physical attributes, personality, hobbies, or past experiences. A tall, small, or thin person might have a name sign with that characteristic. One person may have several descriptive name signs, each given by a different group within the community. If the person is a supervisor at work, the worst player at poker, and a loving father at home, he may have three name signs to reflect these three different characteristics, or he may just have the same name sign in all three situations.

Both descriptive and arbitrary name signs tend to incorporate the first letter of the person's first and/or last name. To avoid confusion, name signs in general are not identical to already existing word signs unless a person's name is also a common word. For example, an individual with the last name of Brown might be given the sign BROWN as a name sign. However, Deaf people tend to try to avoid giving name signs that could be easily misunderstood because they look like other, similar signs.

Whereas in the English language a person has a first, middle, and last name, in ASL a person's name is a one-word unit. A name sign will not change its form into a shorter version, like from Robert to Rob.

A new kind of name sign is showing up in the Deaf community, probably due to hearing adults learning sign language as a second language. This new sign, called a nontraditional name sign, is a blend of the arbitrary and descriptive name signs. An example is the hand-shape S (used to represent the first letter of the person's name) placed next to the eye, twisting the wrist up and down to represent that the person winks a lot. If it was descriptive, it would not use an alphabetical handshape. If it was arbitrary, the location would not be at the eye but at the nearest acceptable location, the temple.

An unwritten rule in Deaf culture is that only Deaf or Hard of Hearing persons can give people name signs. It is taboo for hearing people to give name signs. Some argue that hearing ASL teachers can give name signs for use in class only. The problem with this practice is that students often tend to use those name signs outside of class, which can be a bad thing when members of the Deaf community hear that a hearing person is giving name signs. The one exception to this cultural norm of only Deaf or Hard of Hearing persons giving name signs is when hearing parents who learn ASL and who have deaf children give their children name signs.

Unlike names in spoken languages, which are used to get a person's attention when addressing the person directly, in ASL the waving of the hand vertically with the palm oriented down is used to get people's attention. Thus, there is no need to sign a person's name when directly addressing a person. Therefore, ASL has evolved so that signers generally do not use a person's name sign when conversing directly with that person. Name signs are only used when talking to other people about an individual. This characteristic of the language enables some people in the Deaf community to go years without learning others' names while still being able to converse with those same people.

Not all Deaf people have name signs. Some prefer to always have their names finger-spelled. And, people still fingerspell their names when meeting each other for the first time, even if they have name signs. When meeting a new person, if a person has a name sign, he or she will show the name sign after fingerspelling his or her name. Often, if the sign looks interesting or is a descriptive name sign, the person is asked to explain how and why he or she received that name sign. Short names such as those with four letters or fewer often are just fingerspelled instead of the person receiving a name sign.

A deaf person usually will not have a name sign if he or she is the only deaf person in the community. The same is true for deaf children born to hearing parents. The deaf children do not get a name sign until they are around others from the Deaf community.

A potential downside to name signs is that once they are conferred and made known to the public they generally cannot be changed. The person will continue to be called by the same name until retirement. The good thing about name signs is that over time a sign will undergo morphological changes, and those who did not already know the origin of the name sign will not get its intended meaning. A shift in location or a change in hand configuration is enough to erase the track that leads to the name sign's etymology. A name sign can be changed if social conditions require it. If someone moves into town and finds a person living there with an identical name sign, then the newcomer would have to change it. It is also common for the elder or the person who has had the name sign the longest to keep it. If a Deaf and hearing person had the same name sign, then the hearing person would be expected to change it. It can be done either by modifying the name sign or replacing it with a completely new name sign. A person can also use the ASL name sign modification system. Adding an additional handshape would modify the existing name sign. An example would be adding the first letter of your last name.

Are Sign Languages "Real" Languages?

WRITTEN BY

LISA KOCH

 **L**anguage is a system of symbols used in a uniform way by a number of people who are of the same community, nation, geographical area, or cultural tradition. Language enables people to communicate with one another.

Human language involves both receptive and productive use. Receptive language use occurs during the comprehension or understanding of words and sentences. Productive language use involves idea generation and the articulation of words in speech. Both reception and production utilize the four basic structural components of language: phonology, semantics, grammar, and pragmatics.

Phonology is the system of the sound segments that humans use to build words. Each language has a different set of these segments, or phonemes, and children quickly come to recognize and then produce the speech segments that are characteristic of their native language.

Semantics is the system of meanings that are expressed by words and phrases. In order to serve as a means of communication, words must have a shared or conventional meaning. Picking out the correct meaning for each new word is a major learning task for children.

Grammar is the system of rules by which words and phrases are arranged to make meaningful statements. Children need to learn how to use the ordering of words to mark grammatical functions such as the subject or direct object. Grammar specifies the order in which the symbols of a language may be combined to make up legitimate statements. Human languages have rather relaxed informal grammars that we pick up as children.

Pragmatics is the system of patterns that determine how humans can use language in different social settings for specific conversational purposes. Children learn that conversations customarily begin with a greeting, require turn taking, and concern a shared topic. They come to adjust the content of their communications to match their listener's interests, knowledge, and language ability.

A language is spoken (or signed) according to the rules that have been developed by the community that uses the language. Human communication, either spoken or written, consists of the use of words in a structured and conventional way. Language can also be a nonverbal method of expression or communication.

The American Speech Language Hearing Association (ASHA) states that language is made up of socially shared rules that include the following:

- What words mean (e.g., *star* can refer to a bright object in the night sky or a celebrity)
- How to make new words (e.g., friend, friendly, unfriendly)
- How to put words together (e.g., "Peg walked to the new store" rather than "Peg walk store new")
- What word combinations are best in what situations ("Would you mind moving your foot?" could quickly change to "Get off my foot, please!" if the first request did not produce results)

WHAT IS A "SIGNED" LANGUAGE?

ASL is a visual/gestural language, distinct from English and other spoken languages, from sign languages used in other countries, and from English-based sign systems used in the United States (such as manually coded English systems). ASL is the predominant language used by the American Deaf community. It is used most frequently for face-to-face communication and is learned either as a first or second language. ASL is a fully developed language, one of hundreds of naturally occurring signed languages of the world, with a complex grammatical structure. Consider the diversity of signed languages:

- About 70 million Deaf people use sign language as their first language or mother tongue.
- Each country has one or sometimes two or more sign languages.
- At least 25 sign languages are used in Africa.
- At least 35 sign languages are used in North and South America.
- 41 sign languages are used in Asia and the Asia-Pacific area.
- 44 sign languages used in Europe.
- 18 sign languages are used in the Middle East.

American ASL users are members of American culture. In addition, they participate in a rich and vibrant Deaf culture that has its own history, arts (e.g., dance, theater, poetry), and customs.

Writing systems have been developed for ASL, but none are widely used to record ASL literature. However, a large body of ASL literature is available in movies, videotapes, and CDs.

ASL is a language in and of itself, with its own grammar and vocabulary. ASL is a visual and manual language made up of signs created with the hands, facial expressions, and body posture and movement. ASL maintains conceptually accurate communication.

American Sign Language is not the same as American Sign Language (ASL). ASL is not pantomime or a simple gestural code representing the surrounding spoken language.

ASL is considered its own language due to its unique rules of grammar, which differ from those of English. In stark contrast, manually coded English (MCE) systems are not distinct languages. MCE systems borrow ASL signs but use English sentence structure. Signs have been invented to express components of English grammar not found in ASL. Pidgin Signed English (PSE) falls somewhere in the middle by preserving the conceptual meaning of ASL while using a more English-like word order.

The ASL continuum describes the contrasts between signed languages, including:

- Pidgin Signed English (PSE)
- Manually coded English (MCE)
- English

PSE describes naturally occurring varieties that incorporate ASL signs in a flexible English grammatical order. English is mouthed exactly as spoken when interpreted. Signs are used with an attempt to retain the conceptual meaning of ASL rather than English, so that "right" would be signed different ways depending on its conceptually accurate meaning.

MCE is the term for systems that encode English in manual form. MCE systems borrow ASL signs, but use English sentence structure. These systems of visual English are attempts to precisely represent the English language, both its grammar and vocabulary, through speech reading. Signs are placed in English order, and signs are used to represent English grammatical forms, such as suffixes and prefixes. Many systems of sign English have been developed in response to the desire of some educators to teach English to deaf children. Controversy surrounds the use of the many of these English sign systems. Studies show that MCE, due to its inability to conceptually translate information, may be detrimental to acquiring literacy. Examples of MCE are Signing Exact English (SEE), LOVE, Manual English, Signed English, and many other derivatives.

ASL maintains conceptually accurate communication. It is a language in and of itself, with its own grammar and vocabulary. Over 60 percent of ASL communication depends on expression and facial grammar, with minimal mouth movements. It conveys ideas, information, and emotion with as much range, complexity, and versatility as spoken languages. ASL is the language typically used among Deaf adults. ASL is not encoded English, nor is it universal.

Because ASL has its own grammar system, separate from that of English, it means that ASL grammar has its own rules for phonology, morphology, syntax, and pragmatics.

Are the natural signed languages that are used by many deaf persons throughout the world "real" languages?

Signed languages are indeed "real" languages, as demonstrated by the following sources of evidence:

1. **Linguistic analyses of natural signed languages.** Linguistic analyses of natural signed languages around the world have revealed that they have the same linguistic properties as the world's spoken languages. Like spoken languages, signed languages have evolved naturally. No person (hearing or deaf), actually invented any of the world's signed languages. Like spoken languages, natural signed languages are passed down from one generation of language users to another, and the people who use particular signed languages constitute distinct social and cultural groups. Moreover, signed languages are nonuniversal; that is, there is no single signed language used by all deaf people around the world. They are also nonconcrete; that is, they are not made

up of "concrete pictures," mime, or "gestures in the air." Natural signed languages have the full abstract and expressive capacity, as well as the strict grammatical regularities, of spoken languages.

ASL exhibits grammatical organization at the same three levels found in spoken language: (a) a sublexical level of structuring internal to the sign, identical to the phonetic, phonemic, and syllabic levels of language organization; (b) a level that specifies the precise ways that meaningful units are bound together to form complex signs and signs to form sentences, identical to the morphological and syntactic levels of language organization; (c) a level that specifies the precise ways that sentences are joined into conversational patterns, identical to the discourse and pragmatic levels of language organization.

Complete human languages are not restricted to the speech channel. Signed languages possess all of the linguistic features that have been identified as being the essential, universal features of the world's spoken languages.

2. **Sociolinguistic analyses of natural signed languages.** Signed languages exhibit the same sociolinguistic patterns observed in spoken languages. Like spoken languages, signed languages undergo change over time, and they demonstrate the same types of historical changes that are seen in spoken languages. Natural signed languages demonstrate strikingly similar patterns of change, variation, and social and cultural use that are common to the world's spoken languages.

3. **Biological analyses of the status of natural signed languages in the human brain.** A common misconception is that spoken language is fundamentally superior to signed language or that sign is "inferior" or "secondary" to speech. At the heart of the misconception is the notion that signed languages are biologically inferior to spoken languages. Why is this so? The answer involves a three-tiered set of related assumptions. First, a common quip is that "most people speak, so speaking must be better." I call this the "more is better" assumption. Second, drawing from the observation that "most people speak," people have further assumed that this must "prove" that speech alone has been selected for over the development or evolution of the species (phylogeny). Third, the assumption that speech has been selected for over human evolution has implicitly been used to support the core critical assumption about the biological foundations of human language: the brain must be neurologically set for speech early in the developmental history of individual human organisms (ontogeny).

Deaf children, who are exposed to signed languages from birth acquire these languages on an identical maturational time course as hearing children acquire spoken languages. Deaf children acquiring signed languages from birth do so without any modification, loss, or delay to the timing, content, and maturational course associated with reaching all linguistic milestones observed in spoken language. Beginning at birth and continuing through age three, speaking and signing children exhibit the identical stages of language acquisition.

Researchers have found that hearing children exposed to both signed and spoken languages from birth (e.g. when one parent signs and the other parent speaks) demonstrate no preference for speech whatsoever, even though they can hear. Instead, they acquire both the signed and the spoken language to which they are being exposed on an identical maturational timetable (the timing of the onset of all linguistic milestones occurs at the same time in both the signed and spoken modalities).

Results from studies of early language acquisition provide especially strong evidence relevant to assessing whether signed languages are indeed real languages. Here we see clearly that the prevailing assumption about the biological foundations of human language—indeed, the very assumption upon which notions of the alleged biological superiority of speech over sign rests—is not supported when the relevant studies are conducted. Specifically, no evidence has been found that the newborn brain is neurologically set exclusively for speech in early language ontogeny. No evidence has been found that speech is biologically more "special," more "privileged," or "higher" in status than sign in early language ontogeny. Instead, the key, persistent research finding that has emerged is this: the biological mechanisms in the brain that underlie early human language acquisition do not appear to differentiate between spoken versus signed language input. Both types of input appear to be processed equally in the brain.

Hearing children who are exposed exclusively to signed languages from birth through early childhood (i.e., they receive little or no systematic spoken language input whatsoever), achieve each and every linguistic milestone (manual babbling, "first signs," "first two-signs," and so forth) in signed language on the identical time course as has been observed for hearing children acquiring spoken language and deaf children acquiring signed language. Thus, entirely normal language acquisition occurred in these hearing children (a) without the use of auditory and speech perception mechanisms and (b) without the use of the motoric mechanisms for the production of speech.

What is most interesting about these research findings is that the modality "switch" can be "thrown" after birth regarding whether a child acquires language on the hands or the language on the tongue. Such findings have led me to propose a new way to construe human language ontogeny (see especially Petitto 1993a, 1993b). Speech and sound are not critical to human language acquisition. Instead, there appears to be a stunning, biologically based equipotentiality (the principle of equipotentiality is the idea that the rate of learning is independent of the combination of conditioned and unconditioned stimuli that are used in classical conditioning.) of the modalities (spoken and signed) to receive and produce natural language in ontogeny (Petitto 1994).

Can a signed "language" (manual articulation, visual transmission) possibly have the same sort of complexity, systematicity, and expressive power as a spoken one (vocal tract articulation, auditory transmission)?

Although not all deaf individuals use ASL, ASL is not used exclusively by the deaf. ASL is strongly associated with Deaf ethnic identity and cultural heritage. Ethnicity, as defined by National Council of Social Studies, is characterized by the following:
- Origins that precede or are external to the state (e.g., indigenous or immigrant groups)
- Group membership that is involuntary
- Ancestral tradition rooted in shared sense of peoplehood
- Distinctive value orientations and behavioral patterns
- Influence of the group on the lives of its members
- Group membership influenced by how members define themselves and how they are defined by others

ASL plays an extremely significant role in the identification of an individual as a member of (American) Deaf culture. Before the eighteenth century, deaf people, in general, were unable to learn language formally. They were viewed as 'dumb' and not recognized as persons under the law. Deaf people were also limited to the most menial of work.

Things changed in mid-eighteenth-century France. Abbé de l'Épeé discovered that a community of deaf people in Paris had developed a language. He formed a school in 1755 to teach French and French Sign Language (FSL) to the deaf. In France, deaf people were recognized as having rights according to the Declaration of the Rights of Man and the Citizen.

In the early nineteenth century, Thomas Gallaudet went to England and France to find a way to teach a deaf child. England was oralist: deaf people were required to learn English, and signing was suppressed. France was manualist: the deaf were trained in French and FSL, using FSL as their first language.

Gallaudet persuaded Laurent Clerc, a deaf Frenchman, to return to the United States. In 1817, they established the Connecticut Asylum for the Education and Instruction of Deaf and Dumb Persons (now the American School for the Deaf in Hartford, Connecticut). ASL is therefore a member of the French Sign Language family; other languages in this family include Irish Sign Language (ISL) and Québécois Sign Language (LSQ).

Other sign languages have developed that are not mutually intelligible. ASL is not a form of "signed English"; ASL (as well as other signed languages) is a distinct linguistic system. But does it have the "universal design features" that have been posited on the basis of years of study of spoken languages, such as arbitrariness, systematicity, compositionality, and discreteness/combinatoric patterning?

ICONICITY

Does the perceptible form of a sign match up with the object or action being represented? ASL is more iconic than spoken language, but its iconicity is limited. Moreover, when we take a close look at ASL signs, we can see that they have building blocks that are formally comparable to the building blocks of the corresponding units in spoken languages: words and morphemes.

ASL can similarly be broken down into four basic components:
- Handshape

- Location
- Movement type
- Palm orientation

If any of these components are changed, the meaning of the sign is changed. For example, the signs for UNCLE and COUSIN differ in handshape. The signs for MOTHER and FATHER differ only in location. The signs for THING and CHILDREN as well as SOCK and STAR differ in palm orientation. The signs for PAPER and SCHOOL differ in movement.

The signs for WAIT and FIVE differ only in that WAIT is signed with two hands and FIVE is signed with one hand.

Pronouns used in ASL have compositional (and arbitrary) structure.
- Extended index: NOMINATIVE/ACCUSATIVE
- Flat hand: POSSESSIVE
- Simple point: SINGULAR
- Arc movement: PLURAL

WH- QUESTIONS

Wh- questions in ASL have two interesting features. Wh- words appear on the right periphery instead of the left periphery (at the end of a question, instead of at the beginning). They require "wh- intonation," which is realized through nonmanual syntactic markings (furrowed brow, slight headshake), which can target just the wh- phrase or spread across the sentence to which it is adjoined.

ASL has grammatical complexity and systematicity that is parallel to that of spoken languages. The fact that we see this despite the significant difference in modality suggests that there are deep and unique properties of language at work.

SIGN LANGUAGE AND THE BRAIN

In cases of trauma to the left hemisphere of the brain, speakers of sign languages show language deficits similar to those who speak spoken languages. In one brain imaging study, Pettito et al. showed that sign languages activate the same areas of the left hemisphere as spoken languages, rather than the right hemisphere areas involved in visual cognition.

CONCLUSION

Sign languages have the same kind of structural complexity, systematicity, and expressive power as spoken languages (a familiar refrain). They perform the same social and cultural functions as spoken languages, serving as central vehicles of group identity, pride, and achievement.

The vehicle is not as important as the design!

REFERENCES

Kennedy, Chris. 2007. "Are Signed Languages Real Languages?" PowerPoint presentation for Language Myths and Realities course, http://semantics.uchicago.edu/kennedy/classes/sum07/myths/myths8%5Bsignlgs%5D.pdf.

Klima, Edward, and Ursula Bellugi. 1979. *The Signs of Language*. Boston, MA: Harvard University Press.

Padden, Carol A., and Tom L. Humphries. 1988. *Deaf in America: Voices from a Culture*. Cambridge: Harvard University Press.

Petitto, Laura Ann. 1994. "Are Signed Languages 'Real' Languages? Evidence from American Sign Language and Langue des Signes Quebeoise." *Signpost* (International Quarterly of the Sign Linguistics Association) 7, 3: 1–10.

Valli, Clayton, and Ceil Lucas. 1993. *Linguistics of American Sign Language*. Washington, DC: Gallaudet University Press.

Wilcox, Sherman, and Joy Kreeft Peyton. 1999. "American Sign Language as a Foreign Language." University of New Mexico Center for Applied Linguistics Digest, February, http://www.cal.org/resources/digest/ASL.html.

ASL Grammar Summary

WRITTEN BY

LISA KOCH

What equals "correct grammar" often is determined by group consensus. Consensus occurs when an opinion or decision is reached by a group as a whole. Political or governmental bodies try to "come to a consensus" on issues. Coming to a consensus does not mean that everyone agreed with every aspect of a decision, but rather that the group as a whole was willing to support it. That is how it is with American Sign Language (ASL). Many of the older folks do not always agree with signs used by the younger folks.

The grammar of a language is decided by the group of people who use the language. New grammar rules come into existence when enough members of the group have spoken (signed). One speaks (or signs) a language according to the rules that have been developed by the community that uses the language. ASL is tied to the Deaf community. Members of the Deaf community use their language in a certain way. That "certain way" is what constitutes ASL grammar.

ASL has its own grammar system, separate from that of English. What this means is that ASL grammar has its own rules for phonology, morphology, syntax, and pragmatics. In general, ASL sentences follow a TOPIC–COMMENT arrangement. Another name for the word comment is predicate. A predicate is simply a word or phrase that says something about a topic. In general, the subject of a sentence is the topic. The predicate is the comment.

When discussing past and future events, the time frame is established before the rest of the sentence. This gives us a TIME–TOPIC–COMMENT structure. For example, "Last week I washed my car" would be WEEK-PAST ME WASH MY CAR in ASL.

Like most other languages, ASL has a set of rules that it follows when being signed. You will be tested various times on your knowledge of these rules, because they are key to learning true ASL. An acronym you can use to remember the rules is TRIPSTONCL.

1.   Topic/comment
2.   Rhetorical
3.   Information seeking

4. Pronominalization
5. Simple yes/no
6. Tense with Time
7. Ordering of simple sentences
8. Negation
9. Conditional
10. Long yes/no

TOPIC/COMMENT

In a simple TOPIC–COMMENT sentence, the topic is described first, followed by the comment.
Example: HER MONEY LOST, SHE UPSET.
English: "She's upset that she lost her money."
The topic is described first ("her money was lost"), followed by the comment ("she was upset").

RHETORICAL

In a rhetorical question, the signer asks a question and then answers it.
Example: ME KNOW ASL? YES.
English: "I know ASL."
The signer asked a person a question, and then answered it; by doing so, we know that that person knows ASL.

INFORMATION SEEKING

Simple questions that ask for information can have a variety of sentence structures and sometimes rely on nonmanual signals to distinguish them from declarative sentences.
Example: AGE YOU?
English: "How old are you?"
This question is short and simple, but the sentence structure does not really have much to change though. Normally, nonmanuals are used in all three question situations.

PRONOMINALIZATION

Pronouns are indicated by pointing to either a person or thing that is present or a place in the signing space that is used as a referent point for a person or thing. Pointing is mostly done with the index finger, but eye gazing and other handshapes are sometimes used.
Example: MY BROTHER, HE VISIT ME.

English: "My brother is visiting me."

In this case, the pronominalization was when HE was used. You could either point at the brother or a spot in your signing space to refer to as "he."

SIMPLE YES/NO

These are short yes/no questions. The order of the signs varies.

Example: YOU EXERCISE WANT? (or) YOU WANT EXERCISE?

English: "Do you want to exercise?"

The question is short and the answer would be a yes or a no. The order of the signs could be moved around and mean the same thing.

TENSE WITH TIME

The time sign is placed at the beginning or near the beginning of a sentence.

Example: ME YESTERDAY, STAY HOME.

English: "I stayed home yesterday."

The time sign YESTERDAY is located near the beginning of the sentence.

ORDERING OF SIMPLE SENTENCES

In simple sentences, the verb can be placed before or after the object of the sentence.

Example: ME PLAY GAME. (or) ME GAME PLAY.

English: "I'm playing a game."

The sentence is short and simple, and we can move the verb around and not have it change the meaning of the sentence.

NEGATION

You can negate a thought by placing a negative sign before the verb or by first describing a topic and then signing the appropriate negative sign or giving a negative head shake.

Example: ME NOT WATCH FOOTBALL GAME.

English: "I'm not watching the football game."

In this case, the sign NOT was the negation portion of the sentence, making the sentence negative.

CONDITIONAL

In a conditional sentence, the condition is described first, and then the outcome of the condition is described.

Example: SUPPOSE SHE SEE ME, ME HAVE TO LEAVE.

English: "I will have to leave if she sees me."

In most conditional statements, the sign SUPPOSE is used. The condition is said first ("suppose she sees me"), and then the outcome comes afterward ("I'll have to leave").

LONG YES/NO

Long yes/no questions sometimes use a TOPIC–COMMENT format.

Example: CAT BLACK TREE CLIMB, YOUR?

English: "Is that black cat climbing the tree yours?"

The question is longer than a simple yes/no questions, and the topic is described before the comment (YOUR).

When you listen to someone speak, you listen to the tone and rise or fall of the person's voice (intonation). These variations add meaning to the message. In ASL, these variations are shown by facial and body expression.

Facial movements and body language are a very important part of ASL. Users of ASL tend to use a lot of facial expressions to clarify and extend the meanings of their signs. How you use your face also helps establish if you are asking a question and whether that question is open-ended or if it should be answered with a simple yes or no.

In ASL, facial expressions are an important part of communication. The facial expressions you use while doing a sign will affect the meaning of that sign. When signing QUIET, if an exaggerated or intense facial expression is added, you are signing VERY QUIET. This also works when signing words such as INTERESTING versus VERY INTERESTING, and FUNNY versus VERY FUNNY.

A nonmanual signal is a change in your facial expression; the tilt, shake, or nod of your head; and/or the hunching of one or both shoulders when used to indicate meaning. If such movements are not used to indicate meaning, then they are not signals.

The term nonmanual marker refers to a signal that you do without using your hands that influences (marks) the meaning of something else that you are signing.

A nonmanual marker is always a nonmanual signal, but a nonmanual signal is not always a nonmanual marker. If a nonmanual signal is used as an independent sign, then it is not called a marker. For example, a head shake "no" is not marking some other sign, it simply signals (signing) the meaning of "no." In this case, the nonmanual signal is not a marker; it is a nonmanual "sign."

Declarative statement	Neutral facial expression
Yes/no question	Body forward, head out, eyebrows raised, forehead wrinkled Example: "Are you going to the party?"
Wh- (information) question	Body forward, head out and/or tilted, eyebrows furrowed Example: "Where are you going?"
Rhetorical question	Body back, head tilted, forehead wrinkled, eyebrows raised Example: "I'm late; Why? Because I had a car accident."
Negative statement	Body back, chin down, upper lip up, nose wrinkled Example: "I don't like that girl."
Conditional statement	Head, body, and eye gaze shift If portion: eyebrows raised Then portion: neutral facial expression Example: "If it rains tomorrow, I will go to the movies."

As mentioned earlier, ASL sentences follow a TOPIC–COMMENT arrangement. In general, the subject of a sentence is the topic. The predicate is the comment that says something about a topic.

When discussing past and future events, establish a time frame before the rest of the sentence, which results in the TIME–TOPIC–COMMENT structure.

You need to place the time indicator at the beginning of the sentence to set up the tense and raise your eyebrows. This applies to the past and future tense in ASL. If a tense marker is not used, assume that the signer is referring to the present tense. Once a tense marker is established, it is not necessary to use another tense marker, unless the tense changes.

Time indicators are glossed (i.e., written) as __ti__.

The nonmanual marker used for yes/no questions is glossed as q.

The nonmanual marker is not used until the end of the sentence:

1. Raise eyebrows.
2. Tilt head with shoulders forward.
3. Hold the last sign until the "listener" begins responding.

The nonmanual marker for wh- questions is glossed as whq. In each sentence, the wh-question word is signed at the end of the sentence. Again, notice that the nonmanual marker is not used until the end of the sentence:

1. Squeeze eyebrows.
2. Tilt head with shoulders forward.
3. Hold last sign until listener begins to respond.

The nonmanual marker for rhetorical questions is glossed as rhq and is the same as used for yes/no questions.

1. Raise eyebrows.
2. Tilt head with shoulders slightly forward.

3. Hold the last sign until the listener begins responding.

To affirm that a statement is correct, gloss   y__ to indicate a head nod.

When someone is excited, surprised, or very angry, it is common to show this in ASL by increasing the intensity and the speed of signing. Nonmanual markers are not used to designate exclamation in ASL.

The nonmanual marker used in ASL for negation is glossed as __n__. This nonmanual marker is accompanied by squeezed eyebrows and a head shake. The negative sign NOT can be omitted if using a negative facial expression and the __n__ head nod. Negative prefixes (e.g., un-, im-, in-, dis-) can be replaced with NOT.

Use NOT for negative contractions such as don't or isn't.

Use CAN'T for cannot.

The signs for WON'T and REFUSE are the same as mouthing "won't."

ASL grammar sometimes repeats the subject pronoun at the end of a sentence; for example, "I TEACHER I." This is perfectly acceptable ASL grammar. You can also sign it as "I TEACHER" or "TEACHER I." Think of the repeated pronoun as filling the same function as vocal inflection does for hearing people. It is used when asking questions or emphasizing statements. Don't mouth the repeated pronoun in the same sentence.

In ASL the signs WITH or AND are not needed. For example, the sentence "Do you like cookies and milk" would be "YOU LIKE COOKIES MILK" in ASL.

The indefinite articles a and an and the definite article the are not signed in ASL. They are not needed in ASL discourse to understand the conversation. In addition, signing these words is cumbersome. One exception is if the article is part of the name of a title, such as in THE LONG SUMMER.

English "prefers" the plural, whereas ASL "prefers" the singular. In most cases, you need to change the plural form of an English word to a singular ASL sign. ASL is always singular unless noted otherwise.

Signs can be emphasized by using quantifiers. A signer can "emphasize" that something is plural by:
- Using a number
- Using a demonstrative pronoun
- Duplicating or repeating the sign
- Using a plural pronoun
- Using a classifier

Like English, ASL sentences "should have" a verb. A complete sentence contains a noun and a verb. There are exceptions, however; for example, "Your name?" and "What time?" Also, ASL does not have verb conjugations in many cases.

ASL does not use to-be (state of being) verbs.

Modals are helping or auxiliary verbs, such as NEED TO, SHOULD, MUST, CAN, WOULD, MIGHT, and COULD. A modal can be placed before or after a main verb or before and after for emphasis.

ASL uses present tense verbs for both past and present tenses. The time frame is indicated by the time indicator placed at the beginning of the sentence.

English verbs are conjugated to show tense and number. ASL has no endings or modified verbs.

ASL does not have infinitives. The "to" infinitive marker in combination with a verb should be deleted. Only certain verb signs can be moved in any direction, such as LOOK, SEND, PAY, MEET, GIVE, BRING, MOVE, HELP, TELL, SHOW, CALL, ASK, THROW, DRIVE, and TEACH.

Some verb signs have limited movement in direction, such as GO and COME.

Nondirectional verbs include COMPLAIN, READ, DISCUSS, EAT, WANT, PLAY, NEED, SAY, LIVE, and FEEL.

A noun sign requires multiple movements. A verb sign requires one, slightly more intense, movement. In ASL, an adjective can be placed before or after a noun, or both. If there is more than one adjective, place all adjectives after the noun. An adjective can be signed twice rather than once if placed after a noun.

When languages are in contact with one another, they often "borrow" words from one other as a matter of convenience. One way that ASL has borrowed from English is through the use of fingerspelled loan signs, or lexicalized fingerspelling.

Such borrowing begins with commonly fingerspelled words (usually short words). If a fingerspelled word is used frequently, it may evolve into a sign; in the process it often "loses" some letter handshapes (vowels being most commonly omitted), adds standard sign language phonological parameters (e.g., movement, location and palm orientation, or facial expression), and sometimes takes on a specialized meaning.

Fingerspelled loan signs are commonly marked with a # and then have capital letters to represent the letters used; for example, #JOB, #BANK, #BUSY, #NG (no good), #BACK, #OR, #CAR, #OH, #GAS, #BUS, #HA HA, #EARLY, #DO DO. There are about 75 signs that involve modified fingerspelling and are indicated with the # nonmanual marker. The following are some commonly used fingerspelled loan signs.

1. With some three- or four-letter English words, the first and last letter handshapes are kept and the middle one is deleted/blended out/omitted:

toy	#TY
but	#BT
fix	#FX
yes	#YS
bus	#BS
car	#CR
ball	#BL
tty (teletypewriter)	#TY
hurt	#HT

2. With some four- or five-letter English words, one or more middle letters are deleted.
hurt #HT

what	#W(H)T
bank	#BK or #BNK
club	#CLB or #CB

busy	#BSY
park	#PRK
camp	#CMP
fresh	#FRSH
sissy	#SISY
would	#WOLD or #WLD
when	#W(H)N

3. Other differences occur in terms of:
    A. Location of the sign:
        soon   #SN (chin)
        bullshit   #BS (chin)
    B. Change in palm orientation:
        job   #JB (palm orientation ends inward)
        gas   #GS (palm orientation ends outward)
        toy   #TY (palm orientation ends inward)
        dog   #DG (palm orientation inward)
        so   #SO (palm orientation upward, meaning "so what?")
    C. Movement of the sign:
        early   #ERLY (circular)
        all   #AL (sweep)
        easy   #ESY (downward)
        busy   #BSY (downward)
    D. Manipulation in space (directional verbs):
        back   #BCK
        ask   #AK
        no   #NO
        off   #OF
        knock out   #KO
    E. Two-handed, often with specific movement:
        do   (with circular movement; chores, activities, hobbies, or busy)
        do   #DO ++ (with wh- question facial expression, "What to do?")
        no good   #NG (couldn't do, can't accomplish)
    F. Commonly used two-letter English words:
        if
        go
        or
        oh
        of
        so
    G. Different meaning:
        ex   #X (formerly lived, formerly connected to)
        cool   #COL (meaning level-headed)
        sure   #SRE ("say sure")

Conditional and adverbial clauses begin with the words ALTHOUGH, AS, AS LONG AS, AFTER, BEFORE, DURING, IF, ONCE, SUPPOSE, UNTIL, WHEN, and WHILE. The nonmanual marker for conditional clauses is CC. Always place the conditional clause at the beginning of the sentence. If you use WHEN for a conditional clause, the sign for HAPPEN is required.

Use AND sparingly in ASL. It is usually for emphasizing nouns, not actions.

No periods are used in abbreviated words in ASL.

For months of the year, spell the abbreviation. Only March, April, May, June, and July are spelled out.

Intensifiers include words such as very, quite, rather, more, most, really, somewhat, less, too, and pretty. To imply "very," you need to sign the adjective with increased emphasis and speed along with an increase in facial expression. The two words become one word. You can also sign WOW or REALLY.

The nonmanual marker for topicalization (the topic of a sentence) is t with raised eyebrows and head. Place the main idea at the beginning of an ASL sentence just after the time indicator (ti). There can be only one topic marker in each sentence.

Pronouns are expressed by pointing (called indexing, or IX, in ASL) at the person or object that is present. If the person or object is not present, establish an absent referent (a location in the signing space) for that person or object and index to that location every time you refer to the person or object.

Reflexive pronouns can function as either pronouns or linking verbs.

ASL does not use the person's name when speaking directly to that person (i.e., direct address).

Most people drop prepositions from the ASL sentence structure. As a general rule, prepositions are used only for location.

The regular double movement (DM) or repetitive motion is reduced to a one-time movement for the first part of a compound gloss:

- BOOK STORE: BOOK is signed with a singular movement, not double.
- BOY SCOUT: BOY is signed with a singular movement, not double.
- PEANUT BUTTER: Both PEANUT and BUTTER are signed with a singular movement.
- BOY and GIRL: Both BOY and GIRL are signed with a singular movement.
- SELF is normally moved several times. The movement can, however, be a singular movement for command or for emphasis:
- YOU BRING CHAIR YOURSELF (Command)
- I CAN COOK MYSELF (Emphasis)

A conjunction is a word that joins two or more words, phrases, or clauses. All conjunctions perform the same basic function: gluing things together.

FIND is often translated as "discovered" or "found out":

1. **Gloss:** I GO-THERE VISIT MY BROTHER, FIND HE NOT HOME.
   Translation: "I went to visit my brother to find that he was not at home."
2. **Gloss:** I CALL-TO-MY FATHER, FIND HE IN HOSPITAL.
   Translation: "I called my father and found out he is in the hospital."
3. **Gloss:** I ORDER HAMBURGER, BIT, OPEN, FIND MOUSE THERE.

Translation: "I ordered a hamburger, bit into it, and then opened it only to find a mouse in it."

4. **Gloss:** I SEE PAPER, PICK UP, LOOK-AT FIND IT $20 BILL.
    Translation: "I saw a piece of paper on the ground, picked it up, and looked at it. I discovered it was a $20 bill."

5. **Gloss:** LAST NIGHT, I SIT, STUDY, REACH FOR GLASS, DRINK, FIND GLASS EMPTY.
    Translation: "Last night I was sitting and studying when I reached for a glass and took a drink only to find out that the glass was empty."

HIT is usually used to denote a positive outcome.

6. **Gloss:** I BUY TICKETS LOTTO WEEKLY, HIT YESTERDAY WON.
    Translation: "I buy lotto tickets weekly; yesterday, surprisingly, I won."

7. **Gloss:** I ENTER STORE, DEPRESSED, GET DRINK, GO-THERE BUY, HIT, I 1,000,000 SHOPPER.
    Translation: "I went into the store feeling depressed; I got something to drink and went to the checkout counter. Amazingly, I was the one millionth shopper and won."

8. **Gloss:** I HUNGRY, DON'T-WANT COOK, ARRIVE HOME, ENTER, HIT SMELL-GOOD, MY FRIEND COOK FOR ME. WOW.
    Translation: "I was hungry and didn't want to cook. I arrived home and went in. The house smelled good. My friend had cooked for me. How great!"

9. **Gloss:** I SEE PAPER, PICK UP, LOOK-AT, HIT IT $20 BILL.
    Translation: I saw a piece of paper on the ground, picked it up and looked at it. To my surprise, it was a $20 bill.

10. **Gloss:** I HEAR CLASS CLOSED, I NEED TO GRADUATE, I GO-TO REGISTER, HIT, ONE PLACE LEFT.
    Translation: "I had heard that a class I needed to graduate was closed. I went to sign up for the class and luckily there was one seat left."

HAPPEN is often interchangeable with the conjunction "wrong"; the most neutral, in terms of meaning, of the conjunctions.

11. **Gloss:** I EATING HAPPEN PHONE RANG.
    Translation: "I was eating when the phone rang."

12. **Gloss:** I SLEEPING, HAPPEN ALARM RING.
    Translation: "I was sleeping when the alarm clock went off."

13. **Gloss:** I LOOKING-AT, WORKING, TYPING COMPUTER, HAPPEN SCREEN OFF.
    Translation: I was working on the computer when the screen went blank.

14. **Gloss:** I TALKING-TO FRIEND, HAPPEN MOTHER ENTER ROOM
    Translation: I was talking to a find when my mother entered the room.

15. **Gloss:** LAST NIGHT, I SIT, STUDY, REACH FOR GLASS, DRINK, HAPPEN GLASS DEPLETE.

Translation: "Last night I was sitting and studying when I reached for a glass and took a drink. The glass was empty."

WRONG is often translated as "suddenly."

16. **Gloss:** I DRIVE, WRONG, SEE WARNING LIGHT FOR OIL.
    Translation: "I was driving along. When I looked down, I saw the oil light on."
17. **Gloss:** I TYPING FINISH, PRINTING WRONG BAD PRINT, CAN'T READ.
    Translation: "I had finished typing and was printing the document when the print turned out so bad that it couldn't be read."
18. **Gloss:** I WALKING ALONG WRONG FALL-DOWN.
    Translation: I was walking along. Suddenly, I fell.
19. **Gloss:** I LISTENING MUSIC ON RADIO, HAPPY, WRONG MUSIC STOP.
    Translation: I was happily listening to music on the radio when it suddenly went off.
20. **Gloss:** MY DAUGHTER SINGING WRONG QUIET WHY? SHE KO.
    Translation: "My daughter was singing when all went quiet. She had fallen asleep."

FRUSTRATED is often translated as "but," showing that you were hoping to do something but that there was an "obstacle" to your plan and you were "thwarted" in doing what you wanted to do.

21. **Gloss:** I EXCITED, WANT NEW SHOES, GO TO STORE, FRUSTRATE FIND NONE.
    Translation:
22. **Gloss:** I WANT ICE-CREAM. GO TO FREEZER, OPEN, FRUSTRATE NONE THERE.
    Translation:
23. **Gloss:** I TURN-KEY, WANT GO TO SCHOOL, FRUSTRATE, CAR NOT START. Translation:
24. **Gloss:** I GO-THERE STORE BUY BOOK, FRUSTRATE, NOT THERE.
    Translation: "I went to the store to buy a book, but it wasn't at the store."
25. **Gloss:** I GO-THERE RESTAURANT, HUNGRY, FRUSTRATE, CLOSED.
    Translation: "I went to the restaurant (and I was hungry), but the restaurant was closed so I didn't get to eat there."

Choose your signs according to what you mean rather than finding the English word in an ASL vocabulary list and then signing that ASL sign. For example, consider the word *move* in the sentence above. *Move* can mean to "pack up and change location" or to "inspire." If you go to a typical ASL vocabulary list and find the sign for the word move and then use that sign in your sentence, you may have missed the intended meaning. The sign MOVE expresses the concept of "picking something up, changing its location, and then setting it down again." It also can be used for concepts such as "to relocate to a new house." But it does not mean *inspire*. We use a different sign for inspire. Another example of using conceptually accurate signs would be if you were telling a story about a butterfly you would not sign BUTTER and FLY, rather you would use the ASL sign for BUTTERFLY.

When people sign using conceptually accurate ASL signs but use English syntax (word order), then they are not really "signing ASL." Instead what they are doing might be called "contact signing." Or, if they add signed English prefixes and suffixes, use initialization more heavily, mouth English, and use specific English signs when there is no equivalent ASL sign (instead of just spelling the concept or using a different way of expressing the concept), then they are using Conceptually Accurate Signed English, or CASE. CASE is similar to "contact signing."

SECTION
TWO

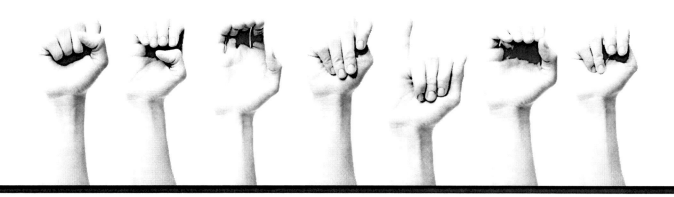

Notable Deaf Men and Women

WRITTEN BY

MICHELLE JAY

NO HEARING PEOPLE HERE!

Deaf people have been more in the spotlight than you know.
There are several famous deaf people who have been the founders of many organizations, been pioneers in deaf education, written books, painted famous artworks, held world records in sports, acted on several well-known television shows, and even started newspapers...

FAMOUS DEAF PEOPLE IN EDUCATION

Alice Cogswell—Alice was the young deaf girl who inspired Thomas Hopkins Gallaudet to devote his life to educating the deaf.

Laurent Clerc—Met Gallaudet in Europe and returned with him to the United States and together, started the first school for the deaf in the US.

I. King Jordan—After the Deaf President Now (DPN) protest, he became the first deaf president of Gallaudet University.

Andrew Foster—The first deaf African-American to graduate from Gallaudet. He also was the founder of many schools for the deaf in Africa.

Dr. Gerard Buckley—President of National Technical Institute for the Deaf, NTID. First alumni to be president of NTID.

Robert F. Panara—The first faculty member at RIT's National Technical Institute for the Deaf, a beloved teacher, founding member of the national Theatre of the Deaf, and honored by the World Federation of the Deaf for his contributions to education and culture.

Rachel C. Mazique—A deaf teacher of English Writing and Miss Deaf America Ambassador.

T. Alan Hurwitz—The tenth president of Gallaudet University who also served as President of the National Technical Institute for the Deaf (NTID) and as Vice President and Dean of the Rochester Institute of Technology (RIT).

Gerilee Gustason—Co-developer of SEE, deaf from a young age (5) due to meningitis, taught at Gallaudet, has PhD in teaching, and adopted a deaf daughter.

Marie Jean Philip—Well-known researcher and advocate for American Sign Language and Deaf Culture.

Ella Mae Lentz—Well known Deaf American author, poet, teacher, and advocate. Widely known in the Deaf community for her poetry, she was awarded the Kappa Gamma Poetry Award at Gallaudet University and is part of the Deaf Bilingual Coalition.

FAMOUS DEAF PEOPLE IN MOVIES AND TELEVISION

Linda Bove—The deaf actress who played "Linda the Librarian" on Sesame Street, as well as many other roles.

Marlee Matlin—The famous deaf actress who won an Academy Award for Best Actress for her debut role in Children of a Lesser God at the age of twenty-one.

Michelle Banks—A famous deaf African-American performer.

Deanne Bray—The star of Sue Thomas: F.B.Eye.

Phyllis Frelich—A very well respected deaf actress who won the Tony Award for Best Actress for her role as Sara in the Broadway version of Children of a Lesser God and acted on shows such as E.R. and Diagnosis Murder as well as Love is Never Silent, the made-for-television movie.

Amy Ecklund—Played Abigail on the soap opera, Guiding Light.

C.J. Jones—A very intelligent and talented African-American deaf actor and comedian. He has performed in many plays, TV shows, and films.

Howie Seago—Starred in the feature film, Beyond Silence.

Anthony Natale—Most famous for his role in Mr. Holland's Opus.

Shoshannah Stern—Best known for playing Holly Brodeen in Threat Matrix, Bonnie Richmond in Jericho, and Megan Graves on Weeds.

Christy Smith—Was the deaf contestant on a season of Survivor.

Terrylene—Played Laura Williams on the TV program, Beauty and the Beast.

Rush Limbaugh—A talk show host who experienced sudden deafness.

Lou Ferrigno—Played the "Hulk" in the original series.

Halle Berry—2001 Best Actress Academy Award winner claims that she has 80% hearing loss in one ear due to domestic abuse.

Kelly Monaco—Actress who plays "Sam" on daytime soap General Hospital once stated that she has some hearing loss due to an accident while portraying a lifeguard on a FOX television program years ago.

Luke Adams—Contestant on The Amazing Race.

Russell Harvard—Well known YouTube star and participated in the hit show CSI.

Herb Larson—Deaf Administrator who also was an actor. Won an Emmy Award for a Television Talk Show, "Off Hand" (co-hosted by Lou Fant through KHJ TV and the Silent Network).

Leslie Nielsen—Starred in many classics - most notably Airplane.

Sean Berdy—A deaf actor, comedian and dancer. He was in Sandlot 2, Legend of the Mountain Man, The Deaf Family, and the hit TV show Switched at Birth.

Tommy Korn—A well known Deaf fashion model and actor and the first ever Mr. Deaf California 2009-2011.

Jane Lynch—Famous actress known for her starring role on the hit TV series Glee. She is deaf in one ear.

Michael Barreca—Deaf actor who played Dummy Hoy in Signs of Time (2008).

Rob Lowe—American actor, completely deaf in right ear.

Robert DeMayo—Deaf actor, educator, ASL consultant, and one of the subjects of See What I'm Saying.

Rhondee Beriault—Deaf actress and dancer. (Quamntum Leap (1991), Alexander Graham Bell: The Sound and the Silence (1992), Reasonable Doubts (1993), I Love You, But (1998)).

Alexander Genievsky—Deaf Russian-born actor, filmmaker, writer, producer, and artist. Founder and President of the non-profit art organization Universal Sign Entertainment.

Katie Leclerc—American actress who has appeared on several television series, including Veronica Mars and Fashion House. In 2011, she received a lead role on the show Switched at Birth, starring as Daphne Vasquez.

Ryan Lane—Deaf actor with a role in the Dummy Hoy documentary and on television shows such as Switched at Birth, Cold Case, and House MD.

Jonathan Kovacs—Former American deaf child actor who was a regular character on The Family Tree and a semi-regular character during season nine of Little House on the Prairie.

Matthew Watkins—Deaf actor who played the deaf son of a doctor on the popular television series, ER.

Holly Hunter—American actress who starred in The Piano for which she won the Academy Award for Best Actress. She received Oscar nominations for her roles in Thirteen, The Firm, and Broadcast News. She's also received two Emmy's and six Golden Globe nominations. Hunter is profoundly deaf in one ear from a bout with mumps during childhood.

Justin LeBlanc—A contestant on the show Project Runway from Season 12.

FAMOUS DEAF MUSICIANS AND PERFORMERS

Paul Stanley—Singer in the rock band KISS was born deaf in one ear.

Evelyn Glennie—A world famous deaf percussionist.

Sean Forbes—Deaf rapper, founder of D-PAN (Deaf Performing Artist Network).

Marko Vuoriheimo "Signmark"—Deaf rapper from Finland and the first deaf person to sign a record deal with an international recording company.

Johnnie Ray—American singer, pianist, and songwriter who was deaf in one ear due to a childhood accident. He was very popular for most of the 1950s and is known to have played a major part in what would become rock and roll.

Ludwig van Beethoven—Was completely deaf for the last part of his life and yet managed to produce some of the greatest music of all time.

James Lee Taylor III—Deaf Rapper from the South Bronx on NY Daily Newspaper and City Limits Magazine. His story has been told in the book Train Go Sorry.

Ayumi Hamasaki—Famous Japanese performer and musician who is deaf in her left ear.

Bob Hiltermann—Founder of Deaf West Theater (Fountain Theater) in North Hollywood, California.

Bernard Bragg—a Deaf performer, writer, director, poet, and artist. He was a founder of The National Theater of the Deaf and is "regarded by many as the leading professional deaf actor in the country."

Iosif Schneiderman—Deaf mime and professional actor who grew up in Russia and has performed all over the world. He directed the grand opening of DeafWay II in 2001 and co-wrote and starred in the internationally acclaimed award winning play, "Deaf Snow White" produced by Cleveland Sign Stage Theatre.

Charlotte Lamberton—The most well known deaf dancer in the 1930s and 1940s, internationally, in Hollywood and on Broadway.

FAMOUS DEAF PEOPLE IN THE MEDIA

Laura C. Redden Searing—First deaf female journalist.

Julius Wiggins—Creator of The Silent News, the newspaper of the Deaf Community.

Thomas J. Cooney, Sr.—Sports Writer for The Silent News publication, Recipient of Thomas Jefferson Award, Points of Light honoree, Grand Marshall for the Helen Keller Parade, A Kentucky Colonel, and, presently, a Motivational Speaker and Advocate for Deaf Awareness, introducing over 1.5 million individuals to Deaf Culture and Signed Languages.

Barry Strassler—Editor of DeafDigest.net and well known sports writer for the deaf community.

Suzanne Robitaille—Deaf American journalist who has worked at BusinessWeek and The Wall Street Journal. She is the author of The Illustrated Guide to Assistive Technology, founder of abledbody.com, and board member of the National Center on Disability and Journalism.

FAMOUS DEAF PEOPLE IN ORGANIZATIONS

Juliette Low—The founder of the Girl Scouts.

Rocky Stone—Founder of Self Help for Hard of Hearing people (SHHH).

Sheri Farnihas—Deaf rights and National Association of the Deaf (NAD) activist.

Opeoluwa Sotonwa—An African-American deaf attorney and literary writer. He currently serves as the Vice President of National Black Deaf Advocates Inc., the nation's civil rights organization of deaf people of color, where he has become a pivotal source of resourcefulness to the NBDA.

George William Veditz—Former president of National Association of the Deaf of the United States and was one of the first to film American Sign Language.

Gregory Hlibok—First person with a disability to be appointed by the FCC to the head of its Disability Rights Office.

FAMOUS DEAF PEOPLE IN SPORTS

Dummy Hoy—The first deaf major-league baseball player.

Shelley Beattie—Professional bodybuilder who once held the record for bench pressing (315 pounds!)

Terrence Parkin—Deaf Olympic swimmer who took home a silver medal in the 2000 Olympics and two gold medals in the 2005 Deaflympics.

James "Deaf" Burke—Famous deaf boxer who was the first boxer to be involved in a fight that resulted in a death.

Curtis Pride—Deaf professional baseball player.

Kenny Walker—Former deaf professional football player.

Matt Hamill—Contestant on The Ultimate Fighter, now UFC fighter. Also three-time NCAA Division III National Wrestling Champion.

Kevin M. Hall—A professional golfer who graduated from Ohio State University and plays in the NGA Tour.

Donna Sue Barker—A Deaf woman who went to Texas School for the Deaf and won many medals in track. She represented the United States in the Deaflympics and traveled to Europe.

Marcus Titus—Swimmer on United States National Swim Team.

Jeffrey "Jeff" Float - Former American swimmer who became the only legally deaf athlete from the USA to win an Olympic gold medal.

Tamika Catchings—Professional basketball player in the WNBA. She played for the University of Tennessee.

LeRoy Colombo—Famous deaf lifeguard entered into the Guinness Book of World Records for saving 907 lives.

Louis Long (aka The Silent Warrior)—Deaf American professional wrestler and founder of Deaf Wrestling Alliance.

Lance Allred—American basketball player, first deaf person to play in the NBA.

Matthew Eby—First deaf professional soccer player in the U.S. Played for Real Maryland FC Professional Soccer in the United Soccer League (USL).

Jim Kyte—The first (and to date, the only) legally deaf National Hockey League (NHL) player.

Bonnie Sloan—First deaf football player in the National Football League (NFL).

Derrick Coleman—First deaf offensive player in the NFL and plays for the Seattle Seahawks.

Ryan Ketchner—Deaf left-handed pitcher who was drafted by the Seattle Mariners.

Paul Wood—First professional deaf cyclist. Competed in Deaflympics seven times and won a total of 11 medals - 5 gold, 4 silver, and 2 bronze.

Ashley Fiolek—Deaf motocross racer.

Kitty O'Neil—Former stuntwoman and racer.

FAMOUS DEAF ARTISTS

Chuck Baird—Well-known deaf artist.
Betty G. Miller—Deaf artist whose work truly edifies the struggles and issues in the deaf community.
Louis Frisino—Well-known deaf painter who painted pictures of realistic-looking animals.
Granville Redmond—Landscape artist whose artwork is worth 6-figures.
Gerald Becker Steffen—Deaf artist at Pike Place Market in Seattle.
Samuel Hudson—African-American deaf artist.
Douglas Tilden—World famous deaf sculptor.
Nancy Rourke—Deaf Artist of expressionist paintings.
Nellie Knopf—Deaf painter (1875-1962).
Ann Silver—Well known deaf graphic designer, advocate for deaf culture art, and one of the founders De'VIA (Deaf View Image Art).
Braam Jordaan—Well known deaf animator.
Joseph Henry Sharp—Famous deaf artist and one of the founding members of the Taos Society of Artists, a group that produced some of the most significant artwork in American history.

FAMOUS DEAF WRITERS

Stevie Platt—The deaf author of the books *Go to the Hill* and *The Last Servant*.
Connie Briscoe—A modern deaf author who became deaf in her 20s.
Jamie Berke—The former About.com Deafness Guide
Sondra McCoy—Author of *Hard Road, Easy Riding: Deaf Biker Lady*.
Henry A. Kisor—Author of *What's that Pig Outdoors?* and other novels based on the Upper Peninsula of Michigan locales.
John Lee Clark—Author of Suddenly Slow: Poems and editor of Deaf American Poetry: An Anthology.
Q. Kelly—Deaf lesbian romance and fiction award-winning writer.
Rie Saito—Famous Japanese hostess who used hitsuden (written communication) to interact with her clients. She wrote the book The Hostess With a Pen.

FAMOUS DEAF-BLIND PEOPLE

Julia Brace—A deaf-blind girl who was born before both Laura Bridgman and Helen Keller. She was successfully educated, but lost the credit as the first to Helen Keller.
Helen Keller—The most well-known deaf-blind girl who successfully learned language.
Laura Bridgman—The deaf-blind girl who was successfully educated before Helen Keller.

OTHER FAMOUS DEAF PEOPLE

Heather Whitestone—First deaf woman to be crowned Miss America.

Rodger Young—Deaf man who faked his Army hearing test in WW2. Won a Posthumous Medal of Honor in the Soloman Islands.

Howard Hughes—Aviator, film producer, engineer, film director, industrialist, and philanthropist.

Robert Weitbrecht—Invented the TTY along with James Marsters who was also deaf.

Cal Rodgers—First deaf pilot in the USA in 1911.

Sue Thomas—Undercover specialist for FBI, the inspiration for the TV series Sue Thomas: FBEye, international speaker, author, founder of Kennels of Levi: EPEC Service Dogs for physically challenged, founder of WaterBrooks a Christian spiritual renewal center, and founder of Sue Thomas Ministries outreach to homeless.

Thomas Alva Edison—American scientist, inventor, and businessman.

Rhulin Thomas—First deaf aviator to fly coast to coast.

John Gotti—Boss of the most powerful organized crime family in the USA. He was deaf in one ear.

Erastus Deaf Smith—Revered Texas scout, guide, and spy and is famous for the important role he played in the Texas Revolution.

Claudia Gordon—First deaf female African American lawyer. She was also the first deaf student to graduate from the American University Washington DC College of Law.

Ginger Jee—Well-respected deaf Disability Rights Advocate in New York tri-state area. Artist and former actress on the television show Criminal Intents. An expert in all disability rights laws and fights for all deaf access across America.

Roberto E. Wirth—Deaf world famous hotelier. Voted into the Hall of Fame of hoteliers as the Best Hotelier of the World in 2005.

Bill Clinton—Former president of the United States has a hearing loss due to age and the time he spent playing the saxophone in his youth.

Keith Nolan—Deaf man well known for fighting to join the US Military.

The Development of Sign Language

WRITTEN BY

DEBORAH CHEN PICHLER

The study of sign language development has become a broad field of inquiry over the last half century, benefiting from approaches across a variety of disciplines, including linguistics, psychology, sociology and neuroscience. An interdisciplinary approach helps us tease apart the myriad of factors that can influence sign language acquisition, such as whether the sign language is being learned as a first or second language, the age at which an individual is exposed to the sign language, the quality of sign language input, and many other variables. Although developmental studies have traditionally focused on the acquisition of American Sign Language (ASL) by deaf children from birth to 4 years, more recent work has begun to explore acquisition at later stages of life, and in other natural sign languages. Only by comparing development across a variety of populations and in multiple sign languages will we have the means to draw solid conclusions about the overall processes by which sign languages are acquired and used.

Sign language acquisition research is still a fairly new discipline, which means that there have been preliminary studies on a great many topics, but comparatively few follow-up studies or attempts to replicate preliminary findings for other populations or sign languages. That said, there are several areas which have enjoyed a higher degree of research attention than others, or which have benefited from parallel investigations across multiple sign languages and/or multiple populations. This chapter will focus on four such areas of research: phonology, non-manual markers, fingerspelling and spatial components of narratives. For readers new to sign language research, Section 1 will provide some background information on the structure and organization of sign languages. Section 2 will survey the literature on the development of sign language as a first language by children, by far the most frequently studied group in the sign language acquisition literature. Section 3 will discuss our four focus areas as they pertain to adult second language learners, before moving on to Section 4, where we will address language decline due to Parkinson's disease. Finally, I will conclude in Section 5 by suggesting some directions for further research.

1   SIGN LANGUAGES: SOME BACKGROUND INFORMATION

Despite the persistent public perception of sign languages as a form of pantomime or simplified English represented manually,[2] sign languages are recognized in today's scholarly literature as fully natural human languages with complex, rule-based organization. There is no universal sign language; deaf communities around the world currently use an estimated 121 national sign languages (Gordon, 2005) that developed and evolved indigenously over time. Although there are many striking similarities across sign languages, some due to historical contact and others due to fundamental iconic properties exploited by visual languages, each sign language possesses a grammatical structure that is distinct both from other sign languages and from local spoken languages. Thus, although ASL and British Sign Language (BSL) both exist in areas where spoken English dominates, they are grammatically distinct from each other and from spoken English.

In order to discuss the development of sign languages, it is necessary to understand the basics of sign language structure. While a detailed exposition on sign language grammar is beyond the scope of this chapter, the following summary of sign phonology, nonmanual markers, fingerspelling and spatial aspects of narratives should serve to orient the reader to the basic focus areas central to this chapter. Readers interested in more detailed descriptions for a variety of sign languages are referred to Lucas, Valli and Mulrooney (2005) for ASL, Sandler and Lillo-Martin (2006) for ASL and Israeli Sign Language (ISL), Sutton-Spence and Woll (1999) for BSL, Meir and Sandler (2007) for ISL and Johnston and Schembri (2007) for Australian Sign Language (Auslan).

1.1 Phonology in Sign Languages

Despite being visual–gestural languages, sign languages nonetheless display the same types of phonological organization found in spoken languages. Signs are composed of distinctive, sublexical parameters traditionally labeled *handshape, movement, location, orientation*, and, for some signs, *nonmanual features* (Stokoe, Casterline, & Croneberg, 1965). The ASL sign illustrated in Figure 9.1, for instance, involves the "5" handshape, with repeated contact (movement) between the thumb of the hand and the chin (location), the palm facing the signer's left (orientation).[3] Each of these sublexical elements, taken on its own, is meaningless, but together they form the ASL sign MOTHER.

Individual sublexical categories such as handshape are themselves complex, made up of component features such as tension, selected fingers, joint specification, etc. Efforts continue in the area of sign language phonetics to identify similar componential features within the other sublexical categories such as movement and location (Johnson & Liddell, unpublished manuscript). These component features are likely candidates for errors across both first and second language learners of sign languages and, as such, represent an important area for further study.

1.2 Nonmanual Features in Sign Languages

Nonmanual features refer to the constellation of facial expressions, eye gaze patterns, and movements of the mouth, head and upper torso accompanying manual signing. These features fall roughly into two categories: grammatical or affective. Grammatical nonmanuals are typically obligatory and linguistically constrained. For example, matrix wh-questions in ASL are articulated with a brow furrow (notated in the following example by the label wh), while topics are articulated with a brow raise (top). Each of these nonmanual features must spread across a specific scope, indicated by the line above the ASL glosses, in order for the utterance to be well formed.

```
              _____ top _____ wh
```
(1) POSS-2 BROTHER, NAME WHAT
    "Your brother, what's his name?"

In contrast, affective nonmanuals, or nonmanuals that convey emotion or affect, are not obligatory in ASL and vary widely across sign production. In the following example, smiling functions as an affective nonmanual feature expressing happiness, but there are no specific timing requirements for its onset or offset, and its omission would not render the utterance ungrammatical.

```
              _____ smile
```
(2) PRO-2 PREGNANT
    "You're pregnant!"

Many nonmanual markers in ASL appear almost iconic in that one can see similarities with relevant affective facial expressions (e.g. the ASL whmarker involves furrowed brows, similar to the affective expression of puzzlement). Indeed, researchers have proposed diachronic paths of development for some nonmanual markers in ASL (Janzen, 1999; MacFarlane, 1998).

With respect to linguistic inquiry of nonmanual signals, research has traditionally focused on the eyes, brows and head. Mouth movements have been investigated, but usually only those associated with specific adverbial or affective nonmanuals (sometimes referred to as mouth gestures, e.g. mouthing "cha" to mean "very large" in ASL) that have no discernible source in spoken words. These are widely accepted as genuine features of signed languages, whereas mouthing of spoken words while signing has often been dismissed as unsystematic artifacts of contact with the dominant spoken language. This idea has been challenged as researchers discover systematic patterns in mouthing distribution and function, indicating that at least some types of mouthing are bona fide elements of sign language phonology (see Brentari, 2001, and Boyes Braem & Sutton-Spence, 2001, for discussion). Still, linguistic mouthing continues to go unmentioned in many studies, particularly those focusing on ASL or language acquisition.

1.3 Fingerspelling in Sign Languages

In ASL and other sign languages, words borrowed from spoken/written language can be represented by spelling them out using a manual alphabet. This practice is known as fingerspelling.

The degree to which fingerspelling is considered an integral part of the language and the prevalence of finger-spelled forms used by skilled signers varies from sign language to sign language. In the French deaf community, for example, fingerspelling is regarded as a foreign component of the sign language, with strong (and somewhat negative) associations to written French; consequently, it is not often used by skilled signers (Michael Filhol, personal communication). In contrast, fingerspelling is an integral part of ASL (Padden, 2006), co-existing productively with signs, not only as a robust mechanism for representing proper names (e.g. T-O-Y-O-T-A) or other vocabulary borrowed from written languages (e.g. S-Y-L-L-A-B-U-S), but also as a source for new compounds (e.g. BLACK+M-A-I-L), abbreviations (e.g. F-L-A for Florida) and initialized signs (e.g. the sign MONDAY uses the M-handshape). Fingerspelling also allows signers to differentiate between potentially ambiguous noun–verb pairs. Padden (2006) cites as an example the ASL sign RENT, which only occurs as a verb. If a signer wants to refer to the noun form, the word is fingerspelled: R-E-N-T. In cases like these, one can perhaps think of finger-spelling as providing a neutral alternative to placing a sign with a strongly associated meaning into a context where that meaning would be inappropriate. A similar principle seems to be at work in compounds like BLACK+MA-I-L. A lexical sign MAIL exists in ASL, but it is highly iconic and calls to mind the action of sticking a stamp onto the corner of an envelope. Given that blackmail has nothing to do with (postal) mail, the use of the sign MAIL in this compound would likely seem quite odd.

1.4 Space and its Use in Narratives

As visual–gestural languages, sign languages have the option of exploiting physical space for linguistic purposes, and they do so in highly effective ways. Personal pronouns in sign languages consist of a pointing gesture directed towards its referent. If the referent is not physically present, the signer can still establish a locus for that referent in the signing space; subsequent pronouns or verbs directed towards that locus are then interpreted as applying to that referent. Spatial mechanisms are particularly effective for depicting complex spatial arrangements that might be difficult or impossible to convey using linear strings of standard lexical signs (i.e. the contours of the coast of Maine). For this reason, they are frequently found in sign narratives, such as the excerpt below, adapted from Reilly (2000, p. 424).

(3) Direct quote of Baby Bear through referential shift. Note: +K indicates eye contact with addressee, –K indicates a gaze shift away from the addressee.

```
_____ topic _____ surprise
_____ +K _____ –K
BABY BEAR LOOK-AT LET'S-SEE MY BOWL
"Baby bear looked at his soup, 'Let's see my bowl.'"
_____ pouting
_____ distress
_____ –K
```

HEY GONE SOUP Cl:1 SOMEONE FINISH EAT ALL "Hey, my soup's gone! Someone ate it all up!"

In this retelling of the story of Goldilocks and the Three Bears, the adult signer begins as narrator, then "takes on" the perspective of Baby Bear through a process known as *referential shift*. Referential shift is the mechanism by which direct quotes are produced in ASL and other sign languages (Emmorey & Reilly, 1998; Engberg-Pedersen, 1993, 1995; Morgan, 1999). Just prior to the shift, this signer (still as narrator) labels the character whose perspective he is about to take on; this label is sometimes accompanied by a point to the locus assigned to that character in signing space. Next, the signer breaks eye contact from his addressee, shifts his head and body to the side, assuming the surprised expression of Baby Bear, and signs that character's utterance. The signer will maintain the character's affective facial expression for the duration of the quoted utterance (in this case, it spans several clauses). While the signer is engaged in referential shift, pronoun reference is interpreted as being from the point of view of the quoted character. Thus the possessive pronoun MY refers to Baby Bear as possessor rather than the signer.

Adults who signed the Goldilocks and the Three Bears story used numerous direct quotes such as the one in (3) and consistently produced head shift and eye gaze in tandem at the beginning of the referential shift function, suggesting these nonmanual changes are obligatory as signals of a shifted perspective (Emmorey & Reilly, 1998; Reilly, 2000). Affective facial expression of the quoted character varied somewhat in its onset point, beginning sometimes with the referential shift and sometimes slightly earlier, but consistently constrained by the length of the quoted material. Rossini, Reilly, Fabretti, and Volterra (1998) note that during dialogues between multiple characters that are already established in space, it is not necessary to label each character before delivering his/her direct quote; changes in nonmanual features are sufficient to signal referential shift from one character to another.

2   CHILD SIGNERS: FIRST LANGUAGE DEVELOPMENT

Before moving on to our discussion of childhood development of sign language, a note on delayed exposure is in order. In the normal case of first language acquisition, children are exposed to their native language(s) from birth. This is, unfortunately, not commonly the case with deaf children, the great majority of whom are born to hearing families who do not know a natural sign language. Delayed exposure to one's first language clearly has a significant impact on the course of development for both first and second languages. Research has demonstrated that deaf children with delayed exposure to a natural sign language display deficits in their grammatical competence and language processing abilities, as well as potential cognitive deficits (for an excellent summary, see Emmorey, 2002, Chapter 6). In a classic comparison of native signers (exposed to ASL from birth by deaf, signing parents), early learners (first exposed to ASL between 4 and 6 years) and late learners (first exposed to ASL after the age of 12) on a number of morphological and syntactic experimental tasks,

Newport (1990) found significant performance gaps between native/early learners and late learners. All subjects had been using ASL as their primary language for 30 years, regardless of age of exposure, ruling out language experience as the source of this difference.

Late-exposed signers also display deficits in phonological processing (Mayberry & Eichen, 1991; Mayberry & Fischer, 1989; Morford & Mayberry, 2000), requiring them to expend more effort to decode and recognize signs than their early-exposed counterparts. This additional demand on the cognitive system slows down access to lexical information, which can in turn impair comprehension. In particular, late learners may experience problems keeping track of spatial referents, as their working memory is already taxed by the task of decoding and recognizing phonological forms (Mayberry, 1995).

In the summary of child sign language development in the next section, I will focus only on native and early-exposed signers. This is in part due to space constraints, and in part due to the widespread opinion that native and early-exposed children provide the clearest picture of "normal" acquisition of sign language. Of course, the notion of "normal" can be turned on its head with respect to deaf children: although one may argue that acquisition from birth represents the ideal and normal pattern observed for all other languages, only a tiny minority of deaf children are born into an environment where such acquisition is possible. Until public policies are enacted to provide all deaf children with early, high-quality access to natural sign languages, the field of sign language acquisition has the charge of elucidating the course of sign development for the overwhelming majority of deaf children who experience delayed exposure to their first language, in addition to the course of "normal" development described below.

Readers interested in more detail on the acquisition of sign language by children (both early- and late-exposed) are referred to the many excellent summaries that now exist on the topic, including Newport and Meier (1985), Emmorey (2002, Chapter 5), Bonvillian (1999) and Lillo-Martin (1999). In the following sub-sections, we will survey a sample of this growing literature, focusing on the four topics described in Section 1.

2.1 L1 Development of Phonology

The development of sign language phonology is observable even before a deaf child begins to sign. Petitto and Marentette (1991) found that deaf babies between 10 to 14 months who had been exposed to sign language from birth produced more complex handshape and movement patterns than age-matched babies exposed only to speech. They called the manual behavior observed in sign-exposed babies *manual babbling*, and noted that frequently recurring patterns from the babbling behavior carried over into the babies' first formal signs. For example, just as speech-exposed babies show a preference for certain classes of consonants (e.g. stop consonants) in both their babbling and their earliest words (Oller, Wieman, Dole, & Ross, 1976), sign-exposed babies favor the same set of handshapes in both their manual babbling and their first signs (cf. also Cheek, Cormier, Repp, & Meier, 2001). Petitto and Marentette (1991) pointed to such similarities between vocal babbling and manual babbling as an argument for abmodality of the human language faculty.

Once a child has begun producing formal signs, we enter the realm of phonology proper. Although reports on early sign phonology exist for a variety of sign languages, most are based on very small data sets, due in part to logistical difficulties in locating sign-exposed children who are available for long-term study. Nonetheless, several patterns of development are observed repeatedly, across studies of different sign languages. Not surprisingly, sign-exposed children produce frequent errors of substitution (usually in the direction of less marked forms), most commonly with respect to hand-shape, and least commonly with respect to location. This general pattern of acquisition has been reported for a variety of sign languages (Conlin, Mirus, Mauk, & Meier, 2000, and Meier, 2006, for ASL, among others; Clibbens & Harris, 1993 for BSL; Karnopp, 2002, for Brazilian Sign Language; von Tetzchner, 1994 for Norwegian Sign Language; Takkinen, 2003 for Finnish Sign Language). This contrast between handshape and location accuracy has several plausible reasons. First, sign locations are fewer in number and more tolerant of variation than sign handshapes, for which a small variation could easily result in a different handshape. Thus, the statistical probability of a handshape error is higher than that of a location error. Second, accurate production of handshapes (e.g. distinguishing the U-handshape from the Rhandshape) involves the fine muscle groups of the fingers, whereas accurate production of location (e.g. distinguishing between contact on the chest and contact on the forehead) involves much larger muscle groups. This same contrast also has potential effects on perception; children may initially have difficulty distinguishing similar handshapes in the input, leading them to substitute a single configuration for multiple targets in their production.

The developing motor skills of young children influence not only hand-shape accuracy, but other aspects of early phonology as well. Richard Meier and his colleagues (Meier, 2006; Meier, Cheek, & Moreland, 2002; Cheek et al., 2001, among others) identified general properties of early motor development that potentially influence the development of sign phonology. Observing that all infants, regardless of language input, produce repeated movements, they predict that sign-exposed children will correctly produce target signs requiring repetition, and incorrectly add repeated movement to target signs that do not.

Infants also have difficulty inhibiting the use of one hand while the other is active, a tendency that leads to sympathetic movement in signs where one hand should normally be held still. Many two-handed signs require the non-dominant "base hand" to remain static, serving as a surface on which the dominant "active hand" acts. For example, the ASL sign for COOKIE, shown in Figure 9.2, is articulated with a twisting motion of the active bent5 handshape (or lax C-handshape) on a static B-handshape base hand.

The tendency to produce sympathetic movement might lead children to articulate COOKIE with identical handshapes (e.g. two bent-5 handshapes) and/or identical movements (e.g. both hands twisting). Cheek et al. (2001) reported just such articulation errors in their data, as well as apparent avoidance of two-handed base-hand signs by their infant subjects, a pattern that has also been observed in Brazilian Sign Language (LSB, Karnopp, 2002), BSL (Morgan, Barrett-Jones, & Stoneham, 2007), and Finnish Sign Language (Takkinen, 2003).

The third and final property of motor development proposed by Meier and colleagues to influence sign phonology is proximalization, the tendency to substitute an articulator close to the torso for one that is further away. Meier (2006) describes errors in which children reliably used a more proximal active joint than was called for in the target sign. For instance, when signing HORSE, which in ASL involves a nodding motion of the hand originating at the first set of knuckles, children produced the nodding motion from the wrist, a more proximal joint. Proximalization errors have been noted in the early development of sign languages besides ASL (Takkinen, 2003, for Finnish Sign Language; Lavoie & Villeneuve, 1999, for Québec Sign Language, or *Langue des Signes Québécoise*, LSQ) and, as we will discuss shortly, has also been identified as a common error in L2 sign production by adult learners (Mirus, Rathmann, & Meier, 2001).

2.2 L1 Acquisition of Nonmanuals

As discussed in Section 1.1, sign language grammars involve not only a manual component, but a nonmanual component as well. With respect to language development, one intriguing question is whether sign-exposed children are sensitive to the similarities that adults see between grammatical nonmanual markers and related affective facial expressions. If they are, they might potentially use affective facial expressions, which are acquired early, by the first year of life (Nelson, 1987), to "break into" the grammatical system of the target sign language. This question has been explored extensively by Judy Reilly and her colleagues over a number of studies (Anderson & Reilly, 1997, 1998; Reilly, 2000; Reilly, McIntire, & Bellugi, 1990a, 1990b, 1991), focusing on a range of ASL grammatical nonmanuals, including those for negation, wh- and yes–no questions, conditionals, topics, and adverbials. Results indicate that although children control affective facial expression early, their development of grammatical nonmanuals is more protracted and problematic, stretching into the fifth year and beyond (Reilly, McIntire, & Bellugi, 1990b; Reilly, 2006).

Reilly and her colleagues argue that their findings point to several generalizations about the acquisition of sign. First, children obey the principle of unifunctionality (Slobin, 1973) in their development of grammatical nonmanuals, initially assuming a one-to-one mapping of grammatical form to function, and resisting marking multiple construction types with the same marker. This point is nicely illustrated by the case of brow raise in Reilly and colleagues' data. Brow raise is a salient feature of several grammatical nonmanuals in ASL, including those for conditionals, yes–no questions, and topics. Prior to the age of 3 years, children have begun producing all three of these constructions, but only yes–no questions are correctly marked with brow raise. Both topics (or, more accurately, proposed objects that are plausible candidates for topics) and conditionals lack the obligatory nonmanual marking. However, the child is still able to mark these two structures, in the case of conditionals, thanks to the availability of lexical markers of conditionality (e.g. the signs SUPPOSE or #IF) that are optional in the adult system. At around 3;0, brow raise is observed marking topic structures, suggesting that children have relaxed their insistence on unifunctionality and are ready to consider using a single marker for more than one function.

Second, children show a "hands before face" bias, treating the hands as the primary articulators of the language. They control the manual component of ASL grammar (e.g. producing signs with the proper form and in proper order) before the nonmanual component, and they choose manual over nonmanual marking in instances when both are available, despite the fact that omission of the nonmanual marker is ungrammatical (e.g. in the case of conditional constructions discussed above).[4] Taken together, these two observations suggest that affective and grammatical nonmanual systems develop independently. Children's early competence in affective facial expression does not lead to smooth and early development of grammatical nonmanuals. The latter begins between 1;6 and 2;0 in most cases, and stretches into the sixth year or later in some special cases (Lillo-Martin, 2000; Reilly, McIntire, & Bellugi, 1990b).

2.3 L1 Acquisition of Fingerspelling

As mentioned in Section 1, fingerspelling is very common in ASL. For children born to deaf, signing parents, fingerspelling is present in their everyday environment. Padden (1991) reports that children as young as 2;0 spontaneously attempt to produce fingerspelled words for common objects such as IC-E or T-V. These early attempts approximate the very salient movement contour of fingerspelled words, but lack a clear internal sequence of individual letter configurations (Akamatsu, 1982; Padden 2006; Padden & LeMaster, 1985). At this age, the children do not yet know how to read or write, but they have begun to develop what Padden calls the "first skill of fingerspelling," learning the types of words represented by fingerspelling, and recognizing common fingerspelled words in the input. The "second skill of fingerspelling" is closely tied to development in English literacy, as it involves recognizing the internal structure of a fingerspelled word as a series of individual hand configurations corresponding to letters of the English alphabet. Full acquisition of fingerspelling requires mastery of both skills, a process that begins early but that stretches well into the school years. Investigations of reading development in deaf children point to a correlation between English reading comprehension skills and the ability to write down fingerspelled words (Padden & Hanson, 2000; Padden & Ramsey, 1998). Other studies have uncovered "indigenous" strategies intuitively employed by native signing parents and teachers that enhance children's access to fingerspelled words (e.g. alternating fingerspelled words with signs related to that word). Such research holds great potential to inform and improve classroom practices in deaf education.

2.4 L1 Acquisition of Spatial Components of Narratives

Before we discuss the narratives produced by child signers, we must briefly look at the development of spatial mechanisms in children's emerging syntax. Much of the early literature on sign language development reports delays in the acquisition of pronouns and verb agreement with respect to spoken language development. Although children are able to direct pronouns and verbs towards present referents between 3;0 and 3;6 (Emmorey, 2002), and understand by 3;0 to 4;0 that non-present referents can be assigned locations in signing space (Bellugi, van Hoek, Lillo-Martin, & O'Grady, 1993; Lillo-Martin, Bellugi, Struxness, & O'Grady, 1985), they are not yet able to themselves direct pronouns and verbs towards non-present referents (Hoffmeister, 1978; Loew, 1984). Lillo-Martin (1999) suggests that the complexities of learning how to associate and maintain referents in space are the source of the observed delay, not a lack of morphological readiness.

The difficulties of establishing and maintaining associations between non-present referents and their loci in space lead to interesting errors, readily apparent in children's development of narratives. Loew (1984) and Bellugi et al. (1993) report that between 3;6 and 5;0, children often lose track of spatial relations over the course of a narrative, either "stacking" multiple referents on the same locus in signing space, or assigning a single referent to more than one loci. The resulting narrative lacks cohesion and leads to viewer uncertainty as to the antecedent of pronouns. This is strikingly similar to what has been reported for early spoken English narratives, in which children produce ambiguous pronouns (Karmiloff-Smith, 1986). In both cases, pronoun reference may be well-formed within an individual sentence, but children under 5;0 seem generally unable to relate coordinate reference across the multiple sentences of a narrative, resulting in a lack of cohesion.

As for referential shift/direct quoting, Loew (1984) reported that the subject in her case study, Jane, was able to use changes in eye contact to mark referential shift by 3;6, although she failed to differentiate between multiple referents or change facial expression at the onset of a new shift. By 4;4 she consistently marked referential shift with eye gaze changes, but was still unable to coordinate multiple spatial referents over the course of a narrative.[5] Jane was finally able to coordinate body shift and eye gaze to signal a shift, as well as to maintain multiple spatial referents across the narrative. However, once engaged in referential shift, she had difficulty assigning pronouns, that is, understanding that a first person pronoun no longer refers to the narrator when produced while quoting another character (Loew, 1984).

A much larger and more controlled study of referential shift was conducted by Reilly and colleagues (Reilly, 2000) on 28 native deaf children ranging in age from 3;0 to 7;0. Their findings were generally in line with those reported by Loew (1984). In particular, eye gaze was used as the earliest indicator of referential shift, employed even by the 3-year-old subjects. All age groups also used affective facial expression in their shifts. However, children younger than 6 years were inconsistent in their use of facial expressions, producing them with incorrect timing or extending the same affective non-manual across the direct quotes of more than one character. Children under 6;0 were also unreliable in their use of labels for quoted characters, compared to adult controls.

A final divergence in the child data from adult controls was the use of the sign SAY to lexically indicate direct quotes. This strategy was used most frequently by the 5-year-old signers, in addition to eye gaze and affective facial expression. Reilly (2000) proposes that the appearance of SAY at 5 years is indication of a linguistic reorganization occurring. While children at 5;0 use affective facial expression in direct quotes, they still do not do so consistently or accurately, so SAY offers them an alternative way to mark these structures. The fact that deaf children apparently invent a new lexical marker for structures that they have difficulty marking nonmanually fits nicely with the findings reported by Reilly and her colleagues for the acquisition of conditionals, summarized earlier in this section.

3   ADULT SIGNERS: SECOND LANGUAGE ACQUISITION OF SIGN LANGUAGE

In contrast to the rich and quickly expanding literature on childhood L1 development in a number of sign languages, there is only a very small and scattered literature on adult L2 signers. As we will see below, this literature focuses mainly on phonological aspects of non-native ASL, and on the ability of native signers to identify non-native signers on the basis of them.

3.1 Phonology in L2 Sign Language

Second language research for spoken languages has identified phonology as one aspect of language for which a critical or sensitive period clearly applies. Studies as early as Scovel (1969) and Oyama (1976) reported that individuals beginning the L2 acquisition process before puberty generally spoke the target language with less "foreign accent" than those who began the process after puberty. Scovel (1981) further demonstrated that native speakers are able to reliably identify a foreign accent by the age of 10.

The concept of "foreign accent" can be broadly defined as non-targetlike phonology, and is thus as applicable to sign languages as it is to spoken languages. Indeed, there has long been a popular perception that skilled signers can identify non-native signers on the basis of their "accent." This claim appeared in an early paper by Cicourel and Boese (1972), but without empirical basis. Kantor (1978) set out to test whether identification of native vs. non-native signers was possible on the basis of simply watching them sign, and whether any particular signer profile (e.g. native deaf vs. native hearing vs. non-native deaf vs. non-native hearing) was more successful than others in detecting non-native accent. Her results showed that native-deaf, native hearing and non-native hearing "judges" (signers who viewed the film clips and were asked to identify the profile of each signer) were all able to identify signers at the extremes of the ASL fluency continuum (i.e. native deaf and non-native hearing signers). Native deaf judges did so with the highest accuracy, followed closely by native hearing judges, then hearing non-native judges. The remaining category of judges, non-native deaf signers, was able to identify fellow non-native deaf signers, but not any other signer profile.

Approaching the data from the perspective of which group was most accurately identifiable across judges, Kantor found that native deaf and nonnative hearing signers were accurately identified the most often by all categories of judges (except the non-native L2 judges); both native hearing and non-native deaf signers were often mislabeled as native deaf. These results led Kantor to two main conclusions regarding "accent" in sign language: (a) the "accent" of native signers is consistent, regardless of hearing status, and

(b) with enough practice, certain signers (i.e. non-native deaf) seem able to escape critical period effects and learn to sign with a native "accent." Kantor also elicited feedback on specific aspects of signing that judges used to determine the hearing/deaf and native/non-native status of signers. The two features most frequently cited by all categories of judges were handshape and facial expression, followed by "rhythm" and choice of signs. Many judges also cited English mouthing as an indication of non-nativeness, and use of "mime" or depictive signing as an indication of nativeness.

A similar study was conducted by Budding, Hoopes, Mueller, and Scar-cello (1995), but with the focus on signers' ability to identify foreign "accent" rather than non-native accent. In this study, deaf native ASL judges watched narratives signed in ASL by deaf individuals who had learned LSQ as a first language (although with significant delays in several cases, as late as 14 years) and ASL much later, as a second language. Half of the judges were informed at the onset that they were about to watch LSQ signers from Quebec. Predictably, these judges were the most likely to report that they noticed a foreign accent. Both sets of judges cited numerous features that contributed to a native accent in ASL, with particular emphasis on effective use of space, nonmanuals and classifier constructions.

Drawbacks of the Kantor (1978) and Budding et al. (1995) studies are that they took on research questions that were very broad and involved a high degree of variation in the content of the video samples (in the case of Kantor, 1978). They also included signers who acquired their L1 later than usual, a population who have since been shown to process and produce signing differently from native signers. As a result, it is difficult to draw strong conclusions from these early studies regarding features that contribute to the perception of non-native accent in sign language.

More recent investigations are more specific in scope and yield more generalizeable conclusions. Mirus et al. (2001) reported proximalization errors in isolated ASL signs produced by hearing L2 learners with no previous experience with sign language, parallel to those they found in infant L1 signing. Proximalization errors were also noted by Rosen (2004) in his examination of phonological errors produced in isolated lexical ASL signs by his L2 subjects. In contrast, native deaf German signers of German Sign Language (*Deutsche GebŠrdensprache*, DGS) who were asked to reproduce isolated ASL signs proximalized much less frequently than hearing L2 signers (Mirus et al., 2001). Mirus et al. conclude that proximalization is not simply the result of an immature motor system, but rather a universal reaction to learning to use the body in a new way. Mirus (personal communication) supports this proposal by pointing out that the awkward "too big" movements of adults skiing for their first time or writing with their non-dominant hand are also due to proximalization.

Rosen (2004) examines phonological errors produced in isolated lexical ASL signs by beginning students of ASL as a second language. After categorizing errors according to the phonological parameter most affected, Rosen attempts to determine whether the errors were caused by a lack of dexterity (i.e. substitutions, displacements, switches and incomplete formation) or incorrect perception by the student (i.e. mirrorizations, parallelizations, and addition or deletion of articulary segments). He concludes that early L2 handshape errors are caused solely by a lack of dexterity, while errors in location, movement and palm orientation are caused by both lack of dexterity and problems in perception.

Chen Pichler (2006) explores the contributions of universal markedness patterns and transfer from L1 (i.e. conventionalized gestures common in American hearing culture) on handshape errors, two potential sources for non-native accent that were not investigated by Rosen (2004). Preliminary results suggest that sign-naïve subjects did sometimes transfer familiar hand-shapes from their gestures to sign, but only for relatively unmarked hand-shapes. Marked handshapes such as R and Y were produced accurately in subjects' gestures ("good luck/cross your fingers" and "call me," respectively), but not in subsequent ASL signs requiring those handshapes. Chen Pichler speculates that naïve signers are generally able to visually extract handshape as an independent component of an unfamiliar sign (thereby facilitating transfer if the handshape is part of their gestural repertoire), but this ability is somehow blocked when the target handshape is highly marked. Thus markedness and transfer may interact to affect L2 sign phonology in ways previously overlooked.

3.2 Nonmanuals and Fingerspelling in L2 Sign Language

There has been very little research on L2 sign development beyond the few studies of L2 sign phonology summarized above. Most are quite general in nature, collecting student and teacher opinions on various aspects of learning sign language as a second language. McKee and McKee (1992) report that adult students of ASL rate nonmanuals and fingerspelling as among the most difficult aspects of ASL to acquire. Difficulties with nonmanual markers are also observed by McIntire and Reilly (1988) in their study of American college students with two to three semesters' worth of ASL classes. Subjects were asked to imitate signed sentences involving a variety of nonmanuals, some linguistic and with specific scope (i.e. grammatical nonmanual markers, adverbial nonmanual markers and nonmanuals associated with specific lexical items) and some paralinguistic with variable scope (i.e. affective nonmanual expressions).

Results indicated that subjects performed better with affective nonmanuals than linguistic nonmanuals. With respect to the latter, less-experienced learners initially employed a gestalt strategy, producing unanalyzed combinations of manual and nonmanual material. More experienced signers had reanalyzed these gestalt combinations and their manual and nonmanual components, but are not able to coordinate them with the correct timing and scope.[6] In some cases, subjects incorrectly reanalyzed adverbial nonmanuals as optional, and omitted them from their imitations. L2 learners exhibited many of the same developmental patterns reported for L1 acquisition of ASL nonmanuals carried out by Reilly and her colleagues (described in Section 2.2).

4   BREAKDOWN OF SIGN LANGUAGE

As we have seen, signing involves not only the hands, but the face and body as well. As the body ages, it is logical to expect that decreased physical strength and dexterity may influence the phonology of signed production. Aging may bring changes to the syntactic and pragmatic components of sign language as well, as signers experience problems with memory or processing. Unfortunately, the process of sign language attrition due to aging has not yet been empirically studied, to my knowledge. However, there is a healthy literature on the effects of disease or damage to the brain on sign language perception and production. These studies, in particular those focusing on sign formation by deaf Parkinson's patients, allow us to begin to understand the process of sign language decline, an important but often neglected counterpart to developmental studies.

4.1 Language Decline: Parkinsonian Signers

Parkinson's disease affects the functioning of the basal ganglia, resulting in profound motor disturbances. Typical symptoms include tremor of limbs, slowed movements and a lack of facial expression. In a series of experiments, Poizner and his colleagues (Brentari & Poizner, 1994; Poizner & Kegl, 1993; Poizner, Brentari, Tyrone, & Kegl, 2000; Tyrone, Kegl, & Poizner, 1999, among others) have demonstrated that the formational features of Parkinsonian signing manifest profound and systematic disruptions. Poizner and his colleagues categorize these errors into two broad categories: reductions and timing disruptions (Brentari & Poizner, 1994).

The most robust type of reduction in Parkinsonian signing is distalization, wherein movement is shifted from the target articulator to one that is further from the torso (this is the opposite effect from proximalization, observed for L2 and young L1 signers). Thus the sign for BETTER, normally signed with an upward diagonal movement of the hand that is articulated at the elbow, is articulated at the wrist and knuckles (Brentari & Poizner, 1994). A secondary effect of distalization is that the entire movement of the sign is contained in a smaller signing space than normal. The reduced signing space may also entail displacement of location. For example, Parkinson's signers often drop signs that normally occur near the face to a more neutral level in front of the lower torso. Another type of reduction targets handshape, specifically, the selected (i.e. active) and unselected (i.e. less active) finger features. Normally, unselected fingers in a given handshape are specified as either fully "open" (extended) or fully "closed." For example, in the "baby-O" handshape, the thumb and index describe a ring configuration, while the unselected fingers (i.e. the rest of the fingers) are fully closed. Brentari and Poizner (1994) noted that Parkinson's signers produced "lax" or imprecise handshapes in which the unselected fingers are somewhere in between open and closed.

Other reductions observed in Parkinsonian signing include shadowing (i.e. assimilation of movement from the dominant hand to the non-dominant hand), deletion of contact (i.e. the dominant hand stops short of its target contact location), and neutralization of orientation (i.e. altering palm orientation towards the mid-sagittal plane). Nonmanual expressions are also affected, appearing dampened or replaced altogether by the rigid, "masked" facial expression characteristic of Parkinson's patients.

Timing disruptions in Parkinsonian signing include excessive pause durations at the beginning of utterances, as well as mechanical acceleration or deceleration of subsequent pauses within the utterance. The normal rhythm of signing is lost, obscuring constituent borders that would normally be marked by brief pauses. Parkinsonian signers also take proportionally longer to effect changes in handshape while the hand is transitioning from one position to another. For instance, the sign for "flood" in ASL is a compound of

WATER, articulated with a W handshape at the chin, and RISE articulated with a variant of the B handshape in front of the torso. In normal production of this compound, the hand changes from the W to the B handshape during the transitional movement from the chin to the area in front of the torso. Brentari and Poizner (1994) report that their control signer executed the W-to-B handshape change within the first 17% of the transitional movement, whereas their Parkinsonian signer took 30% of the transition movement to achieve the same task. Brentari, Poizner, and Kegl (1995) further observed that Parkinsonian signers produced about the same handshape change to movement ratio at word boundaries as they did within words (i.e. between two parts of a compound), giving their signing a monotonous quality.

Together, reduction and timing disruptions have a particularly striking effect on handshapes, and correspondingly, on fingerspelling. Indeed, finger-spelling is particularly vulnerable to the effects of Parkinson's disease, exhibiting not only the lax position of unselected fingers just described, but also blending and feature unraveling, two additional types of reduction. Blending occurs when the selected fingers feature for one letter handshape is combined with that of an adjacent letter handshape. For example, Tyrone et al. (1999) describe an instance of the fingerspelled word P-I-L-L in which the deaf Parkinsonian signer produced P and I simultaneously, coalescing the two handshapes into one. In cases of feature unraveling, a single feature of one letter handshape is decoupled from the others during the transition between letters. For instance, while signing the last two letters of the sequence A-S-L, one Parkinsonian signer waited until the thumb component of the L was almost fully extended before extending the index finger to complete the fingerspelled letter (Tyrone et al., 1999). This lack of coordination can seriously disrupt the flow of the fingerspelled word, since it appeared as though an extra handshape had been inserted between the S and the L.

Poizner and colleagues argue that despite the extensive effects of Parkinson's disease on sign production, the errors produced by this population are phonetic rather than phonological (Brentari & Poizner, 1994). Support for this proposal comes from the fact that the reductions and disruptions in timing discussed above all favor ease of articulation, consistent with documented difficulties that Parkinson's patients have in controlling movement. This is quite a different pattern than is observed for deaf aphasics, for instance, who suffer breakdown at the phonological level of structure. Aphasics are often able to articulate signs clearly and sharply; their errors do not arise from the need to ease articulation, but rather from errors in selecting phonological targets (Corina et al., 1992; Poizner, Klime, & Bellugi, 1987). Aphasics also display serious problems in syntactic or morphological processing and production (paraphasias), not associated with Parkinson's disease; deaf Parkinsonians employ the full range of sentence types, morphological and classifier forms typical of normal signers, and correctly use referential space (Brentari et al., 1995; Kegl & Poizner, 1997; Poizner & Kegl, 1993). Thus it appears that even though Parkinsonian signing is heavily compromised at the production level, their language capacity at the grammatical level is spared, unlike in the case of aphasics.

5   CONCLUSION AND DIRECTIONS FOR FUTURE RESEARCH

In this brief and limited survey, we have seen that sign language development, while certainly rapid and dynamic during the first few years of life, continues to be a worthy object of inquiry through later childhood and into adulthood and old age. We have noted a few developmental patterns that emerge for both child and adult signers, such as a tendency to proximalize movement, and difficulty coordinating manual and nonmanual signals. The fact that we have not noticed more similarities between child and adult language acquisition, or between errors in early development and errors due to aging and language decline, is surely due to a lack of research, rather than any lack of underlying similarities. The field of sign language acquisition is still relatively new, with many unexplored corners.

Certainly, over the last half century we have made great strides in our understanding of sign language development. New technology and experimental methodologies are making it possible to perform studies on younger children than was previously possible, and to probe the regions of the brain where language is controlled. More cross-linguistic investigations are being conducted, making important comparisons between the traditionally well-studied sign languages of Europe and the Americas with sign languages from Asia, Africa, Australia and elsewhere. Still, there are gaps in our research program, some of them quite big, that are still waiting to be filled in.

With respect to childhood development of sign language, three areas in particular stand out as needing further study. The first, development of sign by late-exposed learners, I have already discussed in the beginning of Section 2. The second area is L1 sign language development in later childhood. Some possible candidates for study (using similar studies from the spoken acquisition literature as a guide) include advanced and low-frequency vocabulary, advanced forms of subordination, metaphors, humorous language and figurative speech. A third area that has traditionally been neglected is sign bilingualism. Hearing children are common in deaf families and many of them are bimodal bilinguals, acquiring both signed and spoken language. Yet with a few exceptions (i.e. Petitto & Holowka, 2002; van den Bogaerde, 2000), there have been no large-scale studies on how bimodal bilinguals develop their native languages, how these two languages interact, and how development in each language diverges from development in sign-only or speech-only monolinguals. There have been even fewer studies on bilinguals learning two sign languages at once.

Turning now to adult signers, there are very few studies on the acquisition of sign languages as an L2, either by hearing learners or by deaf signers already proficient in a different sign language. Given the recent rise in popularity of sign languages in schools and universities in the US and elsewhere, it would seem in our best interest to understand the processes underlying second language development of sign languages. On a related note, I know of no studies examining the acquisition of multiple "varieties" or dialects of the same sign language. Sociolinguistic variables such as gender, age, region, socioeconomic status, etc., have been identified as factors contributing to phonological, lexical and syntactic variation in ASL (Lucas, Bayley, & Valli, 2001, 2003) and Australian Sign Language (Schembri, Johnston, & Goswell, 2006), but to my knowledge, there has not been any systematic study on the acquisition of these dialectal differences by native signers: for example, changes in one's original dialect due to prolonged contact with another dialect.

Finally, we know little about the process of sign language attrition, either as a result of the natural aging process, or (in the case of grown hearing children of deaf parents) departure from the signing environment of one's childhood. L1 signers who move to an area where a different sign language is used may also experience attrition to their L1 sign language, as may L2 learners whose exposure to sign language is suspended for a long period of time (e.g. between academic terms at university).

This list of suggested directions for further research is of course far from comprehensive, and it reflects my biases as a linguist studying language acquisition. Still, I hope it will convince students and other future sign language researchers of how much still remains unknown in this field, and how much they stand to contribute, should they choose to pursue it.

NOTES

1. I wish to thank the many colleagues who patiently answered my questions and offered helpful suggestions while I was writing this manuscript: Richard Meier, Ginger Pizer, David Quinto-Pozos, Martha Tyrone, Jenny Singleton, Paul Preston, Michele Bishop, Anne Baker, and Karen Emmorey. Thank you also to Julie Hochgesang for the photo illustrations. All errors are, of course, my own.

2. Signed versions of English such as Signed Exact English (SEE) are artificial systems invented by educators as a way to present English to deaf students. They do not qualify as natural sign languages and are not acquired in the same way as natural sign languages.

3. This is assuming the signer is right-handed, as the majority of signers are. In the case of a left-handed signer, this sign is articulated with the left hand, the palm accordingly facing the signer's right.

4. There is even evidence that deaf parents share the "hands before face" bias, at least in child-directed signing (see Reilly & McIntire, 1991).

5. Note that the inability to maintain multiple spatial referents in one's *production* does not preclude the ability to *comprehend* them in another's signing (cf. the Bellugi et al. (1993) and Lillo-Martin et al. (1999) studies cited earlier).

6. Difficulties in coordinating grammatical nonmanuals with lexical materials have also been reported by Morgan, Smith, Tsimpli, and Woll (2002) in the BSL production of a polyglot savant, Christopher.

REFERENCES

Akamatsu, C. (1982). *The acquisition of fingerspelling in pre-school children.* Unpublished doctoral dissertation, University of Rochester, NY.

Anderson, D., & Reilly, J. (1997). The puzzle of negation: How children move from communicative to grammatical negation in ASL. *Applied Psycholinguistics, 18,* 411–429. Anderson, D., & Reilly, J. (1998). Pah! The acquisition of adverbials in ASL. *Sign Language and Linguistics, 1,* 117–142.

Bellugi, U., van Hoek, K., Lillo-Martin, D., & O'Grady, M. L. (1993). The development of spatialized syntactic mechanisms in American Sign Language. In D. Bishop & K. Mogford (Eds.), *Language development in exceptional circumstances* (pp. 132–149). Edinburgh: Churchill Livingstone.

Bonvillian, J. (1999). Sign language development. In M. Barrett (Ed.), *The development of language.* East Sussex, UK: Psychology Press.

Boyes Braem, P., & Sutton-Spence, R. (Eds.). (2001). *The hands are the head of the mouth: The mouth as articulator in sign languages.* Hamburg: Signum-Verlag. Brentari, D. (Ed.) (2001). *Foreign vocabulary in sign languages.* Mahwah, NJ: Lawrence Erlbaum. Brentari, D., & Poizner, H. (1994). A phonological analysis of a deaf Parkinsonian signer. *Language and Cognitive Processes, 9*(1), 69–100.

Brentari, D., Poizner, H., & Kegl, J. (1995). Aphasic and Parkinsonian signing: Differences in phonological disruption. *Brain and Language, 48,* 69–105.

Budding, C., Hoopes, R., Mueller, M., & Scarcello, K. (1995). Identification of foreign sign language accents by the deaf. In L. Byers & M. Rose (Eds.) *Gallaudet University Communication Forum, Vol. 4* (pp. 1–16). Washington, DC: Gallaudet University Press.

Cheek, A., Cormier, K., Repp, A., & Meier, R. (2001). Prelinguistic gesture predicts mastery and error in the production of first signs. *Language, 77,* 292–323.

Chen Pichler, D. (2006). *Handshape in L2 ASL: Effects of markedness and transfer.* Presented at the 9th Congress on Theoretical Issues in Sign Language Research (TISLR 9), Florianópolis, Brazil.

Cicourel, A., & Boese, R. (1972). Sign language acquisition and the teaching of deaf children. In C. Cazden, V. John, & D. Hymes (Eds.), *Function of language in the classroom.* New York: Teachers College.

Clibbens, J., & Harris, M. (1993). Phonological processes and sign language development. In D. Messer & G. Turner (Eds.), *Critical influences on child language acquisition and development.* London/New York: Macmillan/St Martin's Press.

Conlin, K., Mirus, G., Mauk, C., & Meier, R. (2000). The acquisition of first signs: Place, handshape, and movement. In C. Chamberlain, J. Morford, & R. Mayberry (Eds.), *Language acquisition by eye* (pp. 51–69). Mahwah, NJ: Lawrence Erlbaum.

Corina, D., Poizner, H., Bellugi, U., Feinberg, T., Dowd, D., & O'Grady-Batch, L. (1992). Dissociation between linguistic and nonlinguistic gestural systems: A case for compositionality. *Brain and Language, 43,* 414–447.

Emmorey, K. (2002). *Language, cognition and the brain: Insights from sign language research.* Mahwah, NJ: Lawrence Erlbaum.

Emmorey, K., & Reilly, J. (1998). The development of quotation and reported action: Conveying perspective in ASL. In E. Clark (Ed.), *Proceedings of the Stanford Child Languages Forum* (pp. 81–90). Stanford, CA: Center for the Study of Language and Information Publications.

Engberg-Pedersen, E. (1993). *Space in Danish Sign Language: The meaning and morphosyntax of the use of space in a visual language.* Hamburg, Germany: Signum-Verlag.

Engberg-Pedersen, E. (1995). Point of view expressed through shifters. In K. Emmorey & J. Reilly (Eds.), *Language, gesture, and space* (pp. 133–154). Hillsdale, NJ: Lawrence Erlbaum.

Gordon, R., Jr. (Ed.), (2005). *Ethnologue: Languages of the world* (15th ed.). Dallas, TX: SIL International. Retrieved December 3, 2007, from www.ethnologue.com/.

Hoffmeister, R. (1978). *The development of demonstrative pronouns, locative and personal pronouns in the acquisition of American Sign Language by deaf children of deaf parents*. Unpublished doctoral dissertation, University of Minnesota.

Janzen, T. (1999). The grammaticization of topics in American Sign Language. *Studies in Language, 23*(2), 271–306.

Johnson, R., & Liddell, S. (2008). *Sign language phonetics: Architecture and description*. Unpublished manuscript.

Johnston, T., & Schembri, A. (2007). *Australian Sign Language (Auslan): An introduction to sign language linguistics*. Cambridge, UK: Cambridge University Press.

Kantor, R. (1978). Identifying native and second language signers. *Communication and Cognition, 11*, 39–55.

Karmiloff-Smith, A. (1986). Some fundamental aspects of language development after age 5. In P. Fletcher & M. Garman (Eds.), *Language acquisition* (2nd ed.) (pp. 456–474). Cambridge, UK: Cambridge University Press.

Karnopp, L. (2002). Phonology acquisition in Brazilian Sign Language. In G. Morgan & B. Woll (Eds.), *Directions in sign language acquisition* (pp. 29–53). Amsterdam: John Benjamins.

Kegl, J., & Poizner, H. (1997). Crosslinguistic/crossmodal syntactic consequences of left-hemisphere damage: Evidence from an aphasic signer and his identical twin. *Aphasiology, 11*, 1–37.

Lavoie, C., & Villeneuve, S. (1999). Acquisition du lieu d'articulation en Langue des Signes Québécoise: Etude de cas. In *Variations: le langage en théorie et en pratique. Actes du colloque: Le colloque des étudiants en sciences du langage*. Montreal: University of Quebec at Montreal.

Lillo-Martin, D. (1999). Modality effects and modularity in language acquisition: The acquisition of American Sign Language. In T. Bhatia & W. Ritchie (Eds.), *Handbook of child language acquisition* (pp. 531–567). San Diego, CA: Academic Press.

Lillo-Martin, D. (2000). Aspects of the syntax and acquisition of wh-questions in American Sign Language. In K. Emmorey & H. Lane (Eds.), *The signs of language revisited: An anthology in honor of Ursula Bellugi and Edward Klima* (pp. 401–414). Mahwah, NJ: Lawrence Erlbaum.

Lillo-Martin, D., Bellugi, U., Struxness L., & O'Grady, M. (1985). The acquisition of spatially organized syntax. In E. Clark (Ed.), *Proceedings of the Stanford Child Languages Forum 24* (pp. 70–78). Palo Alto, CA: Stanford University Press.

Loew, R. (1984). *Roles and reference in American Sign Language: A developmental perspective*. Unpublished doctoral dissertation, University of Minnesota.

Lucas, C., Bayley, R., & Valli, C. [in collaboration with Mary Rose, Alyssa Wulf, Paul Dudis, Laura Sanheim, & Susan Schatz]. (2001). *Sociolinguistic variation in ASL* (*Sociolinguistics in deaf communities, Vol. 7*). Washington, DC: Gallaudet University Press.

Lucas, C., Bayley, R., & Valli. C. (2003). *What's your sign for PIZZA? An introduction to variation in ASL*. Washington, DC: Gallaudet University Press.

Lucas, C., Valli, C., & Mulrooney, K. (2005). *Linguistics of American Sign Language* (4th ed.). Washington, DC: Gallaudet University Press.

MacFarlane, J. (1998). *From affect to grammar: Ritualization of facial affect in signed languages*. Paper presented at the Theoretical Issues in Sign Language Research Conference at Gallaudet University.

McIntire, M., & Reilly, J. (1988). Nonmanual behaviors in L1 & L2 learners of American Sign Language. *Sign Language Studies, 61,* 351–375.

McKee, R., & McKee, D. (1992). What's so hard about learning ASL? Students' and teachers' perceptions. *Sign Language Studies, 75,* 129–158.

Mayberry, R. (1995). Mental phonology in language comprehension, or what does that sign mistake mean? In K. Emmorey & J. Reilly (Eds.), *Language, gesture, and space* (pp. 355–370). Hillsdale, NJ: Lawrence Erlbaum.

Mayberry, R., & Eichen, E. (1991). The long-lasting advantage of learning sign language in childhood: Another look at the critical period for language acquisition. *Journal of Memory and Language, 30,* 486–512.

Mayberry, R., & Fischer, S. (1989). Looking through phonological shape to lexical meaning: The bottleneck of nonnative sign language processing. *Memory and Cognition, 17,* 740–754.

Meier, R. (2006). The form of early signs: Explaining signing children's articulatory development. In M. Marschark, B. Schick, & P. Spencer (Eds.), *Advances in sign language development by deaf children* (pp. 202–230). New York: Oxford University Press.

Meier, R., Cheek, A., & Moreland, C. (2002). Iconic versus motoric determinants of the form of children's early signs. In B. Skarabela, S. Fish, & H.-J. Do (Eds.), *BUCLD 26: Proceedings of the 26th Annual Boston University Conference on Language and Development* (pp. 393–405). Somerville, MA: Cascadilla Press.

Meir, I., & Sandler, W. (2007). *A language in space: The story of Israeli Sign Language.* New York: Lawrence Erlbaum.

Mirus, G., Rathmann, C., & Meier, R. (2001). Proximalization and distalization of sign movement in adult learners. In V. Dively, M. Metzger, S. Taub, & A. M. Baer (Eds.), *Signed languages: Discoveries from international research* (pp. 103–119). Washington, DC: Gallaudet University Press.

Morford, J., & Mayberry, R. (2000). A reexamination of "Early Exposure" and its implications for language acquisition by eye. In C. Chamberlain, J. Morford, & R. Mayberry (Eds.), *Language acquisition by eye* (pp. 111–128). Mahwah, NJ: Lawrence Erlbaum.

Morgan, G. (1999). Event packaging in BSL discourse. In E. Winston (Ed.), *Story telling and conversation: Discourse in deaf communities* (pp. 27–58). Washington, DC: Gallaudet University Press.

Morgan, G., Barrett-Jones, S., & Stoneham, H. (2007). The first signs of language: Phonological development in British Sign Language. *Applied Psycholinguistics, 28,* 3–22.

Morgan, G., Smith, N., Tsimpli, I., & Woll, B. (2002). The effects of modality on BSL development in an exceptional learner. In R. Meier, K. Cormier, & D. Quinto (Eds.), *Modality and structure in signed and spoken language* (pp. 422–441). Cambridge, UK: Cambridge University Press.

Nelson, C. (1987). The recognition of facial expressions in the first two years of life: Mechanisms of development. *Child Development, 58,* 889–909.

Newport, E. (1990). Maturational constraints on language learning. *Cognitive Science, 14,* 11–28.

Newport, E., & Meier, R. (1985). The acquisition of American Sign Language. In D. Slobin (Ed.), *The crosslinguistic study of language acquisition* (pp. 881–938). Mahwah, NJ: Lawrence Erlbaum.

Oller, K., Wieman, L., Dole, W., & Ross, C. (1976). Infant babbling and speech. *Journal of Child Language, 3,* 1–12.

Oyama, S. (1976). A sensitive period in the acquisition of a non-native phonological system. *Journal of Psycholinguistic Research, 5*, 261–285.

Padden, C. (1991). The acquisition of fingerspelling in deaf children. In P. Siple & S. Fischer (Eds.), *Theoretical issues in sign language research. Vol. 2, Psychology* (pp. 191–210). Chicago: University of Chicago Press.

Padden, C. (2006). Learning to fingerspell twice: Young signing children's acquisition of fingerspelling. In M. Marschark, B. Schick, & P. Spencer (Eds.), *Advances in sign language development by deaf children* (pp. 189–201). New York: Oxford University Press.

Padden, C., & Hanson, V. (2000). Search for the missing link: The development of skilled reading in deaf children. In K. Emmorey & H. Lane (Eds.), *The signs of language revisited: An anthology in honor of Ursula Bellugi and Edward Klima* (pp. 435–448). Mahwah, NJ: Lawrence Erlbaum.

Padden, C., & LeMaster, B. (1985). An alphabet on hand: The acquisition of finger-spelling in deaf children. *Sign Language Studies, 47*, 161–172.

Padden, C., & Ramsey, C. (1998). Reading ability in signing deaf children. *Topics in Language Disorders, 18*, 30–46.

Petitto, L., & Holowka, S. (2002). Evaluating attributions of delay and confusion in young bilinguals: Special insights from infants acquiring a signed and spoken language. *Sign Language Studies, 3*, 4–33.

Petitto, L., & Marentette, P. (1991). Babbling in the manual mode: Evidence from the ontogeny of language. *Science, 251*, 1493–1496.

Poizner, H., & Kegl, J. (1993). Neural disorders of the linguistic use of space and movement. In P. Tallal, A. Falaburda, R. Llinas, & C. von Euler (Eds.), *Annals of the New York Academy of Science, Temporal Information Processing in the Nervous System. Vol. 682* (pp. 192–213). New York: New York Academy of Science Press.

Poizner, H., Brentari, D., Tyrone, M., & Kegl, J. (2000). The structure of language as motor behavior: Clues from signers with Parkinson's disease. In K. Emmorey & H. Lane (Eds.), *The signs of language revisited: An anthology in honor of Ursula Bellugi and Edward Klima* (pp. 509–532). Mahwah, NJ: Lawrence Erlbaum.

Poizner, H., Klima, E., & Bellugi, U. (1987). *What the hands reveal about the brain.* Cambridge, MA: MIT Press/Bradford Books.

Reilly, J. (2000). Bringing affective expression into the service of language: Acquiring perspective marking in narratives. In K. Emmorey & H. Lane (Eds.), *The signs of language revisited: An anthology in honor of Ursula Bellugi and Edward Klima* (pp. 401–433). Mahwah, NJ: Lawrence Erlbaum.

Reilly, J. (2006). Development of nonmanual morphology. In M. Marschark, B. Schick, & P. Spencer (Eds.), *Advances in sign language development by deaf children* (pp. 262–290). New York: Oxford University Press.

Reilly, J., & Bellugi, U. (1996). Competition on the face: Affect and language in ASL motherese. *Journal of Child Language, 23*, 219–239.

Reilly, J., & McIntire, M. (1991). WHERE SHOE: The acquisition of wh-questions in ASL. *Papers and Reports in Child Language Development, 30*, 104–111.

Reilly, J., McIntire, M., & Bellugi, U. (1990a). FACES: The relationship between language and affect. In V. Volterra & C. Erting (Eds.), *From gesture to language in deaf and hearing children* (pp. 129–141). New York: Springer-Verlag.

Reilly, J., McIntire, M., & Bellugi, U. (1990b). Conditionals in American Sign Language: Grammaticized facial expressions. *Applied Psycholinguistics*, 11(4), 369–392.

Reilly, J., McIntire, M., & Bellugi, U. (1991). BABYFACE: A new perspective on universals of language acquisition. In P. Siple (Ed.), *Theoretical issues in sign language research: Psycholinguistics* (pp. 9–23). Chicago: University of Chicago Press.

Rosen, R. (2004). Beginning L2 production errors in ASL lexical phonology. *Sign Language Studies, 7,* 31–61.

Rossini, P., Reilly, J., Fabretti, D., & Volterra, V. (1998). *Non-manual behaviors in Italian Sign Language.* Paper presented at the Italian Sign Language Conference, Genoa, Italy.

Sandler, W., & Lillo-Martin, D. (2006). *Sign language and linguistic universals.* Cambridge, UK: Cambridge University Press.

Schembri, A., Johnston, T., & Goswell, D. (2006). NAME dropping: Location variation in Australian Sign Language. In C. Lucas (Ed.), *Multilingualism and sign languages: From the Great Plains to Australia* (pp. 121–156). Washington, DC: Gallaudet University Press.

Scovel, T. (1969). Foreign accents, language acquisition and cerebral dominance. *Language Learning, 19,* 245–254.

Scovel, T. (1981). The recognition of foreign accents in English and its implications for psycholinguistic theories of language acquisition. In J.-G. Savard & L. Laforge (Eds.), *Proceedings of the 5th Congress of AILA* (pp. 389–401). Laval, Quebec: University of Laval Press.

Slobin, D. (1973). Cognitive prerequisites for the development of grammar. In C. Ferguson & D. Slobin (Eds.), *Studies of child language development.* New York: Holt, Rinehart, and Winston.

Stokoe, W., Casterline, D., & Croneberg, C. (1965). *A dictionary of American Sign Language on linguistic principles.* Silver Spring, MD: Linstok Press.

Sutton-Spence, R., & Woll, B. (1999). *The linguistics of British Sign Language: An introduction.* Cambridge, UK: Cambridge University Press.

Takkinen, R. (2003). Variations of handshape features in the acquisition process. In A. Baker, B. van den Bogaerde & O. Crassborn (Eds.), *Cross-linguistic perspectives in sign language research: Selected papers from TISLR 2000* (pp. 81–91). Hamburg: Signum.

Tyrone, M., Kegl, J., & Poizner, H. (1999). Interarticulator co-ordination in deaf signers with Parkinson's disease. *Neuropsychologia, 37,* 1271–1283.

van den Bogaerde, B. (2000). *Input and interaction in deaf families.* Published doctoral dissertation, University of Amsterdam. Utrecht: LOT.

von Tetzchner, S. (1994). First signs acquired by a Norwegian deaf child with hearing parents. *Sign Language Studies, 44,* 225–257.

The Ear and Deafness

HOW WE HEAR

WRITTEN BY

AMERICAN SPEECH-LANGUAGE-HEARING ASSOCIATION

Hearing is one of the five senses. It is a complex process of picking up sound and attaching meaning to it. The ability to hear is critical to understanding the world around us.

The human ear is a fully developed part of our bodies at birth and responds to sounds that are very faint as well as sounds that are very loud. Even before birth, infants respond to sound.

HOW DO WE HEAR?

The ear can be divided into three parts leading up to the brain—the outer ear, middle ear and the inner ear.

- The outer ear consists of the *pinna, or auricle,* and the ear canal (*external auditory meatus*). The pinna—the part of the "ear" that we see on each side of our heads—is made of cartilage and soft tissue so that it keeps a particular shape but is also flexible. The pinna serves as a collector of sound vibrations around us and guides the vibrations into the ear canal. It helps us decide the direction and source of sound.
- The middle ear is a space behind the eardrum that contains three small bones called *ossicles.* This chain of tiny bones is connected to the eardrum at one end and to an opening to the inner ear at the other end. Vibrations from the eardrum cause the ossicles to vibrate which, in turn, creates movement of the fluid in the inner ear.
- The inner ear contains the sensory organs for hearing and balance. The *cochlea* is the hearing part of the inner ear. **The cochlea is a bony structure shaped like a snail and filled with fluid.** Movement of the fluid in the inner ear, or *cochlea,* causes changes in tiny structures called *hair cells.* This movement of the hair cells sends electric signals from the inner ear up the auditory nerve (also known as the hearing nerve) to the brain. The brain then interprets these electrical signals as sound.

WHAT IS HEARING LOSS?

When describing hearing loss, we generally look at three categories: type of hearing loss, degree of hearing loss, and configuration of hearing loss. Hearing loss can greatly affect the quality of life for adult and children. Unmanaged hearing loss can have an impact on employment, education, and general well-being.

Hearing loss can be categorized by which part of the auditory system is damaged. There are three basic types of hearing loss: conductive hearing loss, sensorineural hearing loss, and mixed hearing loss.

Conductive hearing loss occurs when sound is not conducted efficiently through the outer ear canal to the eardrum and the tiny bones (ossicles) of the middle ear. Conductive hearing loss usually involves a reduction in sound level or the ability to hear faint sounds. This type of hearing loss can often be corrected medically or surgically.

Sensorineural hearing loss (SNHL) occurs when there is damage to the inner ear (cochlea), or to the nerve pathways from the inner ear to the brain. Most of the time, SNHL cannot be medically or surgically corrected. This is the most common type of permanent hearing loss.

SNHL reduces the ability to hear faint sounds. Even when speech is loud enough to hear it may still be unclear or sound muffled.

Sometimes a conductive hearing loss occurs in combination with a sensorineural hearing loss (SNHL). In other words, there may be damage in the outer or middle ear and in the inner ear (cochlea) or auditory nerve. When this occurs, the hearing loss is referred to as a *mixed* hearing loss.

DEGREE OF HEARING LOSS

Degree of hearing loss refers to the severity of the loss. The table below shows one of the more commonly used classification systems. The numbers are representative of the patient's hearing loss range in decibels (dB HL).

DEGREE OF HEARING LOSS	HEARING LOSS RANGE (DB HL)
Normal	−10 to 15
Slight	16 to 25
Mild	26 to 40
Moderate	41 to 55
Moderately severe	56 to 70
Severe	71 to 90
Profound	91+

Source: Clark, J. G. (1981). Uses and abuses of hearing loss classification. Asha, 23, 493–500.

CONFIGURATION OF THE HEARING LOSS

The configuration, or shape, of the hearing loss refers to the degree and pattern of hearing loss across frequencies (tones), as illustrated in a graph called an audiogram. For example, a hearing loss that only affects the high tones would be described as a high-frequency loss. Its configuration would show good hearing in the low tones and poor hearing in the high tones.

On the other hand, if only the low frequencies are affected, the configuration would show poorer hearing for low tones and better hearing for high tones. Some hearing loss configurations are flat, indicating the same amount of hearing loss for low and high tones.

CAUSES OF HEARING LOSS

Hearing loss can occur at birth (Congenital Hearing Loss), after Birth (Acquired Hearing loss), due to ear infections (otitis media), noise exposure or ototoxic medications.

The term congenital hearing loss means the hearing loss is present at birth. Congenital hearing loss can be caused by genetic or nongenetic factors. Genetic factors (hereditary) are thought to cause more than 50% of all hearing loss. Hearing loss from genetic defects can be present at birth or develop later on in life. Most genetic hearing loss can be described as autosomal recessive or autosomal dominant. Nongenetic factors can account for about 25% of congenital hearing loss.

Acquired hearing loss is a hearing loss that appears after birth. The hearing loss can occur at any time in one's life, as a result of an illness or injury.

Ear infections happen when the middle ear becomes inflamed. The middle ear is the small space behind the eardrum. Ear infections are also called acute otitis media. They can happen in one or both ears.

Loud noise can be very damaging to hearing. Both the level of noise and the length of time you listen to the noise can put you at risk for noise-induced hearing loss. Noise levels are measured in decibels, or dB for short. The higher the decibel level, the louder the noise. Sounds that are louder than 85 dB can cause permanent hearing loss. The hearing system can be injured not only by a loud blast or explosion but also by prolonged exposure to high noise levels.

Certain medications are considered "ototoxic" to the ear. These medications can damage the ear, resulting in hearing loss or ringing in the ear.

There are more than 200 known ototoxic medications (prescription and over-the-counter) on the market today. These include medicines used to treat serious infections, cancer, and heart disease.

Deafhood

A CONCEPT STRESSING POSSIBILITIES, NOT DEFICITS

WRITTEN BY

PADDY LADD

TRADITIONAL CONSTRUCTIONS

Western deaf communities have existed since at least the fifteenth century, but it was not until the first deaf schools were established in the late eighteenth century that large numbers of deaf people were able to congregate, educate each other, develop their own cultures, and form urban communities around such schools. During the Enlightenment period, with its intense interest in the relationship between humanity and language, deaf communities and their sign languages were more positively regarded [1]. This interrelationship between deaf and non-deaf peoples was rooted in beliefs about *Nature*, a crucial and positive concept prior to the Industrial Revolution.

However, during the nineteenth century, through the rise and reification of science and medicine, the development of Social Darwinism and the rapid growth of colonialism, the concept of *Progress* gained hegemony. Unpicking this concept reveals an assumption of the "Manifest Destiny" of the Nordic races—that Man's increasing subordination of Nature to science was both an inevitable stage of human evolution and a virtually unqualified good. Thus Nature itself, its connotations, and, by extension, most non-Nordic peoples, were constructed as "backwards" or retarded on an evolutionary scale, and deaf people's previous association with Nature resulted in their submersion within this category [2].

As a consequence, an intricate medical-educational administrative nexus was established as the means by which deaf communities should be categorized and ruled. This process required the development of a *medical model* of deafness, which stressed that the only way for deaf people to attain full humanity was to integrate with the majority population and forsake contact with their own languages and peoples [3]. Although deaf communities vigorously resisted these policies, it was not until the late twentieth century that their views were heeded, and some changes initiated.

As the twentieth century moved on, the administrators of the medical model adopted the term *disability*, which for the first time placed deaf peoples in an administrative category that included all other "physically impaired" people. This had both positive and negative effects for deaf communities, who were unhappy about such a categorization primarily because of the disability movement's insistence that all disabled children be mainstreamed, which led to the closure of hundreds of deaf schools across the West [4]. By removing deaf children from their much-needed contact with deaf adults and other deaf children, mainstreaming thereby severely damaging deaf people's cultures. Despite numerous worldwide protests, they have been unable to reverse the trend.

THE SOCIAL MODEL AND THE DEAF CULTURO-LINGUISTIC MODEL

By the 1990s disabled people's organizations developed an alternative to the medical model—the *social model*—in which they asserted that the roots of disability lay not within themselves but in the societies that denied them citizenship, and thus "disabled" them [5].

In my book "Understanding deaf culture" [6] I explain deaf people's conception of themselves as a linguistic and cultural minority, and outline how the social model as applied to deaf people contains internal contradictions and how it fails to take on board several key differences in the quality of deaf cultural lives compared with those of persons with disabilities. I emerge with a new *culturo-linguistic model* that enables the deaf experience to be more properly understood, not only as a cultural experience. This model also enables a beginning to the investigation to locate administrative placement with more appropriate groups of oppressed Others. This model offers the term *deafhood*, not only as a refutation of the medical term *deafness*, but as a means by which to capture and set down the historically transmitted value systems by which deaf peoples, as uniquely visuo-gesturo-tactile biological entities, believe they offer a different and positive perspective on what it means to be human.

DEAFHOOD, DEAFNESS, AND ORALISM AS COLONIALISM

These values can be traced back through over 200 years of deaf communities (see later section) and stand in (largely unrecognized) opposition to the deafness models that gained hegemonic control of the administration of those communities. Various concepts and strategies have been attempted in order to overturn those models. The most recent constructs deaf communities as being the victims of a *colonization* process, proposed by Lane [7], then Wrigley [8], but not formalized until Ladd [6]. The essential features of this form of colonization are policies actively intending to eradicate or marginalize sign languages and deaf cultures. The name given to such policies is *oralism*, whose central tenets are described below.

Prior to the hegemony of oralism, which began in the 1880s, sign languages were used in deaf education, deaf schools were founded by deaf people themselves, and deaf teachers and professionals abounded [9]. In the last 120 years oralism has proscribed the use of sign language in deaf education, and removed deaf teachers and deaf adults from the education system in order to try and prevent them from passing down deaf culture to the next generations of deaf children. This policy still continues in most countries today, although in the last 20 years a movement towards reinstating sign language, known as *bilingual* *deaf education,*and which began in Scandinavia, has made some inroads in other countries. (It would be instructive to understand why Scandinavian policies are much more enlightened than those elsewhere, but this subject unfortunately—and significantly—has not been researched.)

Oralism disguises its intent under the rubric of education, claiming that if sign languages and deaf teachers were removed from the system, and deaf children were isolated from each other where possible and taught only by lip-reading, speech, and auditory input, then they would be assimilated into majority societies. This ideology claims that speech can *only* be developed by the removal of those languages and cultures from the deaf child's environment. In order to administer such a system, it denies the existence of the concept of a "deaf child", replacing it by the terms *deafness* and *hearing-impaired,* which focuses on what the child lacks rather than the qualities he or she possesses in potentia. Ultimately it claims that a deaf child is "simply a hearing child who cannot hear" [5].

The consequences of oralism have been severe. Deaf school-leavers worldwide have a reading age of 8¾, sufficient for the headlines of a tabloid newspaper, yet their speech is still almost incomprehensible [10]. This not only affects their ability to gain appropriate employment or further education but deprives them of meaningful relationships with their parents. It instils in them a range of internalized oppressions, from a simple lack of self-confidence or self-belief, through identity crises and self-hatred, to a rate of acquired mental illness double that of non-deaf populations[11].

Inevitably, oralism has also seriously affected the quality of deaf individuals' collective lives in their signing communities. This has been manifested in damage to their traditional cultures [6] and artforms [1], and in their ability to run their own clubs and organizations, which were subsequently taken over by non-deaf peoples and administered, in effect, as deaf colonies [12], with subsequent community divisions which are characteristic of the colonization process [6].

Crucially for students of public health policies, by removing sign languages from the public eye, oralism also resulted in the exclusion of deaf peoples from the twentieth-century's liberal or radical discourses, so that these important avenues of social change were no longer available to them.

DEAFHOOD COVERTLY MAINTAINED

Although driven "underground" in this way, deaf communities nevertheless refused to stop using their own languages and continued to maintain their own existence and culture through deaf clubs, national and international organizations, and the successful raising of hundreds of thousands of non-deaf children in those cultures. The cultural cornerstones of the communities are the 10% of deaf children born to deaf parents who have passed the pre-oralist deafhood inheritance down as many as nine generations, dating back to the 1820s, when records first began [13].

It is a testimony to the determination of deaf people that those local, regional, national, and international communities have continued to exist throughout the oralist century, and re-emerged to win some changes from 1975 onwards (the *deaf Resurgence*)—notably a greater visibility in the media, and a consequent explosion of the numbers of non-deaf people wishing to learn sign languages. It is because of these successes that the contemporary reader has any awareness of sign languages and deaf people, to whatever degree.

Nevertheless, given the exponential increase in academic discourses in the twentieth century, this removal of deaf people has led to the creation of a particularly large "discourse distance" between their own discourses and even the most radical non-deaf discourses. Given the importance of liberal/radical forces in achieving social reform, one can understand why the arguably child-abusive practice of oralism [6] has been allowed to continue without appropriate scrutiny.

THE DEAFHOOD CONCEPT AND POSTCOLONIAL CULTURES

In order, therefore, to create a space in English-language discourses to even begin to bridge this distance, one in which the positive, collective, worldwide deaf experience can be situated, a term other than "*deafness*" is needed. Thus, *deafhood*. There are deaf sign-language terms that capture aspects of the concept. But the primary challenge at this historical moment is to disrupt these powerful deafness discourses in order to be able to enable the beginnings of a deaf counter-narrative.

Given that human beings have a tendency to seek fixity, it is important to state from the outset that deafhood is a process, not a fixed state, a checklist of characteristics that can be used to police whichever ideologies arise to attempt hegemony. Like any other group of humans, deaf children and adults undergo enculturation. One learns to become a member of a culture, and in a similar way a child born deaf, even to deaf parents, has to learn to become "deaf", that is, to become a responsible sign-language-using member of a national community.

There is one crucial difference between this process and majority society enculturation. One can become "English" (for example) over a period of years, and Englishness is then established. The arguments as to what that Englishness might be are contested anew by every generation, and the culture evolves when members of that society seek to extend what Englishness might mean in a future that they imagine for their communities.

But the state of being "English" itself is rarely brought into question, except in times of war when one's behaviour or beliefs can be attacked as "un-English". In intensely ideological states such as the USA, the concept of behaving in an "un-American" way can be used by the military-industrial complex to enforce conformity. But, generally, majority Western society's membership of its own cultures has not been seriously questioned until the rapid rise of concepts of ethnicity following the end of the Cold War.

Minority cultures and *postcolonial cultures*, on the other hand, are constantly challenged to validate their status, not just by external forces but by internal forces also. For example, being "Black" or "Native American", for example, is a state of existence that is continually called into question, hence the derogatory terms "Uncle Tom", "oreo", or "apple" applied to members of those societies who are perceived to side with those external forces. There are few such equivalent pressures for majority cultures.

Moreover, the temptations to try and leave behind one's origins by merging with majority society continue throughout one's life. Maintaining one's "Blackness", therefore, can become a lifetime's struggle. And so it is with deafhood: one not only has to become "deaf", but to maintain that "deaf" identity in the face of decades of daily negations. Precisely what "deaf" means for each group within each generation will vary—but the first criteria of deafhood is that it is a *process* through which each deaf man, woman, and child implicitly explains his/ her existence as a deaf being in the world to him/ herself and to each other. It is the next step that becomes especially interesting—namely the precise epistemological or ontological "content" of those explanations.

DEAFHOOD AND DEAF POSSIBILITIES

Deafhood as a concept is utilized as a way by which to measure *deaf possibilities*. Majority cultures do not have to measure their culture in such ways—they are implicit within their own definitions of "cultural change". But minority cultures that have undergone oppression, especially Black or postcolonial societies, are forced to create and re-create their cultures, often by reference to whatever aspects of their pre-colonized cultures they still retain, in order to identify a "larger" self which once existed.

After 120 years of oppression of sign languages and their users, and the consequent internalized oppression and self-shame, we no longer know very much about whatever larger deaf self existed. Yet to simply proceed from the present historical moment is to limit our understanding of deaf possibilities. One must therefore seek out evidence of pre-oralist deaf selfhood, although very few data presently exist, not least because sign languages have no written form. Perhaps the most important data currently accessible are the writings of French deaf people from Desloges [14] through Massieu and Clerc [15] to the deaf Parisian Banquets held between 1834 and 1880 [16].

Such writings, which span a century, can be regarded as the "tip of the iceberg", since new historical data continue to emerge. In them, seven epistemological principles of deafhood can presently be identified. Briefly summarized, these include the belief that sign languages were not only the equal of spoken languages *but even arguably "superior" in their ability to communicate across national boundaries.* (This ability has much to do with the tremendous grammatical similarities across sign languages.) Deaf people believed that these languages were a gift from God/ Nature, and that they were deliberately placed on earth to manifest the beauty, power, and usefulness of those languages. They regarded non-signing people as "sign-impaired", incomplete beings and offered their languages as a gift to those people to help them become "completed beings" [6].

The extent to which these principles seem remarkable or incredible to the reader can actually be rendered as an indication of the extent to which he or she has "bought into" the medical model that constructs deaf people as incomplete beings who can be helped—but not at any time learned from. In fact evidence is beginning to emerge that communicating with non-deaf babies through signing can enhance their cognitive development and speed up the acquisition of their spoken language [17]. One might ask therefore just what other powerful gains for humanity might be achieved through utilizing the skills of deaf communities.

DEAFHOOD PRINCIPLES IN CONTEMPORARY RESEARCH

I then used these deafhood principles as a basis from which to examine UK deaf culture during the twentieth century, and this approach proved to be fruitful. By mid-century few of those tenets still remained within overt deaf discourses during that time. But in researching the lives of deaf children in residential schools and the lives of deaf adults within deaf clubs during that century, it was possible to identify aspects of deaf belief and behaviour that could nevertheless be described as attempts to maintain deafhood identity [6]. Numbers of these examples operated on a daily, localised level—such as the concept of "1,001 [small] Victories" [6]—where deaf children attempted to subvert the ban on sign languages in numerous "small acts". On reaching adulthood, deaf adults asserted themselves similarly in response to the everyday discrimination of hearing-speaking (*audist*) societies.

However, I also located what can be called "class" divisions within deaf communities, where a deaf "middle class" ran the communities by attributing negative meanings to the term "deaf". Similar patterns can be observed in other colonized and minority cultures, where the striving to be as "white" as possible by a Black bourgeoisie operated in tandem with a derogation (or subsequent rebellious adoption) of the concept of "Nigger", to give one example [18].

In one respect, then, deafhood represents the sum of all the self-explanations of "deaf" presently available to deaf communities. In another—and this is one of the most difficult points to resolve this early in the deafhood decolonization process—there is the impulse towards larger deaf possibilities, which suggests that the process of becoming and maintaining "deaf" could lead to deafhood being used by one group or another to validate ideas about being "more" or less "deaf" at any one point in time. This could for instance become limited by narrow concepts of "deaf nationalism", a problem faced by other decolonizing societies.

To minimize this danger, I suggest a stress on the "deepening" of one's deafhood whilst acknowledging that there is no obvious end to that process. I also stress that the "deaf Nation" concept can, following Berthier [cf. 16], be recognized as essentially an *international* concept, so that individual deaf countries and communities form branches of a global entity. This belief is already widespread, being embodied in the practices (if not the overt discourses) of the 50-year-old World Federation of the Deaf.

Another strategy for avoiding deaf nationalism is to use the deaf culture term in a certain way. By describing what deaf culture has enclosed over the last century, it is possible to view the diminished postcolonial readings as "*deaf cultural traditions*", and to identify the strivings to go beyond these as "*deafhood*". This enables us to make an epistemological break with whatever negative cultural features one considers to have been internalized, and thus to create space for decolonizing praxis—thoughts, beliefs, and actions that interrupt older patterns and aspire towards concepts of a larger deaf self, able to extend the boundaries of what being "deaf" might mean.

A few simple examples may be useful. Deaf cultures are notorious for their members being critical of each other rather than praising (the "horizontal violence" found in other minority cultures). It is possible to demonstrate that this feature is learned from an oralist upbringing, and that deafhood could enclose the possibility of change to a more positive mode of being [6]. The profound devaluation of sign-language skills and deaf arts in some deaf communities can be shown to be similarly learned. By reference to the deafhood concept, a climate of positive valuation of the range and beauty of the language can be encouraged, together with a reorienting of (for example) deaf theatre, so that instead of simply translating non-deaf plays into sign, deaf life and community can become a valid subject for deaf dramatists [6].

In external domains one can demonstrate that deaf ways of thinking and being have long been excluded from deaf education, so that in this present age when deaf people are once more beginning to be admitted to their rightful role in respect of deaf children, there begins a search of the myriad ways in which deafhood might be used to completely reform deaf education. A similar dynamic can be located within deaf mental health services, deaf television and deaf organizations [6].

The concept is also useful when we come to examine other national deaf cultures. Ladd (forthcoming) illustrates that ideas about being "STRONG-DEAF" were constructed differently between the UK and the USA. In the latter, there is a strong valorizing of one's ASL (American Sign Language) skills, on sign-play and creativity, and election of deaf leaders can depend on their ASL rhetorical skills. By contrast in the UK, emphasis on BSL skills and appreciation of BSL aesthetics is little valorized. There is, however, greater emphasis in the UK than in the USA on service to one's community, and to political activity as a manifestation of that service. On the international scene, moreover, American deaf people are seen as notoriously unwilling to socialize with other nations, and it can be argued that this too is a legacy of their own form of American colonialism. In each example, the absence of one or other of these features usually leads one deaf grouping to assert that the other is either "NOT-DEAF" or "LESS-DEAF". The deaf-hood concept, by contrast, enables us to read across those cultures, to say that deafhood is simply constructed differently in each country.

Finally, although the seven principles of French Victorian deafhood have been described as epistemological, it seems probable that they may be ontological principles [19], relating to (as yet unexplored) aspects of existentialism and phenomenology, since many versions of deafhood require the deaf person to answer the question "*Why have I been created deaf in this world ? Is there merely a 'negative', biological answer, or is this biological state simply a manifestation of a larger, possibly spiritual dimension of human existence?*' After all, one can refute scientist arguments that a person is born deaf because of defective features in the body, by pointing out that if any Supreme Being decided to create a signlanguage-using race, it would be necessary also to create the biological conditions that would render such developments possible.

DEAFHOOD, DEAF CULTURE, AND PUBLIC HEALTH

Importantly, deafhood also asserts that attitudes towards deaf by *lay* non-deaf people, that is, hearing people situated *outside* the colonialist administration, and in whose name the system is operated, can be positively influenced, once deaf communities are able to bring their own discourses to public notice, so that they can become allies in the decolonization process.

However, decolonization cannot proceed unless deaf societies clarify for themselves and others what "deaf Culture" is, and how it might operate across the colonized domains, especially deaf education systems. If this is not speedily accomplished—to give but one example—not only will teachers and parents become frustrated, but the admission of deaf people to major positions in education will be greatly slowed, and deaf children consequently negatively affected.

In turn this could lead to oralism regaining hegemony with the next generation of parents of deaf children, especially in view of the vast sums of money from the military-industrial complex (hundreds of millions of dollars worldwide) being invested in "new oralism" via the search for "miracle cures" as is currently manifested in the spread of cochlear implantation of deaf children [7].

Likewise the recent rise of genetic engineering and the concerted attempts to remove deaf genes from human existence poses another major ontological challenge, which cannot be met unless the deaf culturo-linguistic model is properly understood by those wielding power and influence. Were this to be understood, then it could be recognized that such attempts would result in the eventual eradication of over 250 of the world's languages, and thus be in direct contravention of both United Nations and European Union charters of rights.

CONCLUSIONS AND IMPLICATIONS

Thus, although the deafhood decolonizing process is still in its infancy, it offers great potential for serving as a counter-narrative, able to disrupt hegemonic medical and social models. With its potential to embody its "vulnerability as a strength" by informing the academy and society of the benefits of understanding and absorbing some of the cultural features of tactile, visuo-gesturally skilled deaf communities, the biodiversity of human experience can be positively valorized in the coming years.

REFERENCES

1. Mirzoeff N. Silent poetry: deafness, sign and visual culture in modern France. Princeton: Princeton University Press; 1995.
2. Branson J, Miller D. Damned for their difference: The cultural construction of deaf people as disabled. Washington, DC: Gallaudet University Press; 2002.
3. Lane H, Philip F. editors. The language of experience. Cambridge, MA: Harvard University Press; 1984.
4. Lee R. editor. Deaf liberation. Feltham: National Union of the Deaf; 1991.
5. Oliver M. The politics of disablement. Basingstoke: Macmillan; 1990.
6. Ladd P. Understanding deaf culture. Clevedon: Multilingual Matters; 2003.
7. Lane H. The mask of benevolence: Disabling the deaf community. New York: Random House; 1993.
8. Wrigley O. The politics of deafness. Washington, DC: Gallaudet University Press; 1996.
9. Lane H. When the mind hears. New York: Random House; 1984.
10. Conrad R. The deaf school child, language and cognitive function. London: Harper & Row; 1979.
11. Hindley P, Kitson N. Mental health and deafness. London: Whurr Publishers; 2000.
12. Alker D. Really not interested in the deaf? Darwen: Darwen Press; 2000.
13. Lane H, Hoffmeister R, Bahan B. Journey into the deaf world. San Diego, CA: DawnSign Press; 1996.
14. Desloges P. A deaf person's observations about an elementary course of education for the deaf. In: Lane H, Philip F, editors. The language of experience. Cambridge, MA: Harvard University Press; 1979.
15. De Ladebat L. A collection of the most remarkable definitions of Massieu and Clerc. London: Cox & Baylis; 1815.
16. Mottez B. The deaf mute banquets and the birth of the deaf movement. In: Fischer R, Lane H, editors. Looking back, Hamburg: Signum Press; 1993.
17. Garcia J. Sign with your baby: How to communicate with infants before they can speak. Seattle: Northlight Communications; 1999.
18. Gregory D, Lipsyte R. Nigger—an autobiography. New York: Washington Square Press; 1964.
19. Batterbury S, Ladd P, Gulliver M. Reassessing minority language empowerment from a deaf perspective. Deaf Worlds, International Journal of Deaf Studies 2003;19:2.

Who Decides for Us, Deaf People?

WRITTEN BY

HELEN R. THUMANN AND LAURENE E. SIMMS

INTRODUCTION

The purpose of this chapter is to examine certain perspectives and present a defensible analysis of the research that has shaped the destiny of a people who are categorized by society-at-large as being "disabled" or "hearing impaired": the Deaf.[1] Specifically, this chapter attempts to compare educational and social research emerging from pathological versus cultural viewpoints. Given our identities as members of the Deaf community and culture, fluent American Sign Language (ASL) users, former teachers of Deaf children, and current faculty members of Gallaudet University's Department of Education, we have observed and experienced how Deaf people and the Deaf community have been viewed and regarded as "less than." By deconstructing the patriarchal assumptions of Deaf people as deficient, we will address implications of viewing Deaf people through cultural and sociolinguistic perspectives versus medical perspectives. Our intent is to depathologize "Deafness" by showing how a lack of cultural recognition has influenced research on Deaf people. Finally this chapter will discuss implications for researchers when the Deaf community[2] is recognized as a linguistic and cultural minority with a rich and unique heritage that is just as valid as the mainstream culture in which they are expected to try to participate.

Anthropologically, heritage and cultures cannot be rated as one being more or less superior than another. In this view, the difference between Deaf and Hearing people can be seen as cultural differences, not as deviations from a Hearing norm (Woodward, 1982). This also represents a development in research toward the understanding of Deaf society and culture in the United States and toward an understanding of why Hearing society in the United States has been so slow to give up the idea of "Deafness" as a pathological condition and Deaf people as handicapped or disabled individuals.

HISTORICAL TREATMENT OF DEAF PEOPLE: PATHOLOGICAL VIEW VERSUS CULTURAL VIEW

Pathological View

Historically, Deaf people have been viewed though the lens of a medical model and therefore have been labeled as deviants with a pathology (i.e., hearing loss) that must be remediated. This pathological perspective has shaped Deaf education for several centuries and is an outgrowth of more general beliefs about people who are different, which has resulted in labels such as "normal" for those who are not perceived to be disabled versus "handicapped" for those who deviate from the medical model's standards. This view has historically been held by the majority of able-bodied persons who interact with disabled people and parallels how other language minority people such as Native Americans and Mexican Americans have been viewed in the educational system (Ballin, 1930; Davidson, 1996; Lane, 1992; Spindler & Spindler, 1990). The widely held majority view that Deaf people have a medical problem has prohibited the acceptance of American Sign Language as a separate language from English and Deaf Culture as a culture separate from the majority culture (Lane, 1992; Woodward, 1982). The underlying principle of this pathological view is to "fix" Deaf people and Deaf children in particular. The pathological view perpetuates the belief that the ultimate educational goal for Deaf children is to "pass as Hearing."

Deviation from the norm is likely to entail a stigma (Baker & Cokely, 1980; Lane, 1992) which in turn serves to reinforce the paternalistic and patriarchal, colonial assumptions of the political and economical elite (Reinharz, 1992). Critical theory (Freire, 1992; Wink, 2000) challenges these traditional Western assumptions and permits one to deconstruct the pathological view and demonstrate its similarity to patriarchal assumptions found in many other situations involving majority/minority interactions (Woodward, 1982).

However, up to now, critical theory has not impacted the pathological/clinical views of Deaf people held by the Hearing culture. At the 1880 Conference on the Education of the Deaf in Milan, Italy, the pathological view was codified in the field of Deaf education when Hearing participants voted to forbid the use of sign language in the education of Deaf people. This decision not only forbade the use of sign language in schools, it also led to the expulsion of Deaf teachers from classrooms (Gannon, 1981). Prior to this conference about 50% of the teachers of the Deaf in the United States were Deaf (Gannon, 1981). One can still see the long-lasting impact of this decision when looking at the current percentage of Deaf teachers, roughly 16% (Andrews & Franklin, 1996–1997). This numerical change has resulted in Deaf people having practically no input into how Deaf children were and continue to be educated. The central idea put forth at the conference was that speaking, referred to as oralism by the Deaf community, was superior to manual communication or sign language. As a result, school policies and questions about which method of communication to use in the classrooms for Deaf children have been continuously and heatedly debated over the last 170 years. The pathological view has been perpetuated by researchers and educators who have attempted to understand how Deaf people differ from Hearing people and then to provide remediation to eliminate these differences; that is, to have Deaf people communicate orally rather than use sign language.

As we argue in what follows, society's view of the Deaf is pathological; the Deaf self-view is cultural. The pathological view has carried over time to influence: (1) education and language planning for Deaf children; (2) training of teachers of the Deaf; and (3) educational and social research involving Deaf children and adults. The origin of this pathological view

Table 14.1   Chronology of the Historical Treatment of Deaf people

355 B.C.	Aristotle says those "born deaf become senseless and incapable of reason."
800 B.C.– 500 A.D.	Deaf newborns in Greece and Sparta were cast out in pursuit of being "perfect, normal, and healthy."
To 500 A.D.	In Christianity, people believed that Deaf individuals were possessed by the devil.
	The views of the Church held out no hope for deaf people, for the apostle Paul had written that "faith cometh by hearing." (Van Cleve, 1993 p. 7)
1485	Rudolphus Agricola (1443–1485) wrote about a deaf-mute who learns to read and write.
1500	Girolamo Cardano (1501–1576), the first physician to recognize the ability of the deaf to reason.
1600s	Juan Pablo Bonet (1579–1620) published the first book on education of the deaf in Madrid, Spain.
	John Wallis (1616–1703) published *De Loquela,* reported to be the first publication describing a successful method for teaching English and Speech to deaf children.
	Johann Amman (1699–1724), a Swiss medical doctor developed and published methods for teaching speech and lipreading to the deaf called *Surdus Loquens.*
1755	Samuel Heinicke (1712–1790) establishes the first oral school for the deaf in the world in Germany.
	Charles Michel Abbe de l'Epee (1712–1789) establishes the first free school for the deaf in the world in Paris, France.
1800s	On Martha's Vineyard Deaf and Hearing people use sign language to communicate with each other on a daily basis, even during business hours (Groce, 1985).
1817	The first permanent school for the deaf was founded and taught by the first Deaf teacher, Laurent Clerc, in Hartford, Connecticut.
1840's	William Willard, Deaf founder of the Indiana School for the Deaf and graduate of the American School, documented his early analysis of sign language.
1864	Congress founds Gallaudet College (later University) as the first institute of higher education for deaf students.
1880	Birth of the National Association of the Deaf and Deaf Movement; Conference on the Education of the Deaf in Milan, Italy where Hearing participants voted to forbid the use of signs in the education of Deaf people threatening the learning freedom of deaf children and the employment of Deaf teachers.
1891	Gallaudet College adds teacher training program.
1960	William Stokoe's research provided evidence that American Sign Language (ASL) is a true language.
1970's	Birth of English-based sign systems controlled by non-deaf professionals.
1988	The first Deaf president of Gallaudet University, the only Liberal Arts University for deaf and hard of hearing students, was selected. This marks a significant milestone in the civil rights of deaf and disabled individuals.
1990's	Birth of the Bilingual/Bicultural educational movement using ASL and English in the classroom.

Source: Adapted from Gannon, 1981.

can be discovered by analyzing the historical treatment of Deaf individuals, and other individuals, who are "different" for whatever reasons, by the Hearing society at large.

Society's view of the Deaf is an outgrowth of more general binary beliefs about people with differences; for example, "normal" vs. "handicapped." The pathological/clinical view takes the behaviors and values of the majority as the "standard" or "norm" and then focuses on how disabled people deviate from the norm. This view has been historically and traditionally held by the majority of able-bodied persons who interact on a professional basis with people with disabilities. This deviation from the "norm" is likely to entail a stigma (Lane, 1992), which in turn serves to reinforce the patriarchal, colonial assumptions of the political and the economical elite (Reinharz, 1992). Ladd (2003) in defining the colonization of the Deaf community, explains that the Hearing majority colonizes the Deaf community linguistically (as opposed to economically) by imposing "the colonizer's language (in this case English) ... on the colonized" (p. 25). Conversely, the cultural view focuses on the language experiences and values of a particular group of people who happen to be different from the "norm."

This brief chronology shows a gradual shift from viewing Deaf people as "incapable of reason" to capable of learning, and most recently, capable of leading. The pathological/clinical views of Deaf people held by the Hearing culture seem not to have changed significantly over time while the views held by the Deaf Community have changed to a cultural perspective. The most explicit example of this progression can be taken from the history of Deaf Education in the United States.

Oral versus Manual Controversy

School policies and questions about which methods of communication to use in the classrooms for Deaf children have been a subject of controversy over the last 170 years. Until the late 1960s, the debate over language use in teaching had always been between the proponents of the oral (spoken language) method and the manual (sign) method. In 1817 the first school for Deaf children in the United States was founded in Hartford, Connecticut. Students were taught by a Deaf teacher, Laurent Clerc, who used sign language as the method of communication. The trend toward oralism was codified by the 1880 Conference on the Education of the Deaf in Milan, Italy where Hearing participants voted to forbid the use of signs in the education of Deaf people. Gannon (1981) explains that Deaf people are still smarting from the indignity they suffered at that international meeting in 1880 which banned the use of sign language in the teaching of Deaf children and led to the expulsion of Deaf teachers from classrooms. As a result, Deaf people had practically no say in how Deaf children were educated. The oral method of teaching quickly became widespread across both the United States and Europe. The shift to oralism had a profound impact on Deaf teachers, who were considered inferior speech models for their students. Prior to the Milan Conference in 1880, about 50% of the teachers of the Deaf were Deaf. Today only 11% of the teaching force is Deaf. The oral-only method continues to be greatly favored as the method of instruction in the United States and worldwide (Nover, 1993).

Efforts of Alexander Graham Bell

Alexander Graham Bell, inventor of the telephone, which was intended for his Deaf wife, was one of the biggest proponents of the oral movement. In 1883 he presented a paper, "Upon the Formation of a Deaf Variety of the Human Race," before the National Academy of Science in New Haven, Connecticut. Bell wrote, "Those who believe as I do, that the production of a defective race of human beings would be a great calamity to the world, will examine carefully the causes that lead to the intermarriages of the deaf with the object of applying a remedy" (cited in Gannon, 1981, p. 75). He would have razed all residential and day schools for the deaf. Bell believed that "herding" Deaf children under one roof was a cruel thing to do. He broached the possibility of forbidding Deaf–Deaf marriages by law arguing that such marriages would produce Deaf offspring (Gannon, 1981, pp. 75–76). Years later, Mindel and Vernon (1971) challenged Bell's theory by demonstrating that 90 to 95% of Deaf people are born of "normal" Hearing parents and have Hearing children.

George W. Veditz, a Deaf teacher and former President of the National Association of the Deaf (NAD), a political organization, called Alexander Graham Bell the American most feared by Deaf people, saying " ... he comes in the guise of a friend, and [is], therefore, the most to be feared enemy of the American Deaf, past and present" (quoted in Gannon, 1981, p. 77). As a result of the oral movement, which was greatly influenced by Bell, the manual (sign) method was banned from the classroom and the Hearing perspective dominated the education of the Deaf.

Recognition of American Sign Language

By the 1960s the majority of Deaf schools in the United States and worldwide employed the oral method for educating Deaf children. Children who were unsuccessful using the oral method and communicated using ASL were seen as failures, regardless of their intellectual ability. In 1960 William C. Stokoe was the first non-Deaf linguist to apply linguistic science to the study of ASL. He recognized ASL as one of the legitimate human languages. (Only recently have universities, such as the University of Arizona, accepted ASL as fulfillment for the foreign language requirement for graduation.) Also during the 1960s, the Civil Rights Movement, along with advocacy and community groups such as the National Association of the Deaf and Deaf Pride, spurred government action targeting the Deaf and other "handicapped" groups. These groups used ASL as their symbol of Deaf pride and culture in order to campaign for "Deaf awareness/heritage" as well as greater government action in an area where, up to then, little attention had been paid. Recognition of ASL as a language as well as the political empowerment of the Deaf community renewed the struggle for the power to decide their language. However, Hearing, nonnative ASL-using educators still dominate the educational process and seriously affect the lives of Deaf children by denying them the use of ASL in the classroom.

ASL versus English-Based Sign System

The oral–manual controversy moved into a new phase in the 1970s. The issue moved from whether or not to sign with Deaf students to what kind of signing to use. Rather than make use of ASL, groups of researchers and educators (primarily Hearing) created "English-based sign systems" which attempted to make spoken English more visible (Stedt & Moores, 1990). This exemplifies how control of language policy has been in the hands of non Deaf professionals. The use of ASL was seen as insufficient and ineffective for teaching Deaf children. Bornstein, Hamilton, and Sornier (1983) make this view clear:

> Can most deaf children get enough information from these signals (ASL) to learn English well? The answer to this question is a clear and very well documented no. Most deaf children do not learn English well, recent surveys of the educational achievement of older deaf children indicate that, on the average, they equal the reading performance of hearing fourth or fifth graders. Not all deaf students do that well. (p. 2)

Since Stokoe's demonstration that ASL is indeed a true language, more and more signed-language researchers and scholars have made significant contributions to the study of language acquisition. In addition, a number of books on sign languages such as ASL, French Sign Language, British Sign Language, and others have appeared along with a myriad of Deaf-related books on such topics as linguistics, sociolinguistics, language acquisition, second language learning, English as a second language (Andrews, Leigh, & Weiner, 2004; Chamberlain, Morford, & Mayberry, 2000; Ladd, 2003; Lucas, 1989, 2006; Lucas, Bayley, & Valli, 2001, 2003; Metzger, 2000).

Unfortunately, the outcome of the 1880 Milan Conference still profoundly affects daily life in the American Deaf community. Prejudice and discrimination were inherently expressed by parents as well as non-Deaf educators in the decision made at the conference to forbid participation by Deaf educators. The ideas put forth at the conference, that is, that oralism is superior to manual communication, fosters the illusion that Deaf people are in agreement with the concept that every Deaf child should be given a chance to be like a "Hearing, normal child"; this classic bias against ASL is a clear formulation of the hegemony of English and an English-based manual system promoted in schools for the Deaf (Bornstein et al., 1983).

The history of Deaf education indicates that audism, in which a higher value is placed on Hearing and oral/aural perspectives and parallels ableism (Lane, 1992), hearization, which is similar to assimilation in nondominant communities, and domination significantly affects the educational and linguistic lives of Deaf people. An examination of the parties who are playing significant roles in the development of Deaf education reveals exactly what ideology controls this institution. In addition, history indicates that those in Deaf education have not been effective in addressing the concerns of the Deaf community regarding Deaf education (Lane, Hoffmeister, & Bahan, 1996). Language planning is still under the control of Hearing educators. In recent years, some programs, such as Texas School for the Deaf, New Mexico School for the Deaf, Metro Deaf School in Minnesota, and Marathon High School in Los Angeles have adopted a bilingual and bicultural approach. Yet, they are still very controversial and do not easily replace the institutionalized Hearing orientation to Deaf education.

Where do Deaf people stand now? What has been the impact of this history on Deaf education and the quality of life for Deaf children? Where do Deaf people begin the "attack" to change this situation? Unfortunately, the pathological perspective is much more deeply ingrained in the Hearing world than we may realize. It pervades the foundations of education and research.

PATHOLOGICAL PERSPECTIVE MAINTAINED THROUGH EDUCATION AND RESEARCH

In Nover's (1993) discussion of the current state of the education of the Deaf, he points out that most textbooks used in training programs for teachers of the Deaf are written by those who view Deaf people as outsiders and who believe that Deaf children and adolescents should behave like Hearing persons. These courses include many terms that denote pathology, such as: *Hearing impaired, special education, disorders of the language development, diagnosis, correction, improvement, hearing loss, and adaptations of regular curriculum.* Nover further explains that a majority of the courses represent the promotion of an English-only philosophy, which is auditory-based, along with a pathological orientation toward Deaf children. He found that classes could be categorized into three areas: English-only centered orientation (75%); Deaf-centered orientation (e.g., those emphasizing ASL; 12%); and nonrelevant (13%).

Nover (1993) argues that a Deaf-centered orientation would include, for example, courses such as teaching English as a second language, teaching reading skills in a second language, second language writing, language transfer, ASL literature, Deaf culture, Deaf history, cross-cultural issues, bilingual education, and first and second language acquisition and teaching.

The majority of researchers who conduct various studies on the Deaf community have been trained and exposed only to literature that emphasizes the English-only, pathological, and non-Deaf orientation. The pathological perspective is still being perpetuated in the majority of teacher training programs as well as by many of the researchers who study Deaf people.

There is a growing number of researchers who have conducted their research from a Deaf culture perspective. The following section will compare several researchers from both the cultural and pathological perspective in order to clarify the differences between the two groups.

RESEARCH IN THE FIELD OF DEAF EDUCATION

For nearly 200 years the focus of research and education has been Deaf children's inability to hear. From this pathological view, social scientists like Alexander Graham Bell, Bornstein,

Ling, and others have looked at Deaf people as a deviant group with hearing loss and they have consistently compared Deaf students to Hearing "normal" counterparts. To study how one becomes "deviant," social scientists assign labels to demoralize a particular group or individual when behavior is marked as abnormal (Gamson, 1991). Thus, such social scientists who study Deaf people make it clear that Deaf people are not normal and are categorized as deviants from the Hearing society because they do not possess what Hearing people possess: the ability to hear. Gamson and Schiffman point out that the attempts to use labels of abnormalities foster the process of stigmatization (Burawoy et al., 1991). Social scientists assign such labels to Deaf people, and thereby continue to control the stigmatizing and demoralizing power over Deaf people.

Further, in Lane's book, *The Mask of Benevolence* (1992), he argues that so-called "experts" in the scientific, medical, and education fields, while claiming to help Deaf people and their community in fact do them great harm. In other words, social scientists look at themselves as the experts on Deafness while Deaf people see themselves as inferior and are "trained" to become dependent on Hearing people. The majority of the social scientists with the colonizing and pathological attitudes toward Deaf people are still making decisions about Deaf people and enabling the Deaf to depend on them because of the hold over and control they have over so many aspects of the lives of the Deaf. Lane (1992) argues that paternalism and money are inseparable in this transaction. For example, these social scientists with pathological views of Deaf people write the textbooks and materials for use in the teacher education programs for teachers preparing to teach Deaf children. The books on methods of instruction for the Deaf are written by researchers who in turn receive recognition for their expertise and profits for their work. Bornstein's attitude about Deaf children can be seen in his text as he (1990) attempts:

> to offer an authoritative description of manual communication as it is used in the United States. It is designed for professionals who work with Deaf and language-delayed children and adolescents (including some who may hear). It should also be useful for teachers-in-training and interested parents. (p. 253)

Students in teacher preparation programs are taught a pathological view through the books written by Hearing researchers. When these students become teachers of the Deaf, they bring attitudes and a mind-set that Deaf people are, to quote social scientists, "deviants." The main point is that social scientists aim to maintain the professional authority over the description of education and communication. The focus is that the social scientists do not want to relinquish their power over Deaf people.

Thus, while numerous statistical and quantitative studies have documented the failures of Deaf students (Allen, 1986; Braden, 1994; Schirmer, 2003; Trybus & Karchmer, 1977) the work of these social scientists has been used to hinder advancement in education of Deaf children by reinforcing the concept of ableism as well as disability. The pathological perspective is perpetuated in research being conducted by social scientists using traditional approaches from a Hearing orientation. Shapiro (1993) noted that in research nondisabled people use "prettifying euphemisms" (Shapiro, 1993, p. 33) and rely on the stereotype that disabled persons should be an inspiration in their efforts to overcome challenges. To the contrary, Blackwell (1993) in her narrative about her experiences growing up Deaf, considered herself not handicapped and was angry that Deaf people were allowed to believe they were handicapped. Bahan (cited in Wilcox, 1989) proclaims that it is the Hearing world that tells us we are handicapped and disabled. Educators trained to think of Deaf children as handicapped and disabled continue to lower the educational expectations and achievements of Deaf children. In turn, these attitudes encourage Deaf children to believe they are handicapped and disabled in the eyes of the majority of Hearing people and thus will never equalize themselves with Hearing peers.

In contrast to this mainstream view, the work of linguistic and anthropological social scientists in American Sign Language and Deaf Culture has facilitated new perspectives on Deaf people (Baker & Battison, 1980; Baker & Cokely, 1980; Erting and Woodward, 1979; Groce, 1985; Klima & Bellugi, 1979; Liddell & Johnson, 1989; Lucas, 1989; Padden & Humphries, 1988; Stokoe, Casterline, & Croneberg, 1965; S. Supalla, 1990; T. Supalla, 1986; Van Cleve & Crouch, 1989). Johnson, Liddell, and Erting (1989) noted that the low average academic achievement levels are not results of loss of Hearing or learning deficits inherently associated with being Deaf but with the problems in the communication practices of the students' teachers. In her study on teacher communication competency, Baker (1978) stated that teachers using sign language and spoken English simultaneously did not provide comprehensive and complete linguistic input for Deaf children during the instructional time. In contrast, Moores (1991) wrote an editorial in the *American Annals of the Deaf* on teacher morale:

> Teachers of the deaf typically deal with a situation in which their children have normal intellectual potential but academic progress is constrained by limited English and other communication skills. Teachers may see only small incremental growth in standardized test scores from year to year and may mistakenly, in my opinion, hold themselves responsible for what they perceive to be an unsatisfactory rate of progress. (p. 243)

Corbett and Jensema (1981) indicated that the majority of teachers of the Deaf were White, Hearing, and female. Teacher training programs offer courses from a medical perspective as illustrated earlier. Therefore, with the majority of White, Hearing females being responsible for the language and instruction of Deaf children, it is anticipated that those people are already trained in a pathological view of Deaf children. Hence, many educational programs for Deaf children described earlier are still employing old research theories regarding learning English as the first language and espousing a paternalistic attitude toward Deaf people.

In a survey, Woodward and Allen (1987) studied 609 elementary teachers. Eighty-five percent of this predominantly Hearing and female group had minimal skills in ASL. In general the research suggests that the educational programs for the Deaf are being dominated by Hearing educators whose communication has been shown to be insufficient as a means to convey information through instruction. Certified teachers of the Deaf may have had only two or fewer classes in sign language during their teacher education program (Maxwell, 1985). As a result, some Deaf children were put in the position of having to teach ASL to their teachers; therefore, the instructional time for Deaf children often is replaced with teachers learning from the children. Additionally, when teachers (and future teachers) of Deaf children do know how to sign, often their ASL fluency is lacking.

One example of this occurred in March 1992. Gallaudet University placed four student teachers at a residential school for the Deaf in the Midwest where the Bilingual and Bicultural program is used. These four student teachers included three White Hearing women and one who identified herself as Hearing impaired. After observing these student teachers working with children in the class, the teachers and principal at the school determined that the student teachers' sign skills were insufficient. As a result the student teachers were asked to cease their practicum at the school. After returning to Gallaudet they were transferred to another school, one that presumably had lower expectations of the sign skills of their teacher interns. This action helped to convince faculty and administrators at Gallaudet University to change its graduate studies program to include more cultural and linguistic aspects of Deaf people and require students to become knowledgeable and proficient in both areas before they could participate in their practicum. The faculty at Gallaudet changed the curriculum of the Deaf Education program to include a demonstration of sign proficiency for students planning to teach. However, state and professional requirements for obtaining a teacher's license in Deaf Education include coursework that emphasizes the pathological view, not a cultural and linguistic view. In spite of new cultural and linguistic theories that emerged in 1960 and thereafter on ASL and Deaf Culture, only a few schools (e.g. Texas School for the Deaf, California School for the Deaf, Metro Day School for the Deaf) and universities (e.g., Gallaudet University, Lamar University, Boston University) have adopted a cultural and linguistic view as the basis for instruction and hire Deaf people who are trained as ASL and Deaf studies instructors.

DEAF PEOPLE AS RESEARCHERS

Lane (1988) proposed that psychologists involve Deaf people themselves at all levels of research undertaken. Deaf people need to be recruited and trained, and researchers should turn to the Deaf community as advisors and collaborators in collecting analyzing, interpreting, and disseminating results. Kurzman (1991) stated that the ideal is to give subjects a voice in the research; however, he warned that the complex sentences and eloquent works in the researchers' writings may remind the subjects of their inability to communicate in the Deaf individual's way. He suggests that we allow subjects to provide input to correct any mistakes the researcher might have made; to create a sense of cooperation between subjects and researcher in the quest to understand the subjects' world; to empower subjects by making them active members in their own analysis; and to keep writings clear in order to keep the subjects' possible reactions in mind as the research unfolds. Padden and Humphries (1988) note in the introduction to their book, *Deaf in America: Voices from a Culture*, that the traditional way of writing about Deaf people is to focus on their condition, the fact that they do not hear, and to interpret all other aspects of their lives as consequences of this fact. In contrast, a sociolinguistic or cultural approach to research focuses on "normalization" of Deaf people as a linguistic and cultural group.

Lane (1980) reviewed existing literature and found over 350 textbooks and reports that reveal paternalistic attitudes toward Deaf people. Though no similar study has been conducted on the research done on or about Deaf people, such a study would likely reveal the preponderance of Hearing researchers and few (though growing) numbers of Deaf researchers or Deaf/Hearing teams. The perspectives of Hearing researchers may differ from those of Deaf researchers or even those of collaborative groups including both Hearing and Deaf researchers. If the number of research studies done by Deaf social scientists were to increase or surpass the number of studies by Hearing social scientists, would a Deaf perspective eventually reflect a new change in the picture of Deaf people?

Although an increasing number of Deaf researchers with higher levels of sophistication have contributed to the field, we still have to deal with enduring stereotypes, negative interpretations, and inappropriate pathological theoretical suggestions already imposed on Deaf people. When social scientists proclaim their theories, the results are often in conflict with a Deaf perspective. For example researchers continue to compare the English ability of Deaf children with Hearing children for reading and writing competencies, while they ignore ASL as literacy. So, the validity of tests and measurements in English for Deaf children is being challenged by the linguistic and cultural theories. What a researcher in one framework may consider to be problematic and require a remedial solution may count as healthy independence to someone looking from a different perspective. Researchers who hold pathological views would consider the importance of teaching English in the classroom to improve the linguistic and grammatical skills, whereas Deaf people find that they could achieve their learning of English through ASL. Lane (1984) adds "But the deaf did not have, do not have, the final word (in research). The final word as always came from their Hearing benefactors" (p. 413).

While some researchers have included Deaf people in their research (both as participants and collaborators) the involvement of those Deaf people has been greatly restricted. Kannapell (1980), a Deaf researcher in Deaf Studies, in discussing her experience working with Signed English developers (Bornstein et al., 1983) expressed that she was disillusioned by the oppression she experienced from the researchers with whom she worked. She eventually resigned from this work, after she discovered her identity as a Deaf person and began a new endeavor, establishing Deaf Studies at Gallaudet University where she retired as a professor. She was a pioneer in recognizing the ambivalence of Deaf people regarding their own identity and language, which was the subject of her doctoral dissertation. It is possible that Deaf researchers who collaborate with Hearing researchers are either not aware of their rights or accept the fact that they have little or no power over the work. Paternalism can corrupt some members of an oppressed minority, forming a class that conspires with the authority to maintain the status quo (Lane, 1992). Indeed, researchers are likely to approach Deaf people with paternalistic attitudes. The failure to involve Deaf people as active participants in research has been a longstanding issue. However, we are seeing more works of linguistic and anthropological researchers involving Deaf people as collaborative researchers, assistants, and subjects (L. Erting & Pfau,1993; C. Erting, Prezioso,

& Hynes,1990; Lucas & Valli, 1990; Padden & Ramsey,1997; T. Supalla & Newport, 1978). For example, in the 1990s two proposals for Deaf research projects were funded by the U.S. Department of Education, Office of Special Education and Rehabilitative Services. Both proposals were submitted by collaborative Deaf and Hearing researchers; Padden and Ramsey and Supalla and Singleton. Both worked with Deaf professionals at different residential schools for the Deaf. Additionally, research projects like the Signs of Literacy (SOL) and the Visual Language, Visual Learning (VL2) research projects at Gallaudet University bring Deaf and Hearing researchers together to examine issues of language development, education of Deaf children, and literacy.[3]

Reinharz (1992, p. 260) noted that feminist researchers draw on a new "epistemology of insider-ness" that sees life and work as intertwined. Feminist research aims at the following goals: "1) to document the lives and activities of women, 2) to understand the experience of women from their own point of view, and 3) to conceptualize women's behavior as an expression of social contexts" (Reinharz, 1992, p. 51). The research on women contributes significantly to rethinking perspectives of Deaf people. With this new influence on the Hearing perspective of Deaf people, the patriarchal attitudes and stigmatization of Deaf people can perhaps be eradicated. Researchers as experienced insiders are able to understand what Deaf people have to say in a way that no outsider could.

Reinharz also points out that there may be a danger of overgeneralizing women's experiences when researchers fail to differentiate their own experiences from those of other women (p. 262). She suggests that feminist researchers include their personal experiences as an asset for their research, using objectivity and subjectivity to serve each other.

Anthropological research has shown diversity among Deaf people (Lane, 1992; Lucas, 1989; Padden & Humphries, 1988). Deaf researchers may already or will draw on their own personal and cultural experiences to do research, but at the same time carefully differentiate their own experience from the experience of other Deaf people (Kannapell, 1980; Stone-Harris & Stirling, 1987; Suppala, 1992). This is a departure from the traditional homogenizing model of Hearing researchers working on Deaf people and a new approach between Hearing and Deaf researchers as collaborators as well as the Deaf as individual researchers. This emerging trend (Andrews, Leigh, & Weiner, 2004; Kuntze, 2004; Ladd, 2003) will give the opportunity to bring in more Deaf perspectives than the traditional model and will offer more valid descriptions of Deaf people.

In order to depathologize the Deaf community and deconstruct the inherent patriarchal assumptions, it has become necessary to develop new strategies such as revising language and eradicating stigmatizing terms. Woodward (1982) discusses the commonly "take for granted" term, *handicapped,* and notes:

> For if we look more closely at the notion of "handicapped" and its ramifications, we come to a rather unpleasant logical conclusion. *The American Heritage Dictionary* (1976) defines handicapped as a "deficiency, or especially an anatomical, physiological or mental efficiency, that prevents or restricts normal achievement." (p. 133)

If we follow the traditional handicapped classification of Deaf people, they are doomed to failure because they will never achieve (nor do they always want to "achieve") the "normality" of becoming a Hearing person. Most Deaf people will then remain deficient (i.e., according to Hearing society's norms), that is "lacking an essential quality or element; incomplete; defective."

Moreover, another controversial term, *Hearing impaired*, is for Hearing people, a more acceptable and tolerable term, but it is a euphemism for "Deaf." The term *Hearing impaired* has a negative connotation and is no longer an acceptable usage among the World Federation of the Deaf and other organizations, such as the National Association of the Deaf (NAD) and the Registry of Interpreters for the Deaf (RID). Bienvenu (1989) points out that "Hearing impaired" defines Deaf people solely in terms of broken or defective ears and this term tends to be preferred by most of the professionals in the audiological and rehabilitation field who take a narrow medical view of Deaf people. Furthermore, Bienvenu challenges the lack of acceptance and misuse of the term *Deaf* as she asks; "Why is it so hard to accept the word 'deaf'? Is it because it sounds like 'death' which is commonly misused by Hearing people?" (Bradford, 1993).

In *The Bicultural Center Newsletter*, April 1991, Bienvenu considers the use of the term *Deafness* (as in "the field of Deafness") as equally ridiculous and a nonhuman entity. She notes that there is no such thing as the "field of womanness" for women and "field of black-ness" for Black people (p. 1) but the "field of deafness" has been seen as acceptable. There is nothing horrible or undignified about the term *Deaf*, so no sophisticated or polite substitute is needed. Even that cringe-inducing term is less debasing than *non-Hearing*. Perhaps the terms *Deaf* and *non-Deaf* should be something to consider (Bradford, 1993). Bradford further explains that in referring to Deaf people as "non-Hearing" is rather like saying "non-Whites" to describe Blacks; it appears to reduce Deaf people to a sterile, subaverage population.

From within the Deaf community, new vocabularies have emerged for shaping theories. Though many of these terms have been commonly used for several centuries by the Deaf, they need to be replaced for the aforementioned negative connotations. In order to promote better understanding and sustain an endogenous cultural view, the term *Deaf* is preferred over any other as a powerful term, presenting a positive identify, and as another way of being human. "Deaf" implicates a language and culture (Padden & Humphries, 1988). "Deaf" is inclusive. The entry "Deaf" reads in the American Heritage Dictionary of the English language (1992):

> Adj. 1 Partially or completely lacking in the sense of Hearing. 2. Deaf. Of or relating to the Deaf or their culture. 3. Unwilling, refusing to listen: heedless: *was deaf to our objections.* N. (used with a plural verb). 1. Deaf people considered as a group 2. Deaf. The community of deaf people who use American Sign Language as a primary means of communication. (p. 368)

To contrast, from a Deaf perspective, ASL is considered as the primary, dominant language. English should be considered a second language for Deaf people in the United States (Grosjean, 1982). Furthermore, Nover and Ruiz (1992) contend that there is a great need to develop more Deaf-centered or Deaf-informed aspects among such disciplines as psychology, education, anthropology, sociology, and the like before researchers will have accurate and acceptable cultural information regarding Deaf people.

RESULTS AND EFFECTS OF THE PATHOLOGICAL VIEW IN THE EDUCATION OF DEAF PEOPLE

The historical treatment of Deaf people has resulted in a number of detrimental effects on the Deaf Community. To justify the need for a change in Deaf education, however, one only needs to look at a long list of studies by researchers in the field of Deaf Education (Allen, 1994; DiFrancesca, 1972; Hoffmeister, 2000; Padden & Ramsey, 1997; Prinz & Strong 1998; Traxler, 2000; Trybus & Karchmer, 1977; Vernon & Andrews, 1990). These studies showed that 30% of Deaf students in the United States left school functionally illiterate (at grade 2.8 or below on education achievement tests); 60% read at grade levels between 5.3 and 2.9 (DiFrancesca, 1972; Trybus & Karchmer, 1977); and only 5% achieved a 10th-grade level or above (Jensema & Trybus, 1978). Approximately one-half of Deaf high school students were unable to meet the academic requirements for a diploma, exiting instead with a certificate or less (Schildroth et al., 1991). Those who dropped out or aged out of high school programs accounted for 29% of those leaving while only 29% of Deaf students graduated with high school diplomas (Bowe, 2003; Schildroth et al., 1991). Students who did graduate often went on to be unemployed or underemployed when compared to Hearing counterparts (Garay, 2003; Punch, Hyde, & Creed, 2004).

This situation with the education of Deaf individuals has had a severe impact on their ability to make the transition from school to employment, and then to independent living. The importance of education was highlighted by Jones (2004) who found no evidence of significant differences in earnings between Deaf and Hearing individuals, *except* for those with lower levels of educational attainment. A series of surveys conducted by MacLeod (1983, 1984, 1985) revealed employment trends among Deaf/hard-of-Hearing graduates of residential and mainstreamed public school programs. Persons responding to those surveys experienced rates of unemployment higher than the norm for Hearing persons; if employed, they typically found work in blue-collar occupations where they earned a lower salary, demonstrated little upward mobility, and tended to stay at the same job for a long period of time. Furthermore, Dr. Frank R. Turk, former director of North Carolina's Division of Deaf and Hard of Hearing Services, claimed approximately 70% of the nation's Deaf-school graduates receive Supplemental Security Income (SSI). These poor educational and work history outcomes point to an ongoing crisis in the state of Deaf education in the United States.

After this long history of linguistic, cultural, and educational oppression and its resultant impacts on the success of members of the Deaf Community, a grassroots change began. This change, beginning in the Civil Rights era of the 1960s, had its roots in the recognition that the signs that Deaf people were using were not simply visual representations of the local spoken language but, in fact, consisted of a rich language with its own grammar, syntax, history, and culture. This recognition of ASL coincided with the Civil Rights Movement, and the sense of Deaf Civil Rights emerged. The resultant empowerment of the Deaf community sparked a change in how Deaf people saw themselves and led to a critical look at the educational methods used in schools and universities throughout the United States. This growing empowerment continued through the 1980s with the Deaf President Now[4] movement at Gallaudet University. In the 1990s the ASL/English Bilingual Education movement began. These changes reflected a shift from a pathological to a cultural view of Deaf people.

IMPLICATIONS FOR RESEARCH

Through our discussion of opposing perspectives on Deaf people (cultural as compared to pathological), the resultant oppression of Deaf people, and the impact of that oppression on the education of Deaf and hard of hearing children, we have argued that there needs to be more Deaf influence and perspective in the education of Deaf and hard of hearing children. Though there is a growing movement toward ASL/English bilingual education, there continues to be a tremendous need for promoting more Deaf focused research in language use and planning, education, and culture. This research should include exploring the attitude and relations between non-Deaf professionals and the Deaf community in order to gain a better understanding and come to a resolution of this conflict of perspectives (Clifford, 1991; Nover, 1993). Kurzman (1991) notes that it is absurd for social scientists to debate subjects' situations without letting them speak for themselves, even though it has been an historical reality for the Deaf community. For Deaf people to gain more control over the research on Deaf lives, the Hearing people in control should relinquish some of their power by hiring more Deaf researchers and collaborating with them when necessary, to maintain a Deaf perspective in their work. Deaf people should have the right to see and comment on Hearing researchers' work especially in the early stages. Though not all perspectives can be addressed and satisfied by any one project, researchers will gain support from the Deaf community for their projects if the work is shared and criticized by Deaf people as part of the project itself.

Hearing social scientists hiring Deaf people only as assistants for their research perpetuate colonization and perpetuate the current power structure through dominant/dominated relationships. Also, "hiring" implies a power differential, that the Deaf people are doing the "dirty work" and that the research design is Hearing oriented. Collaboration of Deaf and Hearing researchers may contribute to an eradication of pathological views to develop relevant, explanatory theories uniquely fitted to what we are studying and to lived realities of Deaf people. Traditional, antiquated theories may explain a particular view of phenomena colored by biases of researchers. We need to refute these erroneous theories with valid arguments and evidence. Experts in the scientific, medical, and education establishments who purport to serve the Deaf in fact do them great harm when they address the realities of our lives, and portray Deaf people as disabled. Woodward (1982) points out that it is very improbable that Deaf people will even achieve equality unless the Hearing society depathologizies Deafness; that is, unless Hearing society rejects the handicapped classification of Deaf people. After all, Deaf people, like all other human beings simply want liberty, equality, and the pursuit of happiness.

NOTES

1. Many authors use capital "D" Deaf to refer to those who are members of the American Deaf culture and lower case "d" deaf to refer to the audiological condition.

2. In using the term *Deaf culture* or *Deaf community* we do not mean to imply that all Deaf people believe, act, or support the same ideas and beliefs. As with any culture or community, the Deaf community is varied and diverse. With this in mind, however, interviews and research on identity in the Deaf community often find members of the Deaf community as identifying themselves first as Deaf. For example in a survey of Deaf lesbians, it was found that these women consistently identified themselves as Deaf first then as women or lesbians.

3. For additional information on the Signs of Literacy project go to http://sol.gallaudet.edu. For information about the Visual Language, Visual Learning project go to http://vl2.gallaudet. edu.

4. In 1988, the Board of Trustees at Gallaudet University selected Elizabeth Zinser, a Hearing woman with no experience working with the Deaf community, to be the President of Gallaudet. The two other candidates were Deaf men who had long histories of working both at Gallaudet and in the Deaf community. This resulted in a protest which included Gallaudet students, faculty, staff, as well as members of the larger Deaf community. The protesters demanded a Deaf president for Gallaudet and 51% Deaf representation on the Board of Trustees. After a week of protests the Board of Trustees chose I. King Jordan as the first Deaf president of Gallaudet. For a detailed account of the Deaf President Now Movement see Christiansen and Barnartt (1995) and Gannon (1989).

REFERENCES

Allen, T. (1986). Patterns of academic achievement in hearing-impaired students: 1974 and 1983. In A. Schlidroth & Karchmer, M. (Eds.), *Deaf children in America* (pp. 161–206). San Diego, CA: College-Hill Press.

Allen, T. (1994). *Who are the deaf and hard of hearing students leaving high school and entering postsecondary education?* Gallaudet University Center for Assessment and Demographic Studies, Washington, D.C. Unpublished manuscript.

Andrews, J., & Franklin, T. (1996–1997, August). Why hire deaf teachers? *Texas Journal of Audiology and Speech Pathology, 22*(1), 120–131.

Andrews, J., Leigh, I., & Weiner, M. (2004). *Deaf people: Evolving perspectives from psychology, education and sociology.* Boston, MA: Pearson Education.

Baker, C. (1978). How does "sim com" fit into a bilingual approach to education? In F. Caccamise & D. Hicks (Eds), *Proceedings of the second National Symposium in Sign Language Research and Training.* Silver Spring, MD: National Association of the Deaf.

Baker, C., & Battison, R. (Eds.). (1980). *Sign language of the Deaf Community: Essays in honor of William C. Stokoe.* Silver Spring, MD: National Association of the Deaf.

Baker, C., & Cokely, D. (1980). *American Sign Language: A teacher's resource text on grammar and culture.* Silver Spring, MD: T.J. Publishers.

Ballin, A. (1930). *The Deaf Mute howls.* Los Angeles, CA: Grafton

Bienvenu, M. J. (1989, October). An open letter to alumni, students of Gallaudet and friends. *The Bicultural Center News, 18.*

Bienvenue, M. J. (1991, April). *The Bicultural Center Newsletter, 21.*

Blackwell, L.R. (1993). Going beyond the anger. In M. Garretson (Ed.), *Deafness: 1993–2013.* Silver Spring, MD: National Association of the Deaf.

Bornstein, H. (1990). *Manual communications: Implications for education.* Washington, D.C.: Gallaudet University Press.

Bornstein, H., Hamilton, L., & Saulnier, K. (1983). *The comprehensive signed English dictionary.* Washington, D.C.: Gallaudet University Press.

Bowe, F. (2003). Transition for deaf and hard of hearing students: A blueprint for change. *Journal of Deaf Studies and Deaf Education, 8* (4), 485–493.

Braden J. P. (1994). *Deafness, deprivation and IQ.* New York: Plenum.

Bradford, S. (1993, May). What do we call ourselves? *Deaf Life,* 22–26.

Burawoy, M., Burton, A., Arnett Ferguson, A., Fox, K., Gamson, J., Gartrell, N., et al. (1991). *Ethnography unbound: Power and resistance in the modern metropolis.* Berkeley, CA: University of California Press.

Chamberlain, C., Morford, J., & Mayberry, R. (Eds.). (2000). *Language acquisition by eye.* Mahwah, NJ: Erlbaum.

Christiansen, J. and Barnartt, S. (1995). *Deaf President Now! The 1988 revolution at Gallaudet University.* Washington, D.C.: Gallaudet University Press.

Clifford, J. (1990). Notes on (field) notes. In R. Sanjek, (Ed.), *Fieldnotes: The making of anthropology* (pp. 47–70). Ithaca, NY: Cornell University Press.

Corbett, E. , & Jensema, C. (1981). *Teachers of the hearing impaired: Descriptive profiles.* Washington, D.C.: Gallaudet University Press.

Davidson A. (1996). *Making and molding identity in schools.* Albany, NY: State University of New York Press.

DiFrancesca, S. (1972). *Academic achievement test results of a national testing program for hearing impaired students, United States, 1971.* Washington, D.C.: Office of Demographic Studies, Gallaudet College.

Erting, C., Prezioso, C., & Hynes, M. (1990). The interactional context of Deaf mother–infant communication. In V. Voltera & C. Erting (Eds.), *From gesture to language in hearing and deaf children.* Washington, D.C.: Gallaudet University Press.

Erting, C., & Woodward, J. (1979). Sign language and the deaf community. *Discourse Processes, 2,* 183–300.

Erting, L., & Pfau, J. (1993, June). *Becoming bilingual: Facilitating English literacy development using ASL in preschool.* Paper presented at CAID/CEASD Convention, Baltimore.

Freire, P. (1992). *Pedagogy of the oppressed.* New York: Continuum.

Gamson, A. (1991). Silence, death, and the invisible enemy: AIDS activism and social movement "newness." In M. Burawoy, A. Burton, A. Arnett Ferguson, K. Fox, J. Gamson, N A. Gartrell et al. (Eds.), *Ethnography unbound: Power and resistance in the modern metropolis* (pp. 35–57). Berkeley, CA: University of California Press.

Gannon, J. (1981). *Deaf heritage: A narrative history of Deaf America.* Silver Spring, MD: National Association of the Deaf.

Gannon, J. (1989). *The week the world heard Gallaudet.* Washington, D.C.: Gallaudet University Press.

Garay, S. (2003). Listening to the voices of Deaf students: Essential transition issues. *Teaching Exceptional Children, 35*(4), 44–48.

Groce, N. (1985). *Everyone here spoke sign language: Hereditary deafness on Martha's Vineyard.* Cambridge: MA: Harvard University Press.

Grosjean, F. (1982). *Life with two languages: An introduction to bilingualism.* Cambridge, MA: Harvard University Press.

Hoffmeister, R. (2000). A piece of the puzzle: ASL and reading comprehension in deaf children. In C. Chamberlain, J. P. Morford, & R. I. Mayberry (Eds.), *Language acquisition by eye* (pp. 143–164). Mahwah, NJ: Erlbaum.

Jensema, C., & Trybus, J. (1978, August). *Communicative patterns and educational achievement of hearing impaired students* (Series T, Number 2). Washington, D.C.: Gallaudet College, Office of Demographic Studies.

Johnson, R. B., Liddell, S., & Erting, C. (1989). *Unlocking the curriculum: Principles for achieving access in Deal Education* (GRI Working Paper Series, No. 89-3). Washington, D.C.: Gallaudet Research Institute.

Jones, D. (2004, Fall). Relative earnings of deaf and hard-of-hearing individuals. *Journal of Deaf Studies and Deaf Education, 9,* 459–461.

Kannapell, B. (1980). Personal awareness and advocacy in the Deaf Community. In C. Baker & R. Battison (Eds.), S*ign language of the Deaf Community: Essays in honor of William C. Stokoe* (pp. 105–116). Silver Spring, MD: National Association of the Deaf.

Klima, E., & Bellugi, U. (1979). *The signs of language.* Cambridge, MA: Harvard University Press.

Kuntze, M. (2004). *Literacy acquisition and deaf children: A study of the interaction between ASL and written English.* Doctoral dissertation, Stanford University, Stanford, California.

Kurzman, C. (1991). Convincing sociologists: Values and interests in the sociology of knowledge. In M. Burawoy A. Burton, A. Arnett Ferguson, K. Fox, J. Gamson, N. Gartrell, et al. (Eds.), *Ethnography unbound: Power and resistance in the modern metropolis* (pp. 250–270). Berkeley, CA: University of California Press.

Ladd, P. (2003). *Understanding Deaf culture: In search of Deafhood.* Clevedon, UK: Multilingual Matters.

Lane, H. (1980, Spring). *Some thoughts on language bigotry.* A presentation at Gallaudet University.

Lane, H. (1984). *When the mind hears: A history of the Deaf.* New York: Random House.

Lane, H. (1988, February). *Is there a psychology of the Deaf?* A presentation at Gallaudet University.

Lane, H. (1992). *The mask of benevolence: Disabling the Deaf Community.* New York: Alfred A. Knopf.

Lane, H., Hoffmeister, R., & Bahan, B. (1996). *A journey into the Deaf-World.* San Diego, CA: Dawn Sign Press.

Liddell, S., & Johnson, R. (1989). American Sign Language: The phonological base. *Sign Language Studies, 64,* 195–277.

Lucas, C. (Ed.). (1989). *The sociolinguistics of the Deaf Community.* San Diego, CA: Academic Press.

Lucas, C. (Ed.). (2006). *Multilingualism and sign languages: From the Great Plains to Australia.* Washington, D.C.: Gallaudet University Press.

Lucas, C., Bayley, R., & Valli, C. (2001). *Sociolinguistic variation in American Sign Language.* Washington, D.C.: Gallaudet University Press.

Lucas, C., Bayley, R., & Valli, C. (2003). *What's your sign for pizza? An introduction to variation in American Sign Language.* Washington, D.C.: Gallaudet University Press.

Lucas, C., & Valli, C. (1990). Predicates of perceived motion in ASL. In S. Fischer & P. Siple (Eds.), *Theoretical issues in sign language research* (pp. 153–166). Chicago: University of Chicago Press.

MacLeod, J. (1983). *Secondary school graduate follow-up program of the hearing impaired: Fourth annual report.* Rochester, NY: National Technical Institute for the Deaf.

MacLeod, J. (1984). *Secondary school graduate follow-up program of the hearing impaired: Fifth annual report.* Rochester, NY: National Technical Institute for the Deaf.

MacLeod, J. (1985). *Secondary school graduate follow-up program of the hearing impaired: Sixth annual report.* Rochester, NY: National Technical Institute for the Deaf.

Maxwell, M. (1985). Sign language instruction and teacher preparation. *Sign Language Studies. 47,* 173–180.

Metzger, M. (Ed.). (2000). *Bilingualism and identity in Deaf communities.* Washington, D.C.: Gallaudet University Press.

Mindel, B., & Vernon, M. (1971). *They grow in silence: The Deaf child and his family.* Washington, D.C.: American International Printing.

Moores, D. (1991). Teacher morale. *American Annals of the Deaf, 136*(3), 243.

Nover, S. (1993, June). *Our voices. our vision: Politics of Deaf education.* Paper presented at the AID/CEASD Convention, Baltimore.

Nover, S., & Ruiz, R. (1992, June 4–6). *ASL and language planning in Deaf education.* Paper presented at the International Symposium in Celebration of the Centennial of Teacher Education. Gallaudet University, Washington, D.C.

Padden, C., & Humphries, T. (1988). *Deaf in America: Voices from a culture.* Cambridge, MA: Harvard University Press.

Padden, C., & Ramsey, C. (1997). *Deaf students as readers and writers: A mixed mode research approach. Final Report to U.S. Department of Education.* University of California, San Diego. Unpublished manuscript,

Prinz, P. M., & Strong, M. (1998). ASL proficiency and English within a bilingual deaf education model of instruction. *Topics in Language Disorders, 18*(4), 47–60.

Punch, R., Hyde, M., & Creed, P. (2004). Issues in the school-to-work transition of hard of hearing adolescents. *American Annals of the Deaf, 149*(1) 28–38.

Reinharz, S. (1992). *Feminist methods in social research.* New York: Oxford University Press.

Schildroth, A., Rawlings, B, & Allen, T. (1991). Deaf students in transition: Education and employment issues for deaf adolescents. *The Volta Review, 93,* 5.

Schirmer, B. R. (2003, Spring). Using verbal protocols to identify the reading strategies of students who are deaf. *Journal of Deaf Studies and Deaf Education, 8*(2), 157–170.

Shapiro, J. (1993). *No pity: People with disabilities forging a new Civil Rights Movement.* New York: Random House.

Spindler, G., & Spindler, L. (1990). *The American cultural dialogue and its transmission.* New York: Falmer Press.

Stedt, F., & Moores, D. (1990). Manual codes of English and American Sign Language: Historical perspectives and current realities. In H. Bornstein (Ed.), *Manual communications: Implications for education.* Washington, D.C.: Gallaudet University Press.

Stokoe, W. C., Casterline, D., & Croneberg, C. G. (1965). *A dictionary of American Sign Language on linguistic principles.* Washington, D.C.: Gallaudet College Press.

Stone-Harris, R., & Stirling, L. (1987). Developing and defining an identity: Deaf children of Deaf and Hearing parents. In *Proceedings of Social Change and the Deaf. Proceedings of the Second Research Conference on the Social Aspects of Deafness.* Washington, D.C.: Gallaudet University Press.

Supalla, S. (1992). *The book of name signs: Naming in American Sign Language.* San Diego, CA: Dawn Sign Press.

Supalla, T. (1986). The classifier system in American Sign Language. In C. Craig (Ed.), *Noun classification and categorization.* Philadelphia: J. Benjamins.

Supalla, T., & Newport, E. (1978). How many seats in a chair? The derivation of nouns and verbs in American Sign Language. In P. Siple (Ed.), *Understanding language through sign language research.* New York: Academic Press.

Traxler, C. B. (2000). Measuring up to performance standards in reading and mathematics: Achievement of selected deaf and hard-of-hearing students in the national norming of the ninth edition Stanford Achievement Test. *Journal of Deaf Studies and Deaf Education, 5,* 337–348.

Trybus, R. J., & Karchmer, M. A. (1977). School achievement scores of hearing impaired children: National data on achievement status and growth patters. *American Annals of the Deaf, 122,* 62–69.

Van Cleve, J. (1993). *Deaf history unveiled: Interpretations from the new scholarship.* Washington, D.C.: Gallaudet University Press.

Van Cleve, J., & Crouch, B. (1989). *A place of their own: Creating the Deaf Community in America.* Washington, D.C.: Gallaudet University Press.

Vernon, M., & Andrews, J. (1990). *The psychology of deafness.* New York: Longman.

Wink, J. (2000). *Critical pedagogy: Notes from the real world* (2nd ed.). New York: Addison Wesley Longman.

Woodward, J. (1982). *How you gonna get to heaven if you can't talk to Jesus?* Silver Spring, MD: T.J. Publishers.

Woodward, J., & Allen, T. (1987). Classroom use of ASL by teachers. *Sign Language Studies, 54,* 1–10.

Learning about Hearing People in the Land of the Deaf

AN ETHNOGRAPHIC ACCOUNT

WRITTEN BY

AUDREI GESSER

This article is a personal account, grounded in some concepts of postcolonial/cultural studies (Bhabha 1990, 1994; Hall 1992), interactional sociolinguistics (Gumperz 1986; Jacob and Ochs 1995), and in theoretical and methodological ethnographic perspectives (Agar 1980, 1994; Erickson and Shultz 1981; Hammersley and Atkinson 1983; Anzul et al. 1991), describing my journey in the land of the Deaf[1]—Gallaudet University. Even though I came to this place to learn about Deaf people's lives, in relation to their culture(s), language(s) and identity(s), what became more interesting to me during my stay at Gallaudet was hearing people's behavior, which in turn, revealed a lot about Deaf people's lives as well. In this sense, I consider that in some situations both hearing and Deaf individuals might overlap in their cultural, linguistic, and identity experiences.

Therefore, I want to start by stressing the importance of a variable that is important in ethnographic studies—*time*. I believe that *time* might work as a useful "tool," helping us to see things through a different light: changes only occur through the passage of time, and the changes I am referring to have mainly to do with my own personal/academic growth and understanding during this process.

Linked to this view, I follow the notion that the "happenings," i.e., "[any] form, interpretation, stance, action, activity, identity, institution, skill, ideology, emotion, or other *culturally meaningful reality* [italics added]" within any social context (globally or locally) are "co-constructed" through social interaction among the participants (Jacob and Ochs 1995,177), and they are "un-linear" (Bhabha 1990, 1994)—even though the historical narrative has to be told linearly due to written language limitations, the social happenings might overlap. In this sense, the discussion in this ethnographic account (whether speaking about individuals, identities, languages and/or cultures) is composed of layers and levels (and is not characterized by homogeneity) and by *continua* (as opposed to dichotomies). These assumptions become relevant because they help us to escape from an essentialist view[2], and therefore, act against the tendency to construct stereotypes.

ENTERING THE FIELD

I arrived at Gallaudet University as a visiting researcher through the Gallaudet Center for Global Education (CGE),[3] and I was supported by the Brazilian government agency CAPES Foundation (Coordination of Higher Education and Graduate Training). I decided to pursue my research at Gallaudet under an anthropological perspective, because I was interested in broadening my view of Deaf people's lives; Gallaudet University appeared to be the ideal place to pursue this interest. To have a better sense of the institution and the people who comprise it, I decided to live in one of the campus residence halls and take my meals at the cafeteria. I also participated in many of the student academic activities: I took a course in ASL for beginners as a regular student and audited some other classes. Even though my formal status was that of a researcher, I believe that I was identified by my peers as an international hearing graduate student. During my stay at the university, I followed the daily routine of the other students, and my data are derived from that activity.

DATA COLLECTION

This investigation relied on ethnographic research methods. According to Hammersley and Atkison (1983), the primary goal of ethnography is the "detailed description of the concrete experience of life within a particular culture and of social rules or patterns that constitute it" (8). To understand *what* is going *on* in some of the social interactions, I investigated and analyzed the local meaning perspectives of the people involved in the context where interaction occurred (Gumperz 1986; Wardhaugh 1992).

The data for this study, then, were generated from field notes taken during the fall semester of 2004 at Gallaudet University. I kept a journal and, from time to time, I developed expansions of my notes trying to make the "unfamiliar" more "familiar" so that my interpretation could come to an approximation of the "inside" view (Erickson 1986; Agar 1980). Although the data were not recorded or videotaped, there are some points in my discussion in which I paraphrase the participants' comments using quotation marks in order to give them *voice* in the text. In this sense, the data are constructions of the researcher in at least two ways: in relation to the paraphrasing process and in relation to the selection and interpretation of the data themselves.[4]

Since Gallaudet comprises a huge anthropological context, it is not possible to cover all the physical spaces and issues in the ways in which they deserve. Therefore, this discussion is restricted to only some of the interactional moments in which I took part. Sometimes, the amount and quality of data I have generated vary from place to place and from person to person. In other words, the language, identity, and culture issues discussed here arose from some of my interactions with some students, teachers, and staff (whether Deaf, Hard of Hearing or hearing), and they occurred sometimes in the dorms, sometimes in classes, or at the cafeteria.

"YOU HAVE TO USE ASL HERE!": UNDERSTANDING LANGUAGE, IDENTITY AND CULTURAL ISSUES

> Language has fundamentally three roles in bonding a group of speakers to one another and to their culture. It is *a symbol of social identity, a medium of social interaction, and a store of cultural knowledge.* [italics added] (Lane, Hoffmeister, and Bahan 1996,67)

One of the things that first attracted my attention when I arrived at the university was the patience that many Deaf people had with me. My biased view was that they would strongly discriminate against me because of my lack of skill with ASL and because I am hearing. Since I was not able to communicate in sign language, most of them read my lips and mouthed in English and/or used written communication. With some hearing people I used mostly English (oral mode) to communicate—a language that is also foreign to me, but much less foreign than ASL. Yet, in both situations, I sometimes had a weird feeling that Agar (1994) metaphorically refers to in regard to his use of the German language: "I often feel, and still feel, that inside of German, I am driving a powerful car on ice without chains. I move, but God only knows where" (97). As time passed by, and my knowledge of these two languages improved, I was always asking myself how is it possible that I am communicating in these two "foreign and weird" codes and these people actually understand what I'm saying? For sure—I always thought to myself—I am making sense, and therefore, doing something with these two languages. I never lost this feeling.

Since I was not proficient in ASL, I developed a strategy of speechreading in English (again, a very difficult skill for me if compared, for instance, to spoken American English speakers) because I noticed that most people at Gallaudet (even Deaf people) frequently mouth words and whisper in English. I relied strongly on this strategy until I was more proficient in ASL and, thus, more comfortable using signs. I also noticed that even ASL-proficient hearing people rely a lot on speechreading during their interactions with ASL users.

It is very common to see hearing people who are interacting with other hearing people using simultaneous communication (SimCom). Only in very rare situations is the English language not used at all. The use of ASL in public space at Gallaudet by hearing people is more a political-ideological issue, since they see themselves circulating in a context that *a priori* is a Deaf space. Then, the use of *hands*— whether conveying ASL, Signed Exact English (SEE), home signs, foreign sign languages, SimCom, wherever you are, whomever you are talking to—is, somehow, the shared linguistic channel for communication. Due to the fact that many languages co-habit this place, it can be observed that language use is circumstantial and it can occur at every point along a continuum: each language's placement will be influenced by the purpose, the content, and the speakers. Therefore, it can be said that these languages operate in a fluid and unstable medium, in the way that they are formed and transformed continuously during the interactions of the people who are using them. In sum, I agree with Fishman (1999) when he says that "languages are rarely hermetically sealed off from one another, so that they may influence each other somewhat, both orally and in writing, even though on the whole their social functions tend to differ" (156).

Within this sociocultural-linguistic ocean, I experienced moments that made me reflect even more about language, culture, and identity issues. During this time I felt more Brazilian than ever. My Brazilian identity, especially with respect to my accent when speaking English, was always projected and co-sustained by me and by my peers in the course of interaction: *"It is so interesting you have nice insights and still have an accent!"* In addition to stressing the difference conveyed by my accent, this comment, not surprisingly, also represents a belief and (mis)concept about language: a biased view that people who have an accent might be lacking knowledge and or/ intelligence.

One of the richest insights that led me to an understanding of hearing people's cultural assumptions, therefore, emerged from the following episode. A hearing person (very proficient in ASL) approached me in the cafeteria. At the very moment we started talking to each other she said: *"You HAVE TO use ASL, otherwise Deaf people are going to look at you and say 'who is that Brazilian hearing girl who is here at Gallaudet and does not sign?' "*. At the beginning, I was shocked about her comment and I took it personally, because she knew that I could not communicate in ASL at that time. But, what does this comment really tell us? On the one hand, it might show this person's concern with political correctness and a feeling of identification with Deaf people in their struggle for recognition and the survival of ASL (despite the efforts of hearing society to eradicate it). However, I started to reflect carefully upon it, and I asked myself to what extent this comment could also mirror hegemonic thinking based on a monolingual view of language use, which in turn, resembles the discourse of linguistic imperialism. Language is a powerful means to convey ideological baggage. It can be a means of solidarity, resistance, control, manipulation, oppression, as well as a representation of identity within a cultural and a social group (Phillipson 1992).

Looking back on that comment, it seemed to me that some hearing people still behave as the oppressors when it comes to Deaf issues, and how hearing people (especially those people who are fluent/proficient in ASL) oppress other hearing people (less or not proficient in ASL at all)[5]. To check my observations in this regard, I also listened to other hearing people's comments (especially those having contact with ASL for the first time) about their experiences with ASL and about its use in interactions with Deaf and hearing people. Most of these people told me that they felt oppressed but the oppression did not come from Deaf people, instead, it came from hearing people:

> You know ... I am really frustrated and sad with hearing people. They keep saying to me that I have to learn ASL and when I try to communicate they correct me all the time and say that my signs are wrong. When I am with Deaf people it is different. They help me a lot, because they want to communicate. Sometimes, I think that some hearing people just want to show their skills in sign, and they ignore other people who are starting to learn. ... Sometimes, they do not care if you understand

them or not. ... I thought hearing people would help me here, but the help and comprehension is coming from the Deaf. (American hearing person/beginner in ASL)

I then spoke with a Hard of Hearing student who told me that he feels angry with some Deaf people because he thinks that they are behaving in the same way hearing people did in the past when they insist he use ASL on campus. "Why?" he says "If I am in Japan do I have to use Japanese? What about my right of privacy? I can speak both ASL and English, what's the problem if I privilege one over another?"[6]. Even though he has a point, and I do understand his perspective, it is important to keep in mind that there are issues between Hard of Hearing and Deaf people. The Hard of Hearing people's situation, from some Deaf—and even hearing—people's point of view, is a situation of "betweenness"—a sense of belonging to neither culture. Bhabha (1994) refers to this feeling as "unhomeliness"—some people are caught between two cultures, and have the feeling of belonging to neither, which, in turn, leads these people to a sense of cultural displacement. The dilemma then is clear—these individuals feels like they have to pick one of the "sides of the coin."

If this is so, this behavior reflects both a very purist view of identity and culture, and a very negative view of bilingual/bicultural individuals who can live effectively with two languages and cultures. Still, these essentialist attitudes toward language use show, to a certain extent, the need for cohesion in the form of a core identity/culture. This cohesion, in turn, is strongly represented by the language you make use of—a valued and recognized cultural trait within the Deaf minority linguistic group (Lane et al. 1996; Ladd 2003).

As the time passed, I was "affected" by the underlying cultural assumption regarding ASL use, and this perception somehow shaped my reality, which in turn, reinforced my perception (Lane et al. 1996,198). There were some moments when I started to feel obliged to use signs with hearing people. But how could I use ASL if I was not fluent? In order to reduce my anxiety in relation to ASL use, I started to simply wave and move my hands frenetically and randomly while speaking in an attempt to make my hands visible, as if I were "materializing a language" and conveying some sort of meaning through these actions. This was certainly an illusion, but I noticed that for some situations it worked as a way to show my attempt to use signs, and therefore, to diminish my "outsider" status (even though I felt silly doing it; still it was a strategy that I found to lower my anxiety as well as to be seen positively by my hearing peers).

I also observed some hearing people (with almost the same level of ASL proficiency as mine) making an effort to use signs—indeed the conversation could be understood because English was being spoken (signs were used only for a few words, put sporadically in the air, as if trying to fill some gaps—this was indeed, a use of fragmented signs). On the one hand, it was easier for me to understand these people's speech better (in English of course!), because by trying to express themselves in signs, these beginner signers also slowed down their speed in the English language. But I wondered how many Deaf people had suffered and missed information when interacting with hearing people using SimCom because the structure of sign language will always be compromised in favor of the use of an oral language.

I could see that SimCom was being used for a variety of reasons. It might work as a step toward the use of one language only (in this case, ASL). In addition, it might also be a strategy used by some hearing people who are just starting to learn sign language—and here I emphasize how *oral* speech (as opposed to sign) is inherent in hearing people's culture (Gesser 1999) and, therefore, hard to abandon completely. Yet, at other times, it might be a reflection of one's ideology. We would have to look closer to see if it was an attempt to reject and ignore Deaf people's sign language.

Following these comments derived from my data, it is possible to perceive that this imposition of ASL will vary from context to context and from speaker to speaker. But what they tell me so far, specifically in regard to hearing people, has to do with the motivations, beliefs, and/or rationales that might be involved. Some hearing and Hard of Hearing people feel oppressed by their hearing and Deaf peers. Hearing people may have numerous reasons for being militant about ASL use. Some hearing people come to Gallaudet to be immersed in Deaf culture and language. They may have invested a considerable amount in order to have this opportunity to live and study at Gallaudet, and for some this linguistic contact will be unavailable elsewhere, so signing 24 hours a day may be a very important goal. In other cases, hearing people may want to be accepted and recognized in the Deaf community.

"ASL IS THE GOLDEN KEY!": HEARING PEOPLE IN THE SEARCH FOR DEAF PEOPLE'S RECOGNITION AND SOCIAL ACCEPTANCE

It was a hot, sunny day. I entered the cafeteria as usual to have my breakfast. The place was not full. Some people were grouped together at one of the tables watching television. While I was walking to find a table a Hard of Hearing friend of mine waved his hands and invited me to sit with him. We started to chat about topics related to Deaf people, and I asked him about his impressions of hearing people at Gallaudet University. We had a great time discussing this issue, and he finally said to me: "you know, if it was a long time ago, I think that Deaf people would never accept the presence of hearing students here in the same way that they do today, but if you want to live well at Gallaudet University, and if you want to be valued and accepted by deaf individuals, then, **ASL is the golden key!**"

The vignette above is indicative of the overall feeling that rules hearing behavior at Gallaudet. I have observed that most hearing people who arrive here feel as if they were minorities in terms of number and prestige (something they have never experienced before outside this place, at least, in regard to hearing status). In this sense, the social dynamic is reversed: positions, social roles, statuses. This new experience leads these people to adopt a specific behavior pattern where acceptance from Deaf people is what matters most. In this setting, it is possible to perceive a feeling, a desire on the part of hearing people "to be Deaf," which in turn, is the same as "being accepted." Being at Gallaudet University in order to have contact with sign language and Deaf people (despite all true and good intentions) are not, I would say, the only reasons that bring hearing people here. It is more than that. It is, at one level, a search for acceptance, which makes this place work very well as a place for a *therapy session*—it is in this sense a huge *therapist's couch*. It is a place for the legitimization of hearing people's need for recognition and validity in the eyes of Deaf people. So, when I see these people associating only with Deaf people or when I see hearing people grouping themselves only with hearing people they consider "Deaf " in some way, using sign language to communicate among themselves even in situations where no Deaf person is present, and rejecting the use oral language (which is an illusion, since most of these people **mouth** when they are signing, and most hearing people rely on this linguistic device to understand each other), all these, reflect the ideology that to be hearing, at a certain level, is seen here as if it were a *sin*.

And what does this side of the coin show us? It shows us a reflection of a complicated double-movement—the attempt of hearing people to reconstitute themselves as a group that despite the "hearing label," does not want to be associated with the well-known oppression created by ("the evil") hearing people of the past. Therefore, the behavior of these hearing people and their use of language are fluid, unstable, and are revealed in fluctuations between two poles (sometimes being too Deaf at one end of the continuum, and at other times, too Hearing). Hearing people's rejection of the use of oral language in face to face interaction represents both a reaction against the past with respect to the treatment of Deaf people and also the hope for a different perception of hearing people in the future. At the same time, it may be that proficiency or fluency in sign language is not a guarantee of good intentions. History suggests (Fanon 1997; Bhabha 1990, 1994) that language can be a powerful instrument of domination, and the history of Deaf people shows that this observation extends to the oppression of Deaf people by hearing society.

It makes sense for these hearing people to go through this process. Before arriving at Gallaudet University, some hearing people may not have detached from their "Deaf people's caretakers identity." Hearing people may have a sense of being Deaf people's *ambassadors* to hearing society. And if this is the case, I would say that hearing people are "superfluous" at Gallaudet. Put simply, Deaf people do not need hearing people's help, at least, not in *the way* or from the point of view hearing people might think they do—a biased, paternalistic, and/or hegemonic one.

Considering this dynamic, it might be true that there is a *disequilibrium* in the status quo, or, as some would prefer to say, there is a threat to hearing people's established social order (Lane 1992). There is a need for a dislocation from one way of seeing, feeling, and behaving to another. Hearing people's roles and status pass through a redefinition at Gallaudet. Then, it is possible to observe an inversion of behaviors, values and, especially, the construction of other social identities: from "caretakers/gatekeepers" to "dependent," from "majority" to "minority," from "norm" to "exception"—in sum, hearing people become "deviant" in this context.

I say this because at many points during my observations, I asked myself the questions "what is my problem?" and "what is my role here?" I felt so displaced myself that I started to see all hearing people in the same way. In fact, these questions were really tied to my prejudiced view of hearing people since I was attributing exclusively bad motives to hearing people's behavior. These questions arose from my initial judgments of hearing people, but they were also part of my own process of getting their points of view. Regarding this process, I understand Erickson (1992) when he stresses the importance in ethnographic research of making the "unfamiliar" "familiar" and the "familiar" "unfamiliar". He argues that it is only through this movement that one can make sense of "what is inside the black box" (202) of a different culture.

"ENGLISH HAS TO BE PERFECT, BUT ASL CAN BE ANYTHING": GALLAUDET UNIVERSITY AS THE BORDER BETWEEN DIVERSE WORLDS

Gallaudet University is a huge social space where many different people with diverse backgrounds, experiences, and views are grouped together. It is the borderland between different worlds. It is a place where the majority hearing group meets the minority Deaf group in the homeland of the latter. It is where diverse groups are in contact and for this reason, it is a place where ideologies, cultures, and identities collide: Deaf, hearing, Hard of Hearing, black, white, Asian, Blind, Catholic, Jewish, Muslim, Baptist, American, foreign, lesbian, gay, heterosexual, just to cite a few, are in contact. So, we have a microcosm where groups distinguished by gender, nationality, age, ethnic, religious, and sexual orientation are co-habiting in a very peculiar way. Even though their main tie and/or core group identification is that of the audiological condition (and here begins the misconception about the way people make sense of each other, because the label establishes an overgeneralization, suggesting a dichotomy between the "good" and the "evil"), it is the contact itself that accentuates this heterogeneity. Therefore, clashes are inevitable. As a consequence it is possible to see a complex and contradictory interface among these groups.

At one of the lectures I attended at the very beginning of my stay at Gallaudet, I remember one Deaf teacher saying: "English has to be perfect, but ASL can be anything." On the one hand, this statement shows Deaf people's frustration in regard to hearing people's expectation when it comes to Deaf people's English language use. But on the other hand, it also implies a view that most people might have toward ASL—that it is a language with a low social status. It was from this early moment that I started to make sense of this place and understand the meaningful role that Gallaudet plays in the lives of all the people who inhabit its community. Therefore, I see Gallaudet connecting all those different worlds, and all the people who, somehow, are engaged in crossing this path to reach each other—they have to pass through a sort of "therapy session." It is the first step for any sort of transition both at the individual as well as at the societal level. This institution is viewed from the outside as *the land of the Deaf*, which creates the false and illusory expectation that ASL is the only language to be used here. It creates the expectation that all people who are linked to Gallaudet have banished their biased views about Deaf people and their language/culture. It also creates the idea that no discrimination, oppression, or any sort of prejudice will be found. That was what I thought before arriving and spending six months here. It was also the view that many people who are part of this place shared with me:

> You know ... before arriving here, I thought I would not find problems. I thought that everybody here would be sensitive to each other in this context. ... I thought I'd be signing all the time, using only American Sign Language and that I wouldn't be using English at all. I am a little bit frustrated because I wanted to improve my sign skills. (hearing person who is proficient in ASL)

Therefore, all social contexts, the cafeteria, classes, meetings, offices, the dorms, all these contexts are potentially used by individuals to express political and ideological views, but also to adjust to diverse cultural frames. In this sense, Gallaudet University is not only a space for Deaf people's political/educational articulation, and for Deaf people's empowerment, it is also a huge therapy couch for hearing people. ASL plays an important role in the constitution of Deaf society and culture, and hearing people's language use and attitudes about its use are important indicators of social identity. ASL use here is a powerful vehicle for the construction and maintenance of selfhood during social interaction among members of different groups.

CONCLUDING REMARKS

This essay is intended as an account of my experiences of face-to-face interaction at Gallaudet University, including attitudes and observed communication behaviors in relation to language, culture, and identity of Deaf, hearing, and Hard of Hearing people. It attempted to present a broad ethnographic account of the behavior of some hearing and Deaf people as they construct meaningful realities, including my own. In this sense, Gallaudet University was inspiring—my experience there was extraordinarily rich, both as a place to study human behavior in all its diversity and as a place to experience personal growth.

NOTES

1. It is common practice in the specialized Deaf literature to use the capitalized term *Deaf* to refer to a particular group of deaf people who share a language, values and beliefs, and the term *deaf*, with a lower case, to refer to the audiological condition of not hearing. Some might argue that this distinction, even though relevant, is difficult to make because it is not possible to know "at what precise point do deaf become Deaf " (Baynton 1996, 12). Still, I believe that the distinction has to be made, because it mirrors "a movement in the identity of Deaf people that derives from their 'ethnic revival' " (Baker 1999, 122).
2. "Essentialism is the existence of fixed characteristics, given attributes, and ahistorical functions that limit the possibility of change and thus of social organization" (Grosz 1999).
3. I would like to express my deepest gratitude to Dr. Robert E. Johnson who shared his knowledge with me during the development of this project.
4. It is important to stress that even transcription excerpts are, to a certain extent, constructions of the researcher (Atkinson 1993).
5. I believe that it might be true that there is still oppression from hearing people toward Deaf people in some interactions within the Gallaudet University context, but this was not investigated in this study.
6. Keeping to this issue of language oppression/discrimination, I have heard from a Deaf international student that she felt oppressed and discriminated against by some Deaf Americans, users of ASL. Many issues and variables might be involved here. Yet, it would be interesting to investigate the relations among Deaf people who are signers of different sign languages to see if ASL has a prestigious status over other sign languages.

REFERENCES

Agar, M. 1980. *The Professional Stranger.* New York: Academic Press. ———. 1994. *Understanding the Culture of Conversation.* New York: Perennial.

Baker, C. 1999. Sign Language and the Deaf community. In *Handbook of Language and Ethnic Identity,* ed. J. A. Fishman, pp. 122–39. Oxford, U.K.: Oxford University Press.

Baynton, D. C. 1996. *Forbidden Signs: American Culture and the Campaign against Sign Language.* Chicago: University of Chicago Press. Bhabha, H. K. 1990. *Nation and Narration.* New York: Routledge. ———. 1994. *The Location of Culture.* New York: Routledge.

Anzul, M., and Margot Ely, Teri Friedman, Diane Garner, Ann Mccormack Steinmetz. 1991. *Doing Qualitative Research: Circles within Circles.* London: Falmer.

Erickson, F. 1986. Qualitative Methods in Research on Teaching. In *Handbook of Research on Teaching,* ed. M. C. Wittrock, 77–200. New York: Macmillan.

———. 1992. Ethnographic Microanalysis of Interaction. In *The Handbook of Qualitative Research in Education,* ed. M. D. LeCompte, W. L. Millroy, and J. Preissle, 201–25. New York: Academic.

———. 1996. On the Evolution of Qualitative Approaches in Educational Research: From Adam's Task to Eve's. *Australian Educational Researcher* 23 (2): 1–15.

Erickson, F., and J. Shultz. 1981. When Is a Context? Some Issues and Methods in the Analysis of Social Competence. In *Ethnography and Language in Educational Settings,* ed. J. L. Green and C. Wallat, 147–60. Nor-wood, N.J.: Ablex.

Fishman, J. A. 1999. Sociolinguistics. In *Handbook of Language and Ethnic Identity,* ed. J. A. Fishman, 152–63. Oxford: Oxford University Press.

Gesser, A. 1999. Teaching and Learning Brazilian Sign Language (LIBRAS) as a Foreign Language: A Microethnographic Description. Master's thesis, Universidade Federal de Santa Catarina, Florianopolis, Brazil.

Gumperz, J. 1986. Interactional Sociolinguistics in the Study of Schooling. In *The Social Construction of Literacy,* J. Cook Gumperz, 229–52. Cambridge: Cambridge University Press.

Hall, S. 1992. The Question of Cultural Identity. In *Modernity and Its Futures,* ed. S. Hall, D. Held, and T. McGrew, 273–326. Cambridge: Polity Press.

Hammersley, M., and P. Atkinson. 1983. *Ethnography: Principles in Practice.* London: Routledge.

Jacob, S., and E. Ochs. 1995. Co-Construction: An Introduction. *Research on Language and Social Interaction* 28(3): 171–83.

Ladd, P. 2003. *Understanding Deaf Culture: In the Search of Deafhood.* Clevedon, U.K.: Multilingual Matters.

Lane, H. 1992. *The Mask of Benevolence: Disabling the Deaf Community.* San Diego: DawnSign.

Lane, H., R. Hoffmeister, and B. Bahan. 1996. *A Journey into the Deaf-World.* San Diego: DawnSign.

Lanehart, S. L. 1999. African American Vernacular English. In *Handbook of Language and Ethnic Identity,* ed. J. A. Fishman, 221–25). Oxford: Oxford University Press.

Mason, J. 1997. *Qualitative Researching.* London: Sage.

Parasnis, I., ed. 1996. *Cultural and Language Diversity and the Deaf Experience.* Cambridge: Cambridge University Press.

Phillipson, R. 1992. *Linguistic Imperialism.* Oxford: Oxford University Press.

Wardhaugh, R. 1992. *An Introduction to Sociolinguistics.* Oxford Blackwell.

Understanding Deafhood

IN SEARCH OF ITS MEANINGS

WRITTEN BY

ANNELIES KUSTERS AND MAARTJE DE MEULDER

Deafhood is a concept that aims to disrupt medically oriented and oppressive discourses, by offering a deafconstructed model that grows out of deaf people's own ontologies (i.e., deaf ways of being in the world), emphasizing positive, experience-oriented views of deaf people (Ladd, 2003).[1] After the publication in 2003 of Paddy Ladd's book *Understanding Deaf Culture: In Search of Deafhood*, the term became a "buzzword" that appeared to touch many deaf people. It was immortalized in tattoos on deaf peoples' arms and feet and commercialized with Deafhood cups, Tshirts, bags, and buttons (see http://shop. gehoerlosen-jugend .de/). The concept has been used in political meetings and activism, and has been an inspiration for yoga (see http://www.deafhoodyoga.com/), plays (see http://www. deafhoodmonologues .com/), and a charitable organization, the Deafhood Foundation (http:// www .deafhoodfoundation.org/Deafhood/ Home.html). There are (or have been) Deafhood workshops, courses, conferences,[2] reading groups, online discussion groups (e.g., http://www. deafhood discourses.com/), and innumerable vlogs (e.g., http://www.deafhooddis courses. com/) and blogs.

However, the Deafhood concept is not free from criticism. The present article is based on discussions during Deafhood presentations and workshops during which it became clear that many participants struggled with questions linked to the nature of this concept. Since 2008 we have taught Deafhood, combining lecturing with workshops, to small groups of up to 25 people (with a few exceptions) in Finland (invited by the Finnish Deaf Association) and Denmark (invited by the Danish Deaf Association and the Frontrunners international deaf youth leadership training program), giving basic and advanced Deafhood courses of 1 to 3 days. We also have taught Deafhood to larger groups (up to 60 people) during camps organized by the World Federation of the Deaf Youth Section and the European Union of Deaf Youth. In Flanders—which we both are from—we have been teaching in a Deafhood consciousness-raising course, organized yearly by Fevlado (the Flemish Deaf Association) since 2009, taught by deaf people and aimed at deaf people only. It is a course organized on two levels (basic and advanced), spread over 10 months. While the Deafhood concept is the primary starting point and is used as a connecting thread throughout the course, the course takes on diverging subjects such as Deaf history, sign language, Deaf culture, Deaf art, and the future of the Deaf community, all taught by deaf teachers. Signing deaf people of all ages and backgrounds have registered for this course, which has significantly affected these people's selfimage, as we discuss in the present article.

During these short courses, participants have appeared to struggle with the rather vague articulation of the Deafhood concept and with its abstract nature. Therefore, we have often compared Deafhood with "feminism," a comparison that has helped us articulate what Deafhood means, in comparison to and in contrast with feminism. Like Deafhood, feminist theories and ontologies have been powerful, moving people toward selfexploration and activism. Our course participants also have found that published explorations of the Deafhood concept (either academic or nonacademic) have been minimal and that Ladd's own explanations are dispersed over several texts and often difficult to digest. The present article thus stems from a consideration of the participants' feedback and concerns, and, as such, aims to offer an account of the lived experience of Deafhood as a concept, in itself and in comparison to feminist theories.

We start the present article by tracing the Deafhood concept back to Dr. Paddy Ladd (whom we introduce later in the text), arguing that Deafhood is an open-ended concept with an essentialist core, the core being the belief that sign language learning and knowledge and deaf socialization should be available to—and pursued by—every deaf person. We then describe how deaf people have perceived different aspects of the Deafhood concept. Subsequently, the basic tenets of Deafhood are compared to theories of feminist essentialisms. We set out which strands of feminism we are referring to, describe criticisms of Deafhood based on the workshops, and compare and contrast these criticisms with criticisms of certain feminist theories that address the issue of essentialism. We argue that the vagueness and breadth of the Deafhood concept is one of its strengths, although we also find that it is in some respects problematic to combine and unite ontology and liberation theory in one concept. This is because, first, it leads to confusion about what Deafhood actually (and primarily) "means," and second, because it gives the impression that Deafhood is merely or mainly a reactionary concept, implying that the authoring of deaf ontologies is inspired solely by resistance to oppression. However, the ontological dimensions have proved to be most appealing to workshop participants. Hence, we suggest that the ontological aspects of Deafhood need to be situated in the foreground (recognizing that this is liberatory in itself), rather than the liberatory effect of "overcoming (mental) colonialism." Finally, workshop participants have expressed strong concerns about concrete applications of the Deafhood concept. We discuss the question of essentialism inherent in the Deafhood concept below, with regard to concrete, everyday issues in Deaf communities such as the relationship with hearing people, the use of spoken language, and the use of technologies such as amplification and cochlear implants.

DEAFHOOD: EMERGENCE AND ADOPTION

The Deafhood concept was first articulated in 1993 by the British Deaf activist and academic Dr. Paddy Ladd (1993b) in a chapter he contributed to a National Association of the Deaf publication (Ladd, 1993b); the chapter was republished, under a different title, in the proceedings of the Deaf Studies III conference (Ladd, 1993a). He further developed the concept in a dissertation on Deaf culture (Ladd, 1998) he wrote as part of his PhD program at the University of Bristol, in England. Worldwide dissemination of the Deafhood concept came with Ladd's 2003 textbook *Understanding Deaf Culture: In Search of Deafhood*, which was based on his dissertation. In this book, Ladd actually argues for the validation of the Deaf culture concept (even though *Understanding Deaf Culture* is—misleadingly—known as "the Deafhood book"). Still, the Deafhood concept became a buzzword in both the academic and lay communities immediately after the book's publication. While the Deafhood concept came into existence as an academic concept and frames academic programs such as the MSc in Deafhood studies at the University of Bristol and summer courses at Ohlone College in California, it has been, as we mention in the introductory section of the present article, inspiring and compelling to deaf people from many different backgrounds.

Between 2007 and 2011, Ladd's book was translated into Japanese, German, and Spanish; a Portuguese translation is forthcoming. Attempts to translate the book into sign languages have been delayed for years due to lack of funding, but it has been in the process of being translated into American Sign Language (ASL) since 2011 (see the website "Deafhood Discussions," www.deafhood.us/wp). However, in addition to the (written) language, the academic and encyclopedic style of writing in the book is a hurdle to many deaf people, for which Ladd has been criticized. Ladd himself has said that he understands the frustrations, but that the prime aim of his PhD dissertation (and the resulting publication) was to "hit" the hearing academic world and to "prove" the existence of Deaf culture (personal communication, September 12, 2008). When he learned about the success of the Deafhood concept, he started working on a website, the launching of which has been delayed for many years—again due to a lack of funding and personnel.

Because Ladd felt overwhelmed by the heavy demand for Deafhood courses and workshops, he started to delegate this work to people who had experienced his academic training and supervision, among whom are ourselves. Since being his students at the University of Bristol, we have been teaching about Deafhood in different contexts in different European countries since 2008, combining lectures with workshops.

LADD'S EXPLANATION OF DEAFHOOD

Ladd (2003, 2005, 2006) explains Deafhood in several different ways; hence, there is no one clear definition of what Deafhood *is*. One of Ladd's explanations is that Deafhood is an English term to counter other (negative) English terms—such as *hearing impaired* and *deafness*—that describe deaf people within a pathological, medical model, implying that being deaf is a loss and that deaf people therefore are deficient beings in need of a cure. The Deafhood concept, on the contrary, aims to disrupt these medically oriented and oppressive discourses, by offering a deaf-constructed model that grows out of deaf people's own ontologies. The concept does this by emphasizing positive, experience-oriented views of deaf people and by emphasizing deaf people's *possibilities*, to ultimately identify their "larger Deaf selves" (Ladd, 2005, 2006).

This idea is also taken up by Bauman and Murray (2010) as part of their "Deafgain" concept. What Deaf people *gain* are enhanced cognitive skills such as increased peripheral recognition (Bavelier et al., 2000), increased facial recognition (Bettger, Emmorey, McCullough, & Bellugi, 1997), increased spatial cognition (Bellugi et al., 1989), visual alertness, and proficiency in visual learning and in the use of visual languages that are rich in "metaphoric iconicity" (Taub, 2001). In addition to these intrinsic arguments, there are also extrinsic arguments that demonstrate the contribution of deaf people and their language "for the greater good of humanity" (Bauman & Murray, 2010, p. 215). ASL is the second most frequently taught non-English language in 4-year colleges and universities in the United States (Furman, Goldberg, & Lusin, 2007); many hearing people register for sign language courses out of sheer interest, and many of them are fond of this new language. Research also suggests that the cognitive, linguistic, emotional, and intellectual development of hearing children can be improved by the early use of sign language (i.e., "baby signs") between parents and their infants (Garcia, 1999).

Another way the Deafhood concept is used is as a "deconstructive tool for more efficient analysis of oppression" (P. Ladd, personal communication, November 23, 2010). Ladd (2003) perceives deaf people and their communities as, among other things, victims of a colonization process that, through the policy of "pure oralism," has had huge consequences for deaf individual and collective lives. Because of this educational policy, deaf people have experienced high levels of internalized oppression leading to a rate of acquired mental illness double that of the hearing population (Hindley & Kitson, 2000). The damage to deaf people's collective lives has been just as bad (Ladd, 2003, 2005): delayed entry into community life, delayed and reduced exposure to Deaf cultural heritage, damage to traditional cultures and art forms (Mirzoeff, 1995).

Ladd has stated that, as a result, there are destructive patterns that are deeply rooted in Deaf cultures, such as not knowing or realizing positive meanings of being deaf, not realizing that sign languages are genuine languages, having a general suspicion or dislike of hearing people, and having a deeply ingrained tendency to criticize rather than praise each other (Ladd, 2003). About these patterns, Ladd (2006) has written,

> How does one break through the patterns? One step is to realize that they *are* patterns. The next step is to draw a line under Deaf culture as it is presently understood and say, "Yes, these are the Deaf traditions we have inherited following colonization. We respect them but we must also continue to aim to realize a larger Deaf self." (pp. 247–248)

According to Ladd, the Deafhood concept, then, can help deaf people "to have a grasp of what we are aspiring towards and help that process along" (Ladd, 1993a, p. 211). The concept is thus not only designed as an ontology emphasizing "gain" but also as "a consciousness-raising strategy through which SLPs [Sign Language Peoples[3]] can examine their own experiences, reempower themselves, and thus engage in the work of community regeneration" (P. Ladd, personal communication, November 23, 2010).

Deafhood is thus a very broad concept, entailing ontology as well as a liberating, empowering philosophy and a counternarrative in response to hegemonic oralist and colonizing discourses. While one of the strengths of the Deafhood concept seems to be that it recognizes and validates deaf people's ontologies and epistemologies, the fact that it serves as a kind of umbrella concept can be confusing as well, and the inherent essentialism has proved to be controversial. These two issues are addressed in the sections below, starting with a description of our workshops.

THE WORKSHOPS AND DEAFHOOD AS ONTOLOGY

As the Flemish course was taught 10 times over 10 months, and linked to various themes, participants had the time to link the philosophy behind the Deafhood concept to their daily lives. As such, Deafhood became a kind of ontological framework that returned throughout the course. While teaching, we felt that, for many participants, Deafhood was a very compelling term that seems to address them in their deepest being. (In the United States, this aspect has even led to Deafhood yoga courses; see http://www.deaf hoodyoga.com/). A workshop technique we used at the end of our teach ing sessions in Flanders was to place a chair in the middle of the classroom, state that the chair represented Deafhood, and ask people how they would position themselves in relation to this chair.[4] Their answers were revealing:

- The chair as luggage, to take with you on your life journey
- The chair as the seat of a car: Deafhood as a way to start on the path of self-exploration
- Looking at the chair from a distance and moving toward it: Deafhood as a process—"I've found my way, I know where to go."
- The chair as a campfire to give us warmth
- The chair to stand on, to widen your horizon
- Sitting "under" the chair: Deafhood as a second skin
- Sitting on the chair: "I've found my place, I feel good here."

These answers point to the fact that thinking about Deafhood offered the participants opportunities for selfreflection: It opened the way to explore their lives and histories. Participants also said the Deafhood course increased their self-determination and their consciousness about being deaf in this world, and made them more tolerant toward, for example, incomprehension from hearing people. Recognizing a shared gut feeling and shared ontologies also generated a feeling of unity. Last but not least, the course caused a feeling of liberation. For example, one of the participants told us that the course had made him feel free, had given him wings.

However, at the same time, our course and workshop participants have repeatedly told us that they think Deafhood is too broad, too vague, and too hard to summarize, let alone explain to other people. If our participants try to explicate the concept, most of the time they discuss the ontological aspect, the gut feeling, connecting the recognition of this experience to the above-mentioned feeling of freedom. On the other hand, some hearing people who have been working with the Deaf community for a long time, and some deaf people who have not been enrolled in the course (yet), have told us (indirectly) that they feel that the course is a sort of breeding ground for deaf activism and even extremism. For them, the liberatory aspects of the concept have come to the fore, and these have been perceived as militant. This is an example of how the vagueness and wideness of the concept's meaning have the potential to cause misunderstandings.

DEAFHOOD AND ESSENTIALISM, AND FEMINIST ESSENTIALISMS

To summarize the previous sections, it appears that Deafhood is a very broad concept implying deaf ontologies and deaf epistemologies as well as being a liberating, empowering philosophy and a counternarrative toward hegemonic structures and discourses. As such, the Deafhood concept has a lot of similarities with feminisms.[5] Because deaf people can in several respects be compared to women, in that they are "overpowered" by societal structures that are not produced by them or for them, and since they produce their own, different spaces, authoring their own ontologies and epistemologies (Kemp & Squires, 1997), we believe that a comparison might help us to understand and articulate the specific nature of Deafhood and its inherent essentialism.

In the present article, we are not so much looking at feminism from its classical liberal rights perspective or at feminist activism, but rather at feminist trends in the 1980s and 1990s "to denounce totalizing theories, to celebrate difference, recognize 'otherness,' and acknowledge the multiplicity of feminisms" (Kemp & Squires, 1997, p. 4). We focus on the debate between social constructivist and essentialist theories regarding feminisms, citing leading feminists who have commented on the tension between the assertion of the existence of an essential "Womanness" and diverse, fluctuating subjectivities.

When, during our presentations and workshops, participants have asked us questions about Deafhood, these questions have almost always been framed within an essentialist rhetoric: a way of thinking characterized by questions such as "Who can have/can't have Deafhood?" and "Who can experience/can't experience Deafhood?" or "What do you need to do/to be to experience Deafhood?" Many participants have been in search of the core of the Deafhood concept, formulated as a set of characteristics or rules, and thus have thought in essentialist ways. For Ladd, when he was devising the concept, the primary commitment was to those who considered themselves members of Deaf communities and used sign language already; thus, the concept originally did not set out to clarify the abovementioned questions (P. Ladd, personal communication, September 12, 2008). Still, our participants have expressed the belief that it is important to think about those topics with regard to Deafhood, following Ladd's suggestion that the concept is not "finished" and that— perhaps paradoxically—the exploration of its meaning is part of the meaning of the Deafhood concept itself: "What Deafhood might mean within and to different sectors of the community is a valid cultural process in itself" (Ladd, 2003, p. 408).

Deafhood seems to imply the possibility of multiple pathways, but in fact is commencing from an essentialist core: "Deafhood comes from maintaining a clear focus on the seed itself " (Ladd, 2003, p. 407). More specifically, Deafhood is a certain ontological experience that relates to being biologically deaf. Such a focus on a "core" or a "seed" has also been maintained in feminist essentialisms: for example, by subjugating all women to a common essence, stating that there are properties shared by all women, such as being "carers," "passive," "subjected," "emotional." There are different kinds of feminist essentialisms—for instance, biological essentialism (as manifested, for example, by women's possession of a womb and their child-bearing capacity). Other forms of feminisms have been sociological, for example, the belief that all women share similar social conditions or characteristics such as "domestic" or "nurturing" (Stone, 2004). Summarizing, Fuss (1989/1997) wrote that, as such, essentialism in feminist theories "appeals to a pure or original femininity, a female essence, outside the boundaries of the social and thereby untainted (though perhaps repressed) by a patriarchal order" (pp. 250–251). There is a parallel here with the Deafhood concept and the fact that the articulation of deaf people's own ontologies and epistemologies has been repressed by colonialist structures (Ladd, 2003).

Singhellou (2007) compared Deafhood to the "performativity" concept of the well-known feminist Judith Butler, who has argued (Butler, 1990) that gender is not natural but habitual and learned, based on cultural norms of femininity and masculinity. Both the Deafhood concept and the performativity concept are poststructuralist theories, but Singhellou noted that, while Ladd's concept has an essentialist core, Butler's theory can be described as anti-essentialist. Both concepts imply a process of *becoming*, but unlike Butler, Ladd emphasizes that this construction "not only 'permits' a belief in cultural change but actually *suggests directions* towards which that change might orientate itself" (Ladd, 2003, p. 409, our emphasis). Also, while Butler speaks about "gender" in general, encompassing both male and female, Ladd's conception of Deafhood is as a process meant *for deaf people only*. Butler's *becoming* is an open-ended process that is not to be categorized into a binary opposition such as male/female (and thus is anti-essentialist), while Ladd's Deafhood concept is, as suggested by Singhellou, an openended *deaf* becoming.

The suggested direction in which to move onward from this seed—the "deaf becoming"— is the "actualization" of the deaf biological state, by the use of sign language and socialization with other deaf people. The number of potential choices of different ways to experience Deafhood is thereby reduced. When we explained this dimension of the Deafhood concept in our courses, a number of participants felt that the Deafhood concept could be exclusive and divisional and therefore oppressive in a way that is not much different from the d/D categorization, which is exactly a categorization that the Deafhood concept seeks to transcend. After all, our participants stated, because Deafhood implies being biologically deaf, it potentially excludes Codas (children of deaf adults) and possibly people with only a slight hearing loss; and because it implies the use of sign language, it potentially excludes all those deaf people who do not (yet) know or use sign language.

When Ladd (2005) states that all deaf people can experience Deafhood, he implies that those deaf people who do not know sign language could (and should), in order to develop their Deafhood, learn sign language and socialize within the Deaf community:

One learns to become a member of a culture, and in a similar way a child born deaf, even to deaf parents, has to learn to become "deaf," that is, to become a responsible sign language–using member of a national community. (p. 14)

Ladd means that this is not just an option, but indeed the preferred path to follow, and the path that deaf people would follow were they not hampered in the development of their inherent potential (as is so often the case). In the next section, this Deafhood "requirement" of "being/becoming a signing deaf person" is discussed in depth.

(HARD OF) HEARING PEOPLE AND DEAFHOOD

Hirons (2009) believes that if one has to be audiologically deaf to experience Deafhood, this means that the concept is based on—or relies on—a medical deficiency model of deafness, while the Deafhood concept was coined to mean exactly the opposite. We believe that the medical model is confused with a purely biological viewpoint here: Instead of being understood as a "loss," deafness could be regarded as a product of biodiversity. Hirons, however, makes a point when wondering about the point at which someone is "deaf enough" to be able to experience Deafhood. While it could be said that there could be a "continuum with flexible ends," Hirons's aim is in fact not to discuss *which deaf* (or hard of hearing) people can or cannot experience Deafhood, but, more radically, to draw people's attention to *hearing* people such as Codas. If people with a sudden or light hearing loss would be able to experience Deafhood, so she claims, why would it be the case that people with no hearing loss at all—but who grew up in a deaf environment—could not experience Deafhood? Does the mere fact of being deaf have the potential to automatically create a certain consciousness, something one cannot experience when one is hearing?

Some participants in our workshops have felt threatened by the thought that hearing people could experience Deafhood, and we have repeatedly received comments from them such as "There are hearing people who know or learn our language, and who are included in our culture and community; that is fine, but the Deafhood experience? That's ours only." But at the same time, some participants have indicated that they are especially concerned about Codas, whom they associate with Deaf communities, cultures, and even identities, so we decided to look closer at Preston's 1994 book about the experiences of Codas, *Mother Father Deaf: Living Between Sound and Silence*. Participants have been impressed and sometimes even baffled by the excerpts from the book that we shared with them. It appears that some Codas do not emphasize hearing or bicultural identities but see their deaf identity as their "real identity":

When I'm sitting in a room or walking down the street, people look at me and they see this hearing person. That's all they see. But just beneath the surface, there's this deaf person. I'm not talking about hearing loss, I'm talking about a whole way of being. The real me is Deaf. (Preston, 1994, p. 216)

> Deafness is our lifeline. You know, when you're born, they cut the umbilical cord and you're a separate person. Well, with deafness you can never cut the umbilical cord. Those of us who were raised in it, we can never leave it behind. (Preston, 1994, p. 235)

As a result of such experiences and the fact that some Codas never feel fully understood or accepted by either hearing or deaf people, it happens that Codas feel left out or excluded:

> Ten years ago I think that deaf people tried to push me out. ... But I got to the point where I started saying, "Wait a minute! You can't get rid of your kids, and you can't get rid of people that are part of Deaf culture. We are as much a part of Deaf culture. We're not a hearing person coming in and telling you what to do. We're your kids! We grew up in the same household. You cannot deny me that." (Preston, 1994, p. 217)

Two of the quotes from Preston em phasize the natural, biological connection between Codas and their deaf parents; this leads to the question of whether the possibility of experiencing Deafhood can be seen as potentially inherent in the situation in which Codas grow up. The question, then, is which dimension of Deafhood constitutes the core of the concept: the fact of experiencing and overcoming barriers and oppression connected with being deaf—that is, the liberatory dimension—or the visuo-gestural-tactile skills that are also emphasized by the Deaf-gain concept (Bauman & Murray, 2010)—that is, the ontological dimension? This is a difficult issue because, as we have already mentioned, the Deafhood concept incorporates both elements. Oppression experienced by Codas is partially similar to and partially different from oppression experienced by deaf people (Preston, 1994). Regarding the "ontological" aspects of Deafhood, Codas—when given the opportunity to develop their visuo-gestural skills—also have abilities such as well-developed spatial thinking and nativelike command of sign languages (Emmorey, Kosslyn, & Bellugi, 1993; Emmorey et al., 2005).

A suggestion that has often occurred during workshops is that Codas perhaps experience a kind of "Codahood," which could then partially overlap with Deafhood. It has also been suggested that Codas can have a kind of "Deafhood seed" as a potential inherent in the situation in which they grow up, that they can or cannot develop, just like deaf people who did not learn sign language during childhood. Hirons (2009) has more boldly concluded that hearing people (not just Codas) have the potential to experience Deafhood if they support "the deaf cause":

> Fundamentally, if Deafhood is interpreted as a wider struggle for human dignity and empowerment, there seems to be little ideological justification for excluding hard of hearing and what Ladd terms "hearing allies" from the Deafhood process. If Deafhood is interpreted so as to only include audiologically deaf persons within its experience, Deafhood philosophy will simply perpetuate the divisiveness and exclusion found within some sectors of the Deaf community at present. (p. 4)

When arguing why to include hearing people, Hirons thus puts the emphasis on the empowerment or liberation aspects of Deafhood (rather than the ontological aspects). If a comparison may be made with feminist activism, it is imaginable that men could be feminists when they supported the feminist cause, so if Deafhood were seen as a "deaf analogue to feminist activism," a hearing person would indeed be able to experience a personal Deafhood process. But the question whether a man can experience (essential) womanhood/womanness is much trickier and more difficult to answer, especially when the experiences of transvestites and transsexuals are considered. We contend that the ontological experience should not become a "secondary prerequisite" to experiencing Deafhood, but that it is central to it. The sign for *Deafhood* in British Sign Language (made on the stomach) seems to imply an emphasis on ontology: *Deafhood* is not signed as "Deaf emancipation" or "Deaf process," but seems to indicate a "gut feeling." We therefore concur with Gulliver (2009), who criticized Ladd's conceptualization of Deafhood as an explicitly contestatory concept, as a "counternarrative," and as such problematizes the fact that ontology as well as emancipation are brought together in one concept.

To clarify our position: Although we understand our workshop participants' concerns about hearing people and Deafhood and the potential divisiveness of the concept, we believe that *Deafhood* is not an appropriate term to use in analyzing the position of Codas and other hearing people in Deaf communities. Other concepts such as Sign Language Peoples (Batterbury, 2012; Batterbury et al., 2007) and *viittomakielinen*, "Sign Language Persons" (Jokinen, 2001), have the potential to be more useful for doing this. Moreover, it has never been Ladd's intention to devise an allencompassing concept to include hearing people's experiences. The primary focus of the Deafhood concept is on deaf people, and it was devised as a tool for their individual and collective self-exploration.

STRATEGIC ESSENTIALISM

The warnings from Hirons (2009) about the potential divisiveness of the Deafhood concept concur with those of Moi (1989/1997), who stated that essentialism in feminism is oppressive, as it "always plays into the hands of those who want women to conform to predefined patterns of femininity" (p. 247). "The 'feminist subject' has been seen to be just as ethnocentric and exclusive, just as imperialist and bourgeois, as her male counterpart in claiming to speak on behalf of all women" (Gunew, 1988/1997, p. 239). Spelman (1988/1997) explained a further danger of essentialism: "If there is an essential womanness that all women have and have always had, then we needn't know anything about any woman in particular" (p. 236). The particularities of each woman's individual life become unimportant, and thus unessential to the definition of womanhood. Differences between women are obscured and made subordinate to similarities between them. Gunew (1988/1997) suggested that women's accounts should not be regarded as "a chorus of women's voices blended in undifferentiated sisterhood" (p. 241). Summarizing the essentialist and anti-essentialist strands in feminism, Riley (1988/1997) stated that feminism has oscillated between over-feminization and under-feminization, between transcendence and deconstruction, between women as having fluctuating identities or sharing an essential "womanness."

Very similar concerns have been raised by our workshop participants: There is enormous diversity among deaf people, especially with regard to language use and language background, hearing status and use of hearing technologies, and educational background. The Deafhood theory says, though, that deaf people are in essence more visually oriented than hearing people, and therefore *should* be sign language–using people. Disregarding or ironing out inter-individual differences between deaf people, however, seems to threaten this diversity. Hirons (2009) thus rightfully pointed out the dangers of essentialism in Deafhood theory.

However, we regard Hirons's (2009) argument that hearing people can experience a Deafhood process as extremely anti-essentialist. Similarly, Soper (1990/1997) argued that although great care should be taken with essentialism in feminism, the danger of anti-essentialism is extreme particularism and hyper-individualism. Soper stated that politics is a group affair, and that without a common cause, feminist political movements collapse. Similarly, extreme anti-essentialism would be disastrous for Deaf communities, as they are still fighting discrimination in the workplace, social welfare systems, the media, and elsewhere, and are still defending their right to use sign languages in a wide range of contexts, the right to education in sign language, and the right not to choose hearing technology such as cochlear implants (Ladd, 2003). Also, in oralist educational systems, deaf people are divided according to skills in speaking and hearing, and an essentialist concept such as "Deafhood" represents an effort to try to unify them (again).

Therefore, Ladd (2003) poses the idea that the rejection of essentialism is "unfortunate for groups like Deaf communities who are still struggling to conceptualize their postcolonial identity." (p. 217). According to him, the timing of antiessentialist discourses (i.e., their occurrence during the postmodernist era) is ironic:

> At the very moment when the discourse of oppressed groups at last becomes visible and they are able to position themselves as a counter-narrative to White or Hearing supremacy … their discourses risk being dismissed along with the Grand Narratives themselves! (p. 80)

Ladd furthermore argues that people of color or women are in further stages of redefining themselves, "whereas Deaf communities are still either caught up in it or just embarking on resolving it" (p. 418).

With regard to feminist theories, Fuss (1989/1997) argued that a distinction should be made between "'deploying' or 'activating' essentialism and 'falling into' or 'lapsing into' essentialism" (p. 257), explaining that the "danger" of using the concept depends on "*who* is utilizing it, *how* it is deployed, and *where* its effects are concentrated" (p. 267, emphasis in original). This corresponds with Spivak's "strategic essentialism," deployed by Ladd in the creation of his "Deafhood" concept. Ladd emphasizes that he is "mindful of the dangers of falling into essentialism" but defends the essentialism inherent in the Deafhood concept as being "at the least strategically viable for the foreseeable future" (Ladd, 2003, p. 217).

He mentions that he hopes that "others may be able to develop readings which refine and 'deessentialize' this one" (p. 81). Hirons (2009) takes it even further:

> When applied to collectivist cultures, essentialism should not in fact be only strategically deployed when no other option is available, but used as a valid way of understanding a culture through explicitly acknowledging and valuing its collectivist basis. (p. 10)

Regarding the need to be careful with essentialism in feminism, Kanneh (1992/1997) emphasized that it is highly important "to determine *which aspects* of this femininity should be held up for celebration, and to sort out just what would be *the political ramifications* of such a move" (p. 293, our emphasis). She also warned that it is important to distinguish between "an inherent feminine essence" and "the direct results of social marginalization and intolerable sexual visibility" (p. 293). Kanneh criticized those feminists who find women incarcerated in the kitchen and therefore sing the kitchen's praise. These remarks highly correspond with what Ladd explains as being the difference between Deaf culture(s) and Deafhood. Ladd found that destructive consequences of oppression in Deaf cultures are justified or explained away as being part of "*the* Deaf way," "*the* Deaf culture" (Ladd, 2003). With his Deafhood concept, Ladd wants to move away from this way of thinking, allowing and encouraging Deaf cultures to *change,* rather than formulating a deaf analogue to "singing the kitchen's praise." Hence, while the Deaf culture and Deafhood concepts both can be seen as essentialist, interpretations of Deaf culture (such as "*the* Deaf way") are often close ended and static, while Deafhood aims at being open ended and dynamic. In the next section of the present article, we consider what this flexibility on the part of Deafhood could entail.

SPOKEN LANGUAGE, HEARING AIDS, COCHLEAR IMPLANTS, MUSIC: TABOOS?

Ladd's interpretation of Deafhood as an open-ended concept with an essentialist core can be summarized thus: Deaf people's lives should commence from their "Deafhood seed" (i.e. using sign language and developing deaf sociality), and from there can develop in multiple ways, much like a tree with multiple roots and branches, which grows from a single seed. There remain many questions as to the implementation of this interpretation in everyday life, particularly in the areas of communication and technology. During our courses, we have received the following questions: "Does Deafhood mean that you should sign in every context and should not speak?" "Does Deafhood mean that you could/should not enjoy listening to music?" "Does Deafhood mean that you should not use hearing aids or a cochlear implant?" We believe these issues could be seen—at least in some situations and by some people—as referring to "taboos" within the Deaf community. During our workshops, they have often been the subjects of heated debate.

Following Ladd's suggestion that it is part of the Deafhood process to explore destructive or damaging results of discrimination and oppression, we argue that these "taboos" could be added to the list of such negative influences, that is, that they are remnants of feelings of oppression: Through abusive speech training and forced use of hearing aids, speech and hearing devices became associated with oppression. Ladd's implementation of the Deafhood concept seems to suggest an open-ended essentialism with room for spoken language, hearing aids, cochlear implants, and the experience of music as *individual choices* that should be respected. Ladd seems to believe that the focus of activism should be on *oppressive systems* rather than on these individual choices. For example, using spoken language could be regarded as just using another language, rather than a betrayal of Deaf communities or even of the Deafhood concept. The Deafhood philosophy emphasizes the importance of *reflection* on one's acts and attitudes. The contexts are more important than what one actually does: Our course participants often agreed with each other that using spoken language to communicate with one's hearing family or partner is not the same as using spoken language in all-deaf contexts, for example, with the aim of "showing off" speech skills.

In essence, the discussion about taboos focuses on the question of if and how certain proclaimed "hearing things" can get a place in a person's articulation as a deaf person. An important question, then, is, *Why* do we consider whether these things "fit" with being deaf? Is it because many deaf people tend to focus on one aspect of who they are (i.e., their being deaf), and treat this as separate from other facets of who they are (mainstreamed, a woman, Black, Muslim, gay, Belgian, socialist, a teacher, etc.)? According to Hirons (2009), "It is arguable that the Deafhood process appears to entail actualizing the 'Deaf' elements of one's personality over other aspects" (p. 5). We do not believe that the essentialism inherent in Deafhood takes such an overarching form, and do not think that the Deafhood philosophy is implying that constant priority should be given to articulating one's "Deaf identity."

CONCLUSION

The Deafhood concept is a comprehensive philosophy encompassing ontology, epistemology, empowerment, and resistance. It could be argued that Deafhood attempts to embody too many different ideas or dimensions within a single concept, leading to confusion about its very ontologistic or liberatory character. We argue that although the philosophy behind the Deafhood concept has clearly been perceived as liberating, the ontological aspects of Deafhood need to be foregrounded, rather than its emancipatory and activist dimensions; we also argue that Deafhood is a concept primarily aimed at the individual and collective self-exploration of *deaf* people. On the other hand, many compelling philosophies are liable to different interpretations. As Ladd so often emphasizes, exploring the meaning of the Deafhood concept is a valid cultural process in itself, since this exploration leads us to attempts to (better) articulate our ontological experiences as deaf persons. Until now, no other concept has proved to have the same potential.

The present article has offered a tentative starting point in beginning to grasp the origins and meanings of the Deafhood concept. To deepen the Deafhood concept, it is necessary to identify, investigate, and consolidate deaf epistemologies and ontologies. There is a need for further in-depth exploration and analysis of the way the concept is used and understood, and of its individual, social, academic and political implications. For example, it is necessary to understand how the concept is used and understood in academic discourses, by deaf social and political organizations, and by individual deaf people with different backgrounds (with respect to family, education, work environment, deaf socialization, use of signed and spoken languages, and use of hearing technologies). A better understanding of the concept will foster individual and collective self-determination among Deaf communities and will enhance academic discourses not only in Deaf studies but in other social sciences. With regard to the latter, further research is needed into the parallels between the Deafhood concept and other liberatory and ontological concepts and worldviews, not only feminism but also, for example, Black consciousness, LGBT (lesbian, gay, bisexual, and transgender) pride, and the worldviews of people from other linguistic and cultural minorities.

NOTES

1. We use the capital "D" only when referring to theoretical concepts such as "Deaf studies," "Deafhood," "Deaf culture," and "Deaf community" because, in the discipline of Deaf studies, this is the commonly accepted usage. We are reluctant, however, to adopt the politicized and divisive capital "D" with regard to deaf *individuals*. In our eyes, "deaf" with a small "d" does not merely point at an audiological pathology in *opposition* to "Deaf," as is often argued, but should instead be understood as a biological condition to which being a signing person is complementary.
2. "Deafhood: Meeting the Challenges of a Changing World" was held in London July 12–14, 2001.
3. SLPs define themselves through the shared experience of, and membership in, physical and metaphysical aspects of language, culture, epistemology, and ontology (Batterbury, Ladd, & Gulliver, 2007).
4. We thank Maija Koivisto for introducing us to this workshop technique during the 2010 Deafhood weekend in Finland.
5. Kemp and Squires (1997) use the plural form "feminisms" because of the diversity in approach, motivation, method, experiences, positions, and strategies among various types of feminism.

REFERENCES

Batterbury, S. (2012). Language justice for Sign Language Peoples: The UN Convention on the Rights of Persons With Disabilities. *Language Policy, 11*(3), 253–272. doi: 10.1007/ s10993-012-9245-8

Batterbury, S., Ladd, P., & Gulliver, M. (2007). Sign Language Peoples as indigenous minorities: Implications for research and policy. *Environment and Planning, 37*, 2899–2915. doi: 10.1068/ a388

Bauman, D., & Murray, J. (2010). Deaf studies in the 21st century: "Deaf-Gain" and the future of human diversity. In M. Marschark & P. E. Spencer (Eds.), *Oxford handbook of Deaf studies, language, and education* (Vol. 2, pp. 210–225). Oxford, England: Oxford University Press.

Bavelier, D., Tomann, A., Hutton, C., Mitchell, T. V., Corina, D. P., Liu, G., & Neville, H. J. (2000). Visual attention to the periphery is enhanced in congenitally deaf individuals. *Journal of Neuroscience, 20,* 1–6.

Bellugi, U., O'Grady, L., Lillo-Martin, D., O'Grady Hynes, M., Van Hoek, K., & Corina, D. (1989). Enhancement of spatial cognition in deaf children. In V. Volterra & C. Erting (Eds.), *From gesture to language in hearing and deaf children* (pp. 278–298). New York, NY: Springer.

Bettger, J. G., Emmorey, K., McCullough, S. H., & Bellugi, U. (1997). Enhanced facial discrimination: Effects of experience with American Sign Language. *Journal of Deaf Studies and Deaf Education, 2,* 223–233.

Butler, J. (1990). Subjects of sex/gender/desire. In S. Kemp & J. Squires (Eds.) (1997). *Feminisms* (pp. 278–286). Oxford, England: Oxford University Press.

Emmorey, K., Grabowski, T., McCulough, S., Ponto, L. L. B., Hichwa, R. D., & Damasioa, H. (2005). The neural correlates of spatial language in English and American Sign Language: a PET study with hearing bilinguals. *NeuroImage, 24,* 832–840. doi:10.1016/j.neuroimage.2004.10.008

Emmorey, K., Kosslyn, S. M., & Bellugi, U. (1993). Visual imagery and visual-spatial language: Enhanced imagery abilities in deaf and hearing ASL signers. *Cognition, 46,* 139–181.

Furman, N., Goldberg, D., & Lusin, N. (2007). Enrollments in languages other than English in United States institutions of higher education, fall 2006. Retrieved from Modern Language Association of America website: http://www.mla.org/2006_flenrollmentsurvey

Fuss, D. (1997). The "risk" of essence. In S. Kemp & J. Squires (Eds.), *Feminisms* (pp. 250–258). Oxford, England: Oxford University Press. (Original work published 1989)

Garcia, J. (1999). *Sign with your baby: How to communicate with infants before they can speak.* Bellingham, WA: Stratton Kehl.

Gulliver, M. (2009). *DEAF space, a history: The production of DEAF spaces emergent, autonomous, located, and disabled in 18th-and 19th-century France* (Doctoral dissertation, University of Bristol, Bristol, England).

Gunew, S. (1997). Authenticity and the writing cure: Reading some migrant women's writing. In S. Kemp & J. Squires (Eds.), *Feminisms* (pp. 237–241). Oxford, England: Oxford University Press. (Original work published 1988)

Hindley, P., & Kitson, N. (2000). *Mental health and deafness.* London, England: Whurr.

Hirons, S. (2009). *The challenge of essentialism in Deafhood.* Unpublished manuscript.

Jokinen, M. (2001). "The Sign Language Person": A term to describe us and our future more clearly? In L. Leeson (Ed.), *Looking forward: EUD in the third millennium—the deaf citizen in the 21st century* (pp. 50–63). Coleford, England: Douglas MacLean.

Kanneh, K. (1997). Love, mourning, and metaphor: Terms of identity. In S. Kemp & J. Squires (Eds.), *Feminisms* (pp. 292–299). Oxford, England: Oxford University Press. (Originally published 1992)

Kemp, S., & Squires, J. (Eds.). (1997). *Feminisms.* Oxford, England: Oxford University Press.

Ladd, P. (1993a). Deaf consciousness: How Deaf cultural studies can improve the quality of Deaf life. In J. Mann (Ed.), *Deaf Studies III: Bridging cultures in the twenty-first century. Conference proceedings* (pp. 199–223). Washington, DC: Gallaudet University, College for Continuing Education.

Ladd, P. (1993b). The Deafhood papers, volume one. In M. D. Garretson (Ed.), *Deafness: 1993–2013* (pp. 67–72). Silver Spring, MD: National Association of the Deaf.

Ladd, P. (1998). *In Search of Deafhood: Towards an understanding of British Deaf culture* (Doctoral dissertation, University of Bristol, Bristol, England).

Ladd, P. (2003). *Understanding Deaf culture: In search of Deafhood.* Bristol, England: Multilingual Matters.

Ladd, P. (2005). Deafhood: A concept stressing possibilities, not deficits. *Scandinavian Journal of Public Health, 33*(66), 12–17. doi: 10.1080/14034950510033318

Ladd, P. (2006). What is Deafhood and why is it important? In H. Goodstein & J. Davis (Eds.), *The Deaf Way II Reader: Perspectives from the Second International Conference on Deaf Culture* (pp. 245–250). Washington, DC: Gallaudet University Press.

Mirzoeff, N. D. (1995). *Silent poetry: Deafness, sign, and visual culture in modern France.* Princeton, NJ: Princeton University Press.

Moi, T. (1997). Feminist, female, feminine. In S. Kemp & J. Squires (Eds.), *Feminisms* (pp. 246–250). Oxford, England: Oxford University Press. (Originally published 1989)

Preston, P. (1994). *Mother father deaf: Living between sound and silence.* Cambridge, MA: Harvard University Press.

Riley, D. (1997). Am I that name? Feminism and the category of "women" in history. In S. Kemp & J. Squires (Eds.), *Feminisms* (pp. 241–246). Oxford, England: Oxford University Press. (Originally published 1988)

Singhellou, K. (2007). *Rethinking Deaf and female identities: Parallels and challenges* (Master's dissertation, University of Bristol, Bristol, England).

Soper, K. (1997). Feminism, humanism, postmodernism. In S. Kemp & J. Squires (Eds.), *Feminisms* (pp. 286–292). Oxford, England: Oxford University Press. (Originally published 1990)

Spelman, E. (1997). Woman: The one and the many. In S. Kemp & J. Squires (Eds.), *Feminisms* (pp. 235–236). Oxford, England: Oxford University Press. (Originally published 1988)

Stone, A. (2004). Essentialism and anti-essentialism in feminist philosophy. *Journal of Moral Philosophy, 1*(2), 135–153. doi: 10.1177/ 174046810400100202

Taub, S. (2001). *Language from the body: Iconicity and metaphor in American Sign Language.* Cambridge, England: University of Cambridge Press.

SECTION
THREE

Deaf Culture and Cochlear Implants

WRITTEN BY

LISA KOCH

The use of cochlear implants by children deafened before they develop language has aroused heated debate between members of Deaf and hearing cultures. Members of the Deaf culture vigorously oppose implants both as an invasive treatment of dubious efficacy and as a threat to Deaf culture.

People who cannot hear are viewed as either "deaf" or "Deaf." Persons who view themselves as deaf are those who have assimilated into hearing society in spite of their impaired ability to hear. They do not view themselves as members of a separate culture: rather they seek to "fix" their hearing loss.

The term "Deaf" culture is used to discussing the social beliefs, behaviors, art, literary traditions, history and values of those that are affected by deafness. Members of the Deaf culture are bound by their deafness and their shared language: American Sign Language (ASL). Deaf individuals believe that deafness opens them up to membership in a community.

There is a long history of viewing deafness as a deficit condition. The Deaf community has struggled to remove the medicalization of deafness. Whereas hearing people work from the perspective that their hearing status is the norm, deaf people assume their deaf status is the norm.

A conflict arises when an infant is considered for cochlear implantation. Deaf individuals consider this as trying to remove that infant from one cultural group (Deaf) and force them into another cultural group (hearing): to assimilate the infant into a culture different from its "birthright".

The decisions about the medical care of minors traditionally have involved the child's parents. Decisions that the parents make rely on the "best interest" of the child. Consider, however, that parents of most deaf- infants are hearing. Because of this fact, members of the Deaf community believe the parents have no perspective upon which to base their decision regarding cochlear implants.

Without intimate knowledge of the Deaf culture, Deaf individuals believe that hearing parents can't make a "best interest" judgment. They believe hearing parents' that decide to implant deaf children are "ill-informed.

There is an interesting disparity about the concerns of the Deaf community about technology. The Deaf community is concerned about the destruction of the inner ear cochlea during the implantation procedure, prohibiting the use of technology developed in the future. The contralateral ear (that is not implanted) is available when new surgical techniques or new technology evolve and require an intact cochlea.

This disparity regarding the destruction of the cochlea is obvious to many. If their concern is that cochlear implantation will be so successful as to eliminate a culture, then the destruction of the cochlea is irrelevant. If improved surgical techniques will be developed that require an intact cochlea, they deny their argument that Deafness does not need a "fix."

DEAF CULTURE AND COCHLEAR IMPLANTS

The Deaf culture is also concerned about the effect of cochlear implants on their culture. They believe that each deaf child is a means to the culture's end: the survival of the culture, not the child's own end. If all deaf-born infants are implanted and choose the hearing world, then it will be the end of Deaf culture.

Parenthood is a balancing act of dreams and hopes for children and the realization that children will someday be on their own. Members of the Deaf culture believe that any decision that closes the child's right to an open future is not in the best interest of the child. Cochlear implants or any other medical, genetic, or surgical techniques that provide future opportunities should not only be permissible but encouraged.

Because cochlear implants have the potential to reduce the effects of deafness, they are opposed by members of Deaf culture who view efforts to "cure" deafness as an immoral means of killing Deaf culture.

Deaf culture argues that parents should not make decisions about cochlear implants for their deaf children: the child should be allowed to make the decision for themselves when they are old enough. The opposing view, however, is that a child who is deaf who learns to speak and is part of the hearing world during childhood can learn to sign later in life and join the Deaf world. To many members of the Deaf cultural community, cochlear implants represent "the ultimate denial of deafness, the ultimate refusal to let deaf children be Deaf."

Will cochlear implants eliminate deafness? An individual who has an implant is still deaf. The difference is that the ramifications of deafness are significantly reduced. Most children do very well with cochlear implants which reduce the need for special schools, interpreters, and other costly accommodations.

The anger, hostility, and solidarity expressed by the Deaf culturists who choose to reject hearing society and who do not wish to be "hearing" to any degree is understandable. Many people who are deaf continue to live as second class citizens, as indicated by the facts that the average deaf person today reads at a fourth grade level, one in three drops out of high school and only one in five who starts college gets a degree. Deaf adults make 30 percent less than the general population. Their unemployment rate is high, and when they are employed they tend to be "underemployed" in manual jobs for which a strong command of English is not required.

Rejecting hearing society and technology is not the solution to the problems of Deaf people. Deaf people with cochlear implants have a wealth of opportunities and potential life experiences available to them. To deny such opportunities exist based on theories of segregation is indeed illogical.

REFERENCES

Edward Dolnick, "Deafness as **Culture**," Atlantic 272, no. 3 (1993): 37–53.

Felicity Barringer, "Pride in a Soundless World: **Deaf** Oppose Cochlear Implants," New York Times, 16 May 1993.

Roslyn Rosen, "President Rosen on **Cochlear Implants**," NAD Broadcaster, December 1992, p. 6; see also, "The President Signs On," NAD Broadcaster, January 1991, p. 3.

M. Arana Ward, "As Technology Advances, A Bitter Debate Divides the **Deaf**," Washington Post, 11 May 1997.

Bonnie Tucker, "Deaf Culture, Cochlear Implants, and Elective Disability:" Hastings Center Report 28, no. 4 (1998): 6–14.

Cochlear implants, the deaf culture, and ethics: a study of disability, informed surrogate consent, and ethnocide. GA, Hladek. *Monash Bioethics Review* Volume: 21 Issue: 1 (2002-01-01) p. 29–44. ISSN: 1321–2753

Defending Deaf Culture: The Case of Cochlear Implants, Robert Sparrow, The Journal of Political Philosophy: Volume 13, Number 2, 2005, pp. 135–152

Construction of Deafness

WRITTEN BY

HARLAN LANE

SOCIAL PROBLEMS ARE CONSTRUCTED

It is obvious that our society is beset by numerous social problems. A brief historical perspective on four of them reveals something not so obvious: social problems are constructed in particular cultures, at particular times, in response to the efforts of interested parties.

The social problem of alcoholism evidently consists in this: there is a particular segment of the population that suffers from the use of alcohol; these sufferers need specially trained people to help them—for example alcoholism counselors, psychologists and psychiatrists; they need special facilities such as detoxification centers; and special organizations like AA. This understanding of alcoholism is less than fifty years old. Recall that the Temperance Movement of the last century viewed excessive drinking not as a disease but as an act of will; alcoholics victimized their families and imposed on the rest of society. The movement advocated not treatment but prohibition. Some groups favored prohibition and took the moral high ground; other groups felt justified in breaking the law. Special facilities existed then to house and treat many problem groups—mentally ill people, for example—but not people who drank too much. Only recently has a consensus developed that excessive drinking "is" a disease—a matter of individual suffering more than a political dispute. With this shift in the construction of alcoholism and alcoholics—from victimizers to victims—the evident need was for medical research to alleviate suffering; vast sums of money are now devoted to research on alcoholism, and there is now a large treatment establishment with halfway houses, hospital wards, outpatient clinics, and specialized hospitals (Gusfield, 1982).

The discovery of child abuse dates from the 1950s. Radiologists and pediatricians first decried the evidence they were seeing of parents beating their children. The Children's Bureau and the media took up the cause (it is still very present in TV and the newspapers) and made the public aware of this social problem. In the decade that followed, the states passed laws requiring reports of child abuse and providing penalties. Of course, parents

171

did not start beating their children only in the 1950s. Rather, a social consensus emerged in that decade that a problem existed requiring laws, special welfare workers, and special budgetary provisions. In the last century, the major problems associated with children concerned poverty and child labor—a rather different and much more political construction of the problem of improper treatment of children (Gusfield, 1989).

For a very long time, the dominant construction of homosexuality, like that of alcoholism, was a moral one: men and women were making sinful choices; the problem was "owned" by the church. Later psychiatry gave it a new construction: it "is" an illness they claimed that psychiatrists could treat (Conrad & Schneider, 1980). In the third phase, Gays and Lesbians were presented as a minority group; they ask for the same protection as all other groups that are discriminated against based on the circumstances of their birth, such as blacks and women.

Disability, too, has had moral, medical and now social constructions, as numerous articles in this journal have explicated. The Disability Rights Movement has shifted the construct of disability "off the body and into the interface between people with impairments and socially disabling conditions" (Hevey, 1993, p. 426).

Alcoholism has changed from a moral failure to a disease; child abuse from an economic problem to a criminal one; homosexuality from disease to personal constitution to human rights; disability from tragic flaw to social barriers. Social problems, it seems, are partly what we make of them; they are not just out there "lying in the road to be discovered by passers-by" (Gusfield, 1984, p. 38). The particular way in which society understands alcoholism, disability and so forth determines exactly what these labels mean, how large groups of people are treated, and the problems that they face. Deafness, too, has had many constructions; they differ with time and place. Where there were many deaf people in small communities in the last century, on Martha's Vineyard, for example, as in Henniker, New Hampshire, deafness was apparently not seen as a problem requiring special intervention. Most Americans had quite a different construction of deafness at that time, however: it was an individual affliction that befell family members and had to be accommodated within the family. The great challenge facing Thomas Gallaudet and Laurent Clerc in their efforts to create the first American school for the deaf was to persuade state legislatures and wealthy Americans of quite a different construction which they had learned in Europe: Deafness was not an individual but a social problem, deaf people had to be brought together for their instruction, special "asylums" were needed. Nowadays, two constructions of deafness in particular are dominant and compete for shaping deaf peoples' destinies. The one construes deaf as a category of disability; the other construes deaf as designating a member of a linguistic minority. There is a growing practice of capitalizing Deaf when referring specifically to its second construction, which I will follow hereafter.

DISABILITY VS. LINGUISTIC MINORITY

Numerous organizations are associated with each of the prominent constructions of deafness. In the U.S., National organizations primarily associated with deafness as disability include the A. G. Bell Association (4,500 members), the American Speech-Language-Hearing Association (40,000), the American Association of Late-Deafened Adults (1,300), Self-Help for the Hard of Hearing (13,000), the American Academy of Otolaryngology, Head and Neck Surgery (5,600), and the National Hearing Aid Society (4,000). National organizations associated primarily with the construction of Deaf as a linguistic minority include the National Association of the Deaf (20,000), the Registry of Interpreters for the Deaf (2,700), and the National Fraternal Society of the Deaf (13,000) (Van Cleve, 1987; Burek, 1993).

Each construction has a core client group. No one disputes the claim of the hearing adult become deaf from illness or aging that he or she has a disability and is not a member of Deaf culture. Nor, on the other hand, has any one yet criticized Deaf parents for insisting that their Deaf child has a distinct linguistic and cultural heritage. The struggle between some of the groups adhering to the two constructions persists across the centuries (Lane, 1984) in part because there is no simple criterion for identifying most childhood candidates as clients of the one position or the other. More generally, we can observe that late deafening and moderate hearing loss tend to be associated with the disability construction of deafness while early and profound deafness involve an entire organization of the person's language, culture and thought around vision and tend to be associated with the linguistic minority construction.

In general, we identify children as members of a language minority when their native language is not the language of the majority. Ninety percent of Deaf children, however, have hearing parents who are unable to effectively model the spoken language for most of them. Advocates of the disability construction contend these are hearing-impaired children whose language and culture (though they may have acquired little of either) are in principle those of their parents; advocates of the linguistic minority construction contend that the children's native language, in the sense of primary language, must be manual language and that their life trajectory will bring them fully into the circle of Deaf culture. Two archetypes for these two constructions, disability and linguistic minority, were recently placed side by side before our eyes on the U. S. television program, "Sixty Minutes." On the one hand, seven-year-old Caitlin Parton, representing the unreconstructed disability-as-impairment: presented as a victim of a personal tragedy, utterly disabled in communication by her loss of hearing but enabled by technology, and dedicated professional efforts (yes, we meet the surgeon), to approach normal, for which she yearns, as she herself explains. On the other hand, Roslyn Rosen, then president of the National Association of the Deaf, from a large Deaf family, native speaker of ASL, proud of her status as a member of a linguistic minority, insistent that she experiences life and the world fully and has no desire to be any different (*Sixty Minutes*, 1992).

PROFESSIONAL INFLUENCE OVER CONSTRUCTIONS

Organizations espousing each construction of deafness compete to "own" the children and define their needs. Their very economic survival depends on their success in that competition. Which construction of a social problem prevails is thus no mere academic matter.

There is a body of knowledge associated with construction A and a quite different body with construction B; the theories and facts associated with construction A have been studied by the professional people who grapple with the social problem; they are the basis of their specialized training and professional credentials and therefore contribute to their self-esteem; they are used to maintain respect from clients, to obtain federal and state funding, to insure one's standing in a fraternity of like professionals; they legitimate the professional person's daily activities. Professionals examine students on this body of knowledge, give certificates, and insert themselves into the legal and social norms based on their competence in that body of knowledge. Whoever says A is a mistaken construction is of course not welcome. More than that, whoever says A is a construction is not welcome, for that implies that there could be or is another construction, B, say, which is better. What the parties to each construction want is that their construction not be seen as a construction at all; rather, they insist, they merely reflect the way things are in the world (cf. Gusfield, 1984).

These "troubled-persons industries," in the words of sociologist Joseph Gusfield, "bestow benevolence on people defined as in need" (Gusfield, 1989, p. 432). These industries have grown astronomically in recent decades (Albrecht, 1992). The professional services fueled by the disability construction of deafness are provided by some administrators of schools and training programs, experts in counseling and rehabilitation, teachers, interpreters, audiologists, speech therapists, otologists, psychologists, psychiatrists, librarians, researchers, social workers, and hearing aid specialists. All these people and the facilities they command, their clinics, operating rooms, laboratories, classrooms, offices and shops, owe their livelihood or existence to deafness problems. Gusfield cites the story about American missionaries who settled in Hawaii. They went to do good. They stayed and did well (Gusfield, 1989).

The troubled-person professions serve not only their clientele but also themselves, and are actively involved in perpetuating and expanding their activities. Teachers of the Deaf, for example, seek fewer students per teacher and earlier intervention (Johnson *et al,* 1989). American audiologists have formally proposed testing of the hearing of all American newborns without exception. The self-aggrandizement of the troubled-persons professions when it comes to Deaf people is guided by a genuine belief in their exclusive construction of the social problem and their ability to alleviate it. Some of their promotional methods are readily seen; for example, they employ lobbyists to encourage legislation that requires and pays for their services. Other measures are more subtle; for example, the structural relation between the service provider and the client often has the effect of disempowering the client and maintaining dependency.

LESSONS FROM SERVICES FOR BLIND PEOPLE

The history of services to blind people illustrates some of the pitfalls of the professionalization of a social problem. Workshops for blind people have large budgets, provide good income for sighted managers, and have a national organization to lobby for their interest. Blind people, however, commonly view sheltered workshops as a dead end that involves permanent dependency. The editor of the journal *Braille Monitor* says that "professional" is a swear word among blind people, "a bitter term of mockery and disillusionment" (Vaughan, 1991). A light-house for the blind was raked over the coals in that journal for having one pay scale for blind employees and a higher one for sighted employees performing the same work; moreover, the blind employees were paid below minimum wage (Braille Monitor, 1989). The National Accreditation Council for Agencies Serving the Blind and visually Handicapped (NAC) was disowned by organizations of blind people for its efforts to keep blind people in custodial care, its refusal to hear blind witnesses, and its token representation of blind people on the board; the Council rebutted that it had to consider the needs of agencies and professionals and not just blind people. For decades blind people picketed the NAC annual meetings (Braille Monitor, 1973; Jernigan, 1973; Vaughan, 1991).

A conference convened to define the new specialization of mobility trainer for the blind concluded that it required graduate study to learn this art and that "the teaching of mobility is a task for the sighted rather than a blind individual" (quoted in Vaughan, 1991, p. 209). This approach was naturally challenged by blind consumers. At first, the American Association of Workers with the Blind required normal vision for certification; then this was seen as discriminatory, in violation of section 504 of the Rehabilitation Act of 1973. So the criteria were changed. To enter the training program, the student must be able to assess the collision path of a blind person with obstacles nearly a block away. As it turns out, the functions claimed to be essential to mobility teaching just happen to require normal vision. Needless to say, blind people have been teaching blind people how to get about for centuries (Olson, 1981).

Workers with blind people view blindness as a devastating personal tragedy although blind people themselves commonly do not. Said the president of the National Association of the Blind "We do not regard our lives ... as tragic or disastrous and no amount of professional jargon or trumped up theory can made us do so" (Jernigan quoted in Olson, 1977, p. 408). As sociologist R. A. Scott explains in his classic monograph, *The Making of Blind Men,* the sighted professionals believe that the blind man's only hope for solving his problems is to submit to their long-term program of psychological services and training. To succeed, the blind man is told, he must change his beliefs about blindness, most of all, his belief that he is basically fine and only needs one or two services. The cooperative client is the one who welcomes all the services provided; the uncooperative client is the one who welcomes all the services provided; the uncooperative client is the one who fails to realize how many and great his needs are—who is in denial. The troubled-persons industries thus stand the normal relation between needs and services on its head: services do not evolve purely to meet needs; clients must recognize that they need the services provided by the professionals. Scott comments that it is easy to be deluded about the reality of these special needs. There are always a few blind clients who can be relied on to endorse these beliefs in the profound need for professional services. These blind individuals have been socialized, perhaps since childhood, to the professional construction of blindness. They confirm that blind people have the needs the agency says they have (Scott, 1981).

So it is with deafness. In much of the world, including the United States, deaf people are largely excluded from the ranks of professionals serving deaf children. In many communities it just happens that to be a teacher of deaf children you must first qualify as a teacher of hearing children, and deaf people are excluded as teachers of hearing children. In other communities, it just happens that to become a teacher of deaf children the candidate who is most capable of communicating with them is disbarred because he or she must pass an examination couched in high register English without an interpreter. And as with services for blind people, many of the professions associated with the disability construction of deafness insist that the plight of the deaf child is truly desperate—so desperate, in fact, that some professionals propose implant surgery followed by rigorous and prolonged speech and hearing therapy. The successful use of a cochlear implant in everyday communication calls on a prior knowledge of spoken language (Staller *et al*, 1991) that only one child candidate in ten possesses (Allen *et al*, 1994); this has not, however, deterred professionals from recruiting among the other ninety percent; it is doubtful that the cochlear-implant industry would survive, certainly not flourish, if it sold its services and equipment only to the core clientele for the disability construction.

As with service providers for blind people, the troubled-persons industry associated with deafness seeks total conformity of the client to the underlying construction of deafness as disability. In the words of an audiology textbook: "One is not simply dealing with a handicapped child, one is dealing with a family with a handicap" (Tucker & Nolan, 1984 quoted in Gregory & Hartley, 1991, p. 87). The text goes on to state: "This concept of 'total child' being child plus hearing aids is one which parents may need time to come to terms with and fully accept." The profession wants to intervene in that family's life as early as possible and seeks to provide "a saturation service" (Tucker & Nolan, 1984 quoted in Gregory & Hartley, 1991, p. 97).

The criteria for disability, presented as objective, in fact conform to the interests of the profession (Oliver, 1990). Audiologic criteria decide which children will receive special education, so the audiologist must be consulted. In most countries of the world, audiology and special education are intimately related; the role of special education is to achieve as far as possible what audiology and otology could not do—minimize the child's disability. Writes one audiologist: "Education cannot cure deafness; it can only alleviate its worst effects" (Lynas, 1986, quoted in Gregory & Hartley, 1991, p. 155). Parents generally have little say about the right educational placement for their child; neither are there any functional tests of what the child can understand in different kinds of classrooms. Instead, audiologic criteria prevail, even if they have little predictive value. For example, the academic achievement scores of children classified as severely hearing-impaired are scarcely different from those of children classified as profoundly hearing impaired (Allen, 1986). Research has shown that some children categorized as profoundly hearing impaired can understand words and sentences whereas others do not even detect sound (Osberger *et al*, 1993). Likewise, Scott states that the official definition of blindness is "based upon a meaningless demarcation among those with severely impaired vision" (Scott, 1981, p. 42).

THE MAKING OF DEAF MEN

The family that has received "saturation services" from the deafness troubled-persons industry will participate in socializing the deaf child to adapt the child's needs to those of the industry. A recent handbook for parents with implanted children states: "Parents should accept a primary role in helping their child adjust to the implant. They must assume responsibility for maintaining the implant device, for ensuring that the child is wearing it properly, and assuring that the auditory speech stimulation occurs in both the home and school" (Tye-Murray, 1992, p. xvi). "The child should wear the implant during all waking hours" (Tye-Murray, 1992, p. 18). Ultimately, the child should see the implant as part of himself, like his ears or hands. The handbook recounts enthusiastically how one implanted schoolchild, told to draw a self portrait, included the speech processor and microphone/transmitter in great detail: "This self-portrait demonstrated the child's positive image of himself and the acceptance of his cochlear implant" (Tye-Murray, 1992, p. 20).

The construction of the deaf child as disabled is legitimized early on by the medical profession and later by the special education and welfare bureaucracy. When the child is sent to a special educational program and obliged to wear cumbersome hearing aids, his or her socialization into the role of disabled person is promoted. In face-to-face encounters with therapists and teachers the child learns to cooperate in promoting a view of himself or herself as disabled. Teachers label large numbers of these deaf children emotionally disturbed or learning disabled (Lane, 1992). Once labeled as "multiply handicapped" in this way, deaf children are treated differently—for example, placed in a less demanding academic program where they learn less, so the label is self-validating. In the end, the troubled-persons industry creates the disabled deaf person.

DEAF AS LINGUISTIC MINORITY

From the vantage point of Deaf culture, deafness is not a disability (Jones & Pullen, 1989). British Deaf leader Paddy Ladd put it this way: "We wish for the recognition of our right to exist as a linguistic minority group ... Labeling us as disabled demonstrates a failure to understand that we are not disabled in any way within our own community" (Dant & Gregory, 1991, p.14). U. S. Deaf scholar Tom Humphries concurs: "There is no room within the culture of Deaf people for an ideology that all Deaf people are deficient. It simple does not compute. There is no "handicap" to overcome ... (Humphries, 1993, p. 14). American Deaf leader MJ Bienvenu asks: "Who benefits when we attempt to work in coalition with disability groups? ... How can we fight for official recognition of ASL and allow ourselves as "communication disordered" at the same time?" And she concludes: "We are proud of our language, culture and heritage. Disabled we are not!" (Bienvenu, 1989, p. 13).

Nevertheless, many in the disability rights movement, and even some Deaf leaders, have joined professionals in promoting the disability construction of all deafness. To defend this construction one leading disability advocate, Vic Finkelstein, has advanced the following argument based on the views of the people directly concerned: Minorities that have been discriminated against, like blacks would refuse an operation to eliminate what sets them apart, but this is not true for disabled people "every (!) disabled person would welcome such an operation" *(Finkelstein's exclamation point)*. And, from this perspective, Deaf people, he maintains, "have more in common with other disability groups than they do with groups based upon race and gender" (Finkelstein, 1991, p. 265). However, in fact American Deaf people are more like blacks in that most would refuse an operation to eliminate what sets them apart (as Dr. Rosen did on "Sixty Minutes"). One U. S. survey of Deaf adults asked if they would like an implant operation so they could hear; more than eight out of 10 declined (Evans 1989) When the magazine *Deaf Life* queried its subscribers, 87 percent of respondents said that they did not consider themselves handicapped.

There are other indications that American Deaf culture simply does not have the ambivalence that, according to Abberley, is called for in disability: "Impairment must be identified as a bad thing insofar as it is an undesirable consequence of a distorted social development, at the same time as it is held to be a positive attribute of the individual who is impaired" (Abberley, 1987, p. 9). American Deaf people (like their counterparts in many other nations) think cultural Deafness is a good thing and would like to see more of it. Expectant Deaf parents, like those in any other language minority, commonly hope to have Deaf children with whom they can share their language, culture and unique experiences. One Deaf mother from Los Angeles recounted to a researcher her reaction when she noticed that her baby did not react to Fourth of July fireworks: "I thought to myself, 'She must be deaf.' I wasn't disappointed; I thought, 'It will be all right. We are both deaf, so we will know what to do' (Becker, 1980, p. 55). Likewise an expectant Deaf mother in Boston told the *Globe*, "I want my daughters to be like me, to be deaf" (Saltus, 1989, p. 27). The Deaf community, writes Paddy Ladd, "regards the birth of each and every deaf child as a precious gift" (quoted in Oliver, 1989, p. 199) Deaf and hearing scholars expressed the same view in a 1991 report to the U. S. National Institutes of Health; research in genetics to improve deaf people's quality of life is certainly important, they said, but must not become, in the hands of hearing people, research on ways of reducing the deaf minority (Padden, 1990).

Finkelstein acknowledges that many Deaf people reject the label "disabled" but he attributes it to the desire of Deaf people to distance themselves from social discrimination. What is missing from the construction of deafness is what lies at the heart of the linguistic minority construction: Deaf culture. Since people with disabilities are themselves engaged in a struggle to change the construction of disability, they surely recognize that disabilities are not "lying there in the road" but are indeed socially constructed. Why is this not applied to Deaf people? Not surprisingly, deafness is constructed differently in Deaf cultures than it is in hearing cultures.

Advocates of the disability construction for all deaf people, use the term "deaf community" to refer to all people with significant hearing impairment, on the model of "the disability community." So the term seems to legitimate the acultural perspective on Deaf people. When Ladd *(supra)* and other advocates of the linguistic minority construction speak of the Deaf community, however, the term refers to a much smaller group with a distinct manual language, culture, and social organization.[1] It is instructive, as American Deaf leader Ben Bahan has suggested, to see how ASL speakers refer to their minority; one term can be glossed as DEAF-WORLD. The claim that one is in the DEAF-WORLD, or that someone else is, is not a claim about hearing status at all; it is an expression of that self-recognition or recognition of others that is defining for all ethnic collectivities (Johnson & Erting, 1989). It is predictive about social behavior (including attitudes, beliefs and values) and language, but not about hearing status. All degrees of hearing can be found among Deaf people (it is a matter of discussion whether some hearing people with Deaf parents are Deaf), and mostpeople who are hearing-impaired are not members of the DEAF-WORLD.

In ASL the sign whose semantic field most overlaps that of the English "disability" can be glossed in English LIMP-BLIND-ETC. I have asked numerous informants to give me examples from that category: they have responded by citing (in literal translation) people in wheelchairs, blind people, mentally retarded people, and people with cerebral palsy, but no informant has ever listed DEAF and all reject it when asked. Another term in use in the Boston area (and elsewhere), which began as a fingerspelled borrowing from English, can be glossed D-A. My informants agree that Deaf is not D-A. The sign M-H-C (roughly, "multiply-handicapped") also has some currency. When I have asked Deaf people here for examples of M-H-C, DEAF-BLIND has never been listed, and when I propose it, it is rejected.

Other important differences between culturally Deaf people and people with disabilities come to light when we consider these groups, priorities. Among the preconditions for equal participation in society by disabled persons, the U.N. *Standard Rules* (1994) list medical care, rehabilitation, and support services such as personal assistance. "Personal assistance services are the new top of the agenda issue for the disability rights movement," one chronicler reports (Shapiro, 1993, p. 251). From my observation, Deaf people do not attach particular importance to medical care, not place any special value on rehabilitation or personal assistance services,[2] not have any particular concern with autonomy and independent living. Instead, the preconditions for Deaf participation are more like those of other language minorities: culturally Deaf people campaign for acceptance of their language and its broader use in the schools, the workplace, and in public events.

Integration, in the classroom, the workforce and the community, "has become a primary goal of today's disability movement" (Shapiro, 1993, p. 144). School integration is anathema to the DEAF-WORLD. Because most Deaf children have hearing parents, they can only acquire full language and socialization in specialized schools, in particular the prized network of residential schools; Deaf children are drowning in the mainstream (Lane, 1992). While advocates for people with disabilities recoil in horror at segregated institutions, evoking images of Willowbrook and worse, the Deaf alumni of residential schools return to their alma mater repeatedly over the years, contribute to their support, send their Deaf children to them, and vigorously protest the efforts of well-meaning but grievously ill-informed members of the disability rights movement to close those schools. These advocates fail to take account of language and culture and therefore of the difference between imposed and elective segregation. Where people with disabilities cherish independence, culturally Deaf people cherish interdependence. People with disabilities may gather for political action; Deaf people traditionally gather primarily for socializing. Deaf people marry Deaf people 90 percent of the time in the U. S. (Schein, 1989).

With the shift in the construction of disability has come an emphasis on the bonds that unite people with disabilities to the rest of society with whom they generally share not only culture but also ranges of capacities and incapacities (cf. Barton, 1993). "We try to make disability fixed and dichotomous," writes Zola, "but it is fluid and continuous" (Zola,1993, p.24). More than 20 percent of the noninstitutionalized population of the U.S. has a disability, we are told, and over 7.7 million Americans report that hearing is their primary functional limitation (Dowler & Hirsch, 1994). This universalizing view, according to which most people have some disability at least some of the time, is strikingly at odds with the DEAF-WORLD, small, tightly knit, with its own language and culture, sharply demarcated from the rest of society: there is no slippery slope between Deaf and hearing. "Deaf people are foreigners," wrote an early president of the National Association of the Deaf, "[living] among a people whose language they can never learn" (Hanson, cited in Van Cleve & Crouch, 1989, p. ix).

It is significant that the four student leaders who led the uprising known as the Gallaudet Revolution, were Deaf children of Deaf parents, deeply imbued with a sense of DEAF-WORLD, and natively fluent in ASL. One of them explained to *USA Today* the significance of the Revolution as it relates to the construction of deafness: "Hearing people sometimes call us handicapped. But most—may be all deaf people—feel that we're more of an ethnic group because we speak a different language ... We also have our own culture ... There's more of an ethnic difference than a handicap difference between us and hearing people" (Hlibok, 1988, p. 11a). The new Deaf president of Gallaudet sought to explain the difference in the underlying construction in these terms: "More people realize now that deafness is a difference, not a deficiency" (Jordan, quoted in Gannon, 1989, p. 173).

So there is no reason to think that Paddy Ladd, Tom Humphries and MJ Bienvenu are being insincere when they claim that Deaf people are not disabled. Quite the contrary: since all are leaders of Deaf communities and are steeped in deaf culture, they advance the construction of deafness that arises from their culture. Mr. Finkelstein could have been tipped off to this very different construction by observing how various groups choose to be labeled: disability groups may find labels such as "disabled" or "motorically-impaired" or "visually handicapped" distasteful and reserve for themselves the right to call someone a "crip," but Deaf culture embraces the label "Deaf" and asks that everyone use it, as in The National Association of the Deaf and The World Federation of the Deaf. It seems right to speak of "the Deaf" as we speak of "The French" or "The British." It is alien to Deaf culture on two counts to speak of its members as "people with hearing-impairment." First, it is the troubled-persons industry for deafness that invented and promoted the label in English "hearing-impaired" (Ross & Calvert, 1967; Wilson *et al*, 1974; Castle, 1990). Second, the "people with" construction implies that the trait is incidental rather than defining, but one's culture is never an incidental trait. It seems to be an error in ordinary language to say, "I happen to be Hispanic," or "I happen to be Deaf"; who would you be, after all, if you were you and yet not Hispanic, or not Deaf? But it is acceptable to say, "I happen to have a spinal cord injury."

Deaf cultures do not exist in a vacuum. Deaf Americans embrace many cultural values, attitudes, beliefs and behaviors that are part of the larger American culture and, in some instances, that are part of ethnic minority cultures such as African-American, Hispanic-American, etc. Because hearing people have obliged Deaf people to interact with the larger hearing society in terms of a disability model, that model has left its mark on Deaf culture. In particular, Deaf people frequently have found themselves recipients of unwanted special services provided by hearing people. "In terms of its economic, political and social relations to hearing society, the Deaf minority can be viewed as a colony" (Markowicz & Woodward,

1978, p. 33). As with colonized peoples, some Deaf people have internalized the "other's" (disability) construction of them alongside their own cultural construction (Lane, 1992). For example, they may be active in their Deaf club and yet denigrate skilled use of ASL as "low sign"; "high sign" is a contact variety of ASL that is closer to English-language word order. The Deaf person who uses a variety of ASL marked as English frequently has greater access to wider resources such as education and employment. Knowing when to use which variety is an important part of being Deaf (Johnson & Erting, 1989). Granted that culturally Deaf people must take account of the disability model of deafness, that they sometimes internalize it, and that it leaves its mark on their culture, all this does not legitimize that model—any more than granting that African-Americans had to take account of the construction of the slave as property, sometimes internalized that construction, and found their culture marked by it legitimizes that construction of their ethnic group.

Neither culturally Deaf people nor people with disabilities are a homogeneous group.[3] Many of the differences between the two that I have cited will not apply to particular subgroups or individuals; nevertheless, it should be clear that cultural Deafness involves a constellation of traits quite different from those of any disability group. Faced with these salient differences, those who would argue that Deaf people are "really" disabled, sometimes resort instead to arguing that they are "really not" like linguistic minorities (Fishman, 1982). Certainly there are differences. For example, Deaf people cannot learn English as a second language as easily as other minorities. Second and third generation Deaf children find learning English no easier than their forbears, but second and third generation immigrants to the U. S. frequently learn English before entering school. The language of the DEAF-WORLD is not usually passed on from generation to generation; instead, it is commonly transmitted by peers or associates. Normally, Deaf people are not proficient in this native language until they reach school age. Deaf people are more scattered geographically than many linguistic minorities. The availability of interpreters is even more vital for Deaf people than for many other linguistic minorities because there are so few Deaf lawyers, doctors and accountants, etc. Few Deaf people are in high-status public positions in our society (in contrast with, say, Hispanics), and this has hindered the legitimation of ASL use (Kyle, 1990,1991; Parratt Slipping, 1991). However, many, perhaps all, linguistic minorities have significant features that differentiate them: Members of the Chinese-American community are increasingly marrying outside their linguistic minority but this is rare for ASL speakers. Many Native American languages are dying out or have disappeared; this is not true of ASL which is unlikely ever to die out. Spanish-speaking Americans are so diverse a group that it may not be appropriate to speak of the Hispanic community in the U. S. (Wright, 1994). Neither the newer strategy of citing what is special about the ASL-speaking minority nor the older one of minimizing ASL itself hold much promise of discrediting the construction of deafness as linguistic minority.

It is undeniable that culturally Deaf people have great common cause with people with disabilities. Both pay the price of social stigma. Both struggle with the troubled-persons industries for control of their destiny. Both endeavor to promote their construction of their identity in competition with the interested (and generally better funded) efforts of professionals to promote *their* constructions. And Deaf people have special reasons for solidarity with people with hearing impairments; their combined numbers have created services, commissions and laws that the DEAF-WORLD alone probably could not have achieved. Solidarity, yes, but when culturally Deaf people allow their special identity to be subsumed under the construct of disability they set themselves up for wrong solutions and bitter disappointments.

It is because disability advocates think of Deaf children as disabled that they want to close the special schools and absurdly plunge Deaf children into hearing classrooms in a totally exclusionary program called inclusion. It is because government is allowed to proceed with a disability construction of cultural Deafness that the U. S. Office of Bilingual Education and Minority Language Affairs has refused for decades to provide special resources for schools with large numbers of ASL-using children although the law requires it to do so for children using any other non-English language. It is because of the disability construction that court rulings requiring that children who do not speak English receive instruction initially in their best language have not been applied to ASL-using children. It is because of the disability construction that the teachers most able to communicate with Britain's Deaf children are excluded from the profession on the pretext that they have a disqualifying disability. It is because lawmakers have been encouraged to believe by some disability advocates and prominent deaf figures that Deaf people are disabled that, in response to the Gallaudet Revolution, the U. S. Congress passed a law, not recognizing ASL or the DEAF-WORLD as a minority, but a law establishing another institute of *health,* The National Institute on Deafness and Other Communications Disorders *[sic],* operated by the deafness troubled persons industry, and sponsoring research to reduce hereditary deafness. It is because of the disability construction that organizations *for* the Deaf (e.g., the Royal National Institute for the Deaf) are vastly better funded by government that organizations *of* the Deaf (e.g., the British Deaf Association).

One would think that people with disabilities might be the first to grasp and sympathize with the claims of Deaf people that they are victims of a mistaken identity. People with disabilities should no more resist the self-construction of culturally Deaf people, than Deaf people should subscribe to a view of people with disabilities as tragic victims of an inherent flaw.

CHANGING TO THE LINGUISTIC MINORITY CONSTRUCTION

Suppose our society were generally to adopt a disability construction of deafness for most late-deafened children and adults and a linguistic minority construction of Deaf people for most others, how would things change? The admirable Open University course, Issues *in Deafness* (1991) prompted these speculations.

1. Changing the construction changes the legitimate authority concerning the social problem. In many areas, such as schooling, the authority would become Deaf adults, linguists and sociologists, among others. There would be many more service providers from the minority: Deaf teachers, foster and adoptive parents, information officers, social workers, advocates. Non-Deaf service providers would be expected to know the language, history, and culture of the Deaf linguistic minority.

2. Changing the construction changes how behavior is construed. Deaf people would be expected to use ASL (in the U. S.) and to have interpreters available; poor speech would be seen as inappropriate.

3. Changing the construction may change the legal status of the social problem group. Most Deaf people would no longer claim disability benefits or services under the present legislation for disabled people. The services to which the Deaf linguistic minority has a right in order to obtain equal treatment under the law would be provided by other legislation and bureaucracies. Deaf people would receive greater protection against employment discrimination under civil rights laws and rulings. Where there are special provisions to assist the education of linguistic minority children, Deaf children would be eligible.

4. Changing the construction changes the arena where identification and labeling take place. In the disability construction, deafness is medicalized and labeled in the audiologist's clinic. In the construction as linguistic minority, deafness is viewed as a social variety and would be labeled in the peer group.

5. Changing the construction changes the kinds of intervention. The Deaf child would not be operated on for deafness but brought together with other Deaf children and adults. The disability construction orients hearing parents to the question, what can be done to mitigate my child's impairment? The linguistic minority construction presents them with the challenge of insuring that their child has language and role models from the minority (Hawcroft, 1991).

OBSTACLES TO CHANGE

The obstacles to replacing a disability construction of deafness for much of the concerned population with a linguistic minority construction are daunting. In the first place, people who have little familiarity with deafness find the disability construction self-evident and the minority construction elusive. As I argue in *The Mask of Benevolence* (Lane, 1992), hearing people led to reflect on deafness generally begin by imagining themselves without hearing—which is, of course, to have a disability but not to be Deaf. Legislators can easily grasp the disability construction, not so the linguistic minority construction. The same tendency to uncritically accept the disability model led *Sixty Minutes* to feature a child from among the nine percent of childhood implant candidates who were deafened after learning English rather than from the 91 percent who do not identify with the English-speaking majority (Allen *et at*, 1994). Not only did the interviewer find the disability construction of deafness easier to grasp but no doubt the producers thought heir millions of viewers would do likewise. Social problems are a favorite theme of the media but they are almost always presented as private troubles—deafness is no exception—because it makes for more entertaining viewing.

The troubled-persons industry associated with deafness—the "audist establishment" (Lane, 1992)— vigorously resists efforts to replace their construction of deafness. Audist policy is that ASL is a kind of primitive prosthesis, a way around the communication impasse caused by deaf peoples' disability. The audists control teacher training programs, university research facilities, the process of peer review for federal grant monies, the presentations made at professional meetings, and publications in professional journals; they control promotion and through promotion, salary. They have privileged access to the media and to law-making bodies when deafness is at issue. Although they lack the credibility of Deaf people themselves, they have expert credentials and they are fluent in speaking and writing English so law and policy makers and the media find it easier to consult them.

When a troubled-persons industry recasts social problems as private troubles it can treat, it is protecting its construction by removing the appearance of a social issue on which there might be political disagreement. The World Health Organization, for example, has medicalized and individualized what is social; services are based on an individualized view of disability and are designed by professionals in the disability industry (Oliver, 1991). The U. S. National Institute on Deafness and Other Communications Disorders proclaims in its very title the disability construction of deafness that it seeks to promote. The American Speech-Language Hearing Association, for example, has the power of accrediting graduate programs for training professionals who work with Deaf people; a program that deviated too far from the disability construction could lose its accreditation; without accreditation its students would not be certified; without the promise of certification, no one would enter the training program.

Some of the gravest obstacles to broader acceptance of the linguistic minority model come from members of the minority itself. Many members of the minority were socialized in part by professionals (and parents) to adopt a disabled role. Some Deaf people openly embrace the disability construction and thus undercut the efforts of other Deaf people to discredit it. Worse yet, many opportunities are provided to Deaf people (e.g., access to interpreters) on the condition that they adopt the alien disability construction. This double blind—accept our construction of your life or give up your access to equal citizenship—is a powerful form of oppression. Thus, many members of the DEAF-WORLD endorsed the Americans with Disabilities Act with its provisions for deaf people, all the while believing they are not disabled but lending credence to the claim that they are. In a related double blind, Deaf adults who want to become part of the professions serving Deaf people, find that they must subscribe to audist views of rehabilitation, special education, etc.

Exponents of the linguistic minority construction are at a further disadvantage because there is little built-in cultural transmission of their beliefs. The most persuasive advocates for Deaf children, their parents, must be taught generation after generation the counter-intuitive linguistic minority construction because most are neither Deaf themselves nor did they have Deaf parents.

A further obstacle arising within the DEAF-WORLD to promoting the linguistic minority construction concerns, ironically, the form that much Deaf political activism takes. Ever since the first congresses of Deaf people organized in response to the Congress of Milan in 1880, Deaf leaders have appeared before friendly Deaf audiences to express their outrage—to preach to the converted. Written documents—position papers, articles and proceedings—have similarly been addressed to and read by primarily the DEAF-WORLD. It is entirely natural to prefer audiences with whom one shares language and culture, the more so as Deaf people have rarely been permitted to address audiences comprised of hearing professionals. Admittedly, preaching to the converted has value—it may evoke fresh ideas and it builds solidarity and commitment. Advocates of the disability construction do the same; childhood implant conferences, for example, rigorously exclude the voices of the cautious or frankly opposed.

I hope it may be allowed, however, to someone who has been invited to address numerous Deaf audiences and is exasperated by the slow pace of reform to point out that too much of this is an obstacle to true reform because it requires effort, permits the illusion that significant action has been taken, and yet changes little since Deaf people themselves are not responsible for the spread of the disability construction and have little direct power to change its range of application. What part of the battle is won when a Deaf leader receives a standing ovation from a Deaf audience? In the tradition of Deaf activism during the International Congress on the Education of the Deaf in Manchester in 1985, and during the Gallaudet Revolution, the past year have seen a striking increase in Europe of Deaf groups turning outward and presenting their views to hearing people and the media uninvited, particularly in opposition to cochlear implant surgery on Deaf children (Lane, 1994).

PRODUCTION CHANGE

Despite all the obstacles, there are powerful social forces to assist the efforts of the DEAF-WORLD to promote the linguistic minority construction. The body of knowledge developed in linguistics, history, sociology, and anthropology (to mention just four disciplines) concerning Deaf communities has influenced Deaf leadership, bureaucratic decision-making, and legislation. The civil rights movement has given great impetus to the belief that minorities should define themselves and that minority leaders should have a significant say in the conduct of minority affairs. Moreover, the failure of the present predominant disability construction to deliver more able deaf children is a source of professional and public embarrassment and promotes change. Then, too, Deaf children of Deaf parents are frequently insulated against the disability construction to a degree by their early language and cultural acquisition within the DEAF-WORLD. These native ASL-users have important allies in the DEAF-WORLD, among hearing children of Deaf parents, and among disaffected hearing professionals. The Gallaudet Revolution did not change the disability construction on a large scale but it led to inroads against it. Growing numbers of schools, for example, are turning to the linguistic minority construction to guide their planning, curricula, teacher selection and training.

Numerous organizations have committed extensive effort and money to promoting the disability construction. What can the national associations of the Deaf do to promote the linguistic minority construction? Publications like the British Deaf Association *News* or the National Association of the Deaf *Deaf American* are an important step because they provide a forum for national political discussion. However, the discussion has lacked focus.

In addition to a forum, such associations need an explicit political agenda and a plan for implementing it. Such an agenda might include, illustratively, building a greater awareness of the difference between hearing-impairment and cultural Deafness; greater acceptance of the national sign language; removal or reduction of language barriers; improving culturally sensitive health care. Nowhere I know of are such agendas made explicit—given priorities, implementation, a time plan. If these were published they could provide the needed focus for the debate. Commentary on the agenda and plan would be invited as well as rebuttals to the commentaries in subsequent issues. Such agendas, plans and debates are buttressed by scholarship. An important resource to develop is a graduate program in public administration or political science focused on the DEAF-WORLD and the promotion of the linguistic minority construction.

NOTES

1. Padden (1980) makes a distinction between a deaf community, a group of Deaf and hearing individuals who work to achieve certain goals, and a Deaf culture, to which Deaf members of that community belong.

2. In an effort to retain the disability construction of deafness, it has been suggested that sign language interpreters should be viewed as personal assistants. However, the services of these highly trained professionals are frequently not personal but provided to large audiences and they "assist" hearing people as well as, and at the same time as, Deaf people. Nor is interpreting between any other two languages (for example, at the United Nations) considered personal assistance.

3. I am not contending that there is a unitary homogenous DEAF-WORLD. My claims about Deaf culture are best taken as hypotheses for further verification, all the more as I am not a member of the DEAF-WORLD. My means of arriving at cultural principles are the usual ones for an outsider: encounters, ASL language and literature (including stories, legends, anecdotes, poetry, plays, humor, rituals, sign play), magazines and newspaper stories, films, histories, informants, scholarly studies, and the search for principles of coherence. See Stokoe (1994) and Kyle (1990).

REFERENCES

Albrecht, G. L. (1992) *The Disability Business: Rehabilitation in America* (Newbury Park CA, Sage).

Aberley, P. (1987) The concept of oppression and the development of a social theory of disability, *Disability, Handicap and Society,* 2, pp. 5–19.

Allen, T. E. (1986) Patterns of academic achievement among hearing-impaired students: 1974 and 1983, in: A. N. Schildroth & M. A. Karchmer (Eds.) *Deaf Children in America* (San Diego, College-Hill).

Allen, T. E., Rawlings, B. W. & Remington, E. (1994) Demographic and audiologic profiles of deaf children in Texas with cochlear implants, *American Annals of the Deaf,* 138, pp. 260–266.

Barton, L. (1993) The struggle for citizenship: the case of disabled people, *Disability, Handicap and Society,* 8, pp. 235–248.

Becker, G. (1980) *Growing Old in Silence* (Berkeley, University of California Press).

Bienvenu, M. J. (1989) Disability, *The Bicultural Center News,* 13 (April), p. 1.

Braille Monitor (1973) NAC—unfair to the blind, *Braille Monitor,* 2, pp. 127–128.

Braille Monitor (1989) Blind workers claim wages exploitative, *Braille Monitor,* 6, p. 322.

Burek, D. M. (Ed.) (1993) *Encyclopedia of Associations* (Detroit, Gale Research).

Castle, D. (1990) Employment bridges cultures, *Deaf American,* 40, pp. 19–21.

Conrad, P. 8c Schneider, J. (1980) *Deviance and Medicalization: from Badness to Sickness* (Columbia, OH, Merrill).

Cant, T. & Gregory, S. (1991) Unit 8. The social construction of deafness, in: Open University (Eds.) *Issues in Deafness* (Milton Keynes, Open University).

Dowler, D. L. & Hirsh, A. (1994) Accommodations in the workplace for people who are deaf or hard of hearing, *Technology and Disability,* 3, pp. 15–25.

Evans, J. W. (1989) Thoughts on the psychosocial implications of cochlear implantation in children, in: E. Owens & D. Kessler (Eds.) *Cochlear Implants in Young Deaf Children* (Boston, Little, Brown).

Finkelstein, V. (1991) We are not disabled, 'you' are, in: S. Gregory & G. M. Hartley (Eds.) *Constructing Deafness* (London, Pinter).

Fishman, J. (1982) A critique of six papers on the socialization of the deaf child, in: J. B. Christiansen (Ed.) *Conference highlights: National Research Conference on the Social Aspects of Deafness,* pp. 6–20 (Washington, DC, Gallaudet College).

Gannon, J. (1989) *The Week the World Heard Gallaudet* (Washington, DC, Gallaudet University Press).

Gregory, S. & Hartley, G. M. (Eds.) (1991) *Constructing Deafness* (London, Pinter).

Gusfield, J. (1982) Deviance in the welfare state: the alcoholism profession and the entitlements of stigma, in: M. Lewis (Ed.) *Research in Social Problems and Public Policy,* Vol. 2 (Greenwich, CT, JAI press).

Gusfield, J. (1984) On the side: practical action and social constructivism in social problems theory, in: J. Schneider & J. Kitsuse (Eds.) *Studies in the Sociology of Social Problems* (Rutgers, NJ, Ablex).

Gusfield, J. (1989) Constructing the ownership of social problems: fun and profit in the welfare state, *Social Problems,* 36, pp. 431–441.

Hawcroft, L. (1991) Block 2, unit 7. Whose welfare?, in: Open University (Eds.) *Issues in Deafness* (Milton Keynes, Open University).

Hevey, D. (1993) From self-love to the picket line: strategies for change in disability representation, *Disability, Handicap and Society,* 8, pp. 423–430.

Hlibok, G. (1988) Quoted in *USA Today,* 15 March, p. 11a.

American Sign Language: Our Natural Language

"THE NOBLEST GIFT"

WRITTEN BY

GALLAUDET UNIVERSITY

George W. Veditz, the seventh president of the National Association of the Deaf, called sign language "the noblest gift God has given to deaf people."

Sign language traces its recorded history back to some Benedictine monks in Italy around A.D. 530. These monks had taken vows of silence and, it is believed, created a form of sign language in order to communicate their daily needs. Sign language has been passed down through the centuries. Pedro Ponce de Leon, also a Benedictine monk, used sign language to teach his deaf pupils. When the Abbé de l'Epée started his school for the deaf in Paris, he learned French Sign Language from deaf people, modified it to approximate spoken French, and used this variety of sign language to instruct his students.

Thomas Hopkins Gallaudet was introduced to signs used in de l'Epée's school when he visited the Paris Institution at the invitation of Abbé Sicard, de l'Epée's successor. It was the French Sign Language which Laurent Clerc and Gallaudet brought back with them to America in 1816. Of course, signs already existed in America before Clerc's arrival; historical records support that fact. A family friend, observing John Brewster, the deaf portraitist, wrote on December 13, 1790, that Brewster could "write well and converse in signs." That statement was made 26 years before the arrival of Clerc. A recent article about predominantly deaf communities on Martha's Vineyard, off the coast of Massachusetts, traces the use of sign language on the island back to the mid-18th century. Dr. James Woodward, a linguist at Gallaudet College, who has studied both American Sign Language and French Sign Language, estimates that approximately 60 percent of American signs are of French origin.

Clerc, Gallaudet, and the teachers and students at the Hartford School most likely combined the French signs with American signs. From the Hartford School, American Sign Language spread to other schools for the deaf. Sign language then enjoyed widespread use in the education of the deaf until the 1860s.

The heavy emphasis early schools placed on manual communication was one of the reasons that led to the establishment of pure oral schools in this country. Some parents and educators felt that no effort was made, or little attention given, to teach articulation in these schools. The establishment of pure oral schools in this country in the 1860s forced the manual schools to change, as did the Milan resolution 20 years later. At the second International Congress on Education of the Deaf meeting in Milan, Italy, in September 1880, those present voted to outlaw the use of sign language in the education of deaf children in favor of the pure oral method. The U.S. delegation and an educator from Great Britain opposed the move but were heavily outvoted. One writer described the meeting as having an atmosphere rivalling religious fervor. Prevailing conditions in the education of the deaf in Europe at this time had much influence on the action taken. Mismanagement of schools for the deaf, the flagrant practice of nepotism, lack of training programs, and little or no accountability had resulted in a drastic decline in the quality of many educational programs. As usual, sign language was blamed as the cause. As a result of the meeting at Milan, education of the deaf in America became more oral. Some schools became pure oral schools while others became "combined" schools. The latter system was born as a result of disagreement with the pure oral philosophy. Rather than surrender the use of sign language, these schools added speech and speechreading for the beginning pupils while retaining signs and fingerspelling in the more advanced and vocational classes. This approach became known as the combined system. These two different approaches, oral or combined, began a heated controversy in this country that was to rage for decades and become what was commonly called, "The War of Methods."

THE WAR OF METHODS

No history of deaf America, unfortunately, would be complete without mention of this war.

Why the controversy? Why the division among educators in the field of deafness? Why did it have to happen to deaf children, who, with their communication handicap, need input so badly? Perhaps one of the reasons is because deaf individuals look so normal. A blind child, or a paraplegic, for example, has a visible handicap. There is no escaping the disability. But a deaf person's deafness is invisible. It is possible, to a point, to hide deafness. Deafness remains unseen until some act gives the deaf person away—the use of sign language, for example, or the failure to respond when spoken to from behind, or wearing a hearing aid. No parents want to admit that their child is handicapped or different from other healthy children. Usually, the parents' first instinct on learning that their child is deaf is to search for a cure, a miracle, or a remedy that would make their child normal. The word "normal" almost always enters into conversation with hearing parents of a deaf child. The oral philosophy holds out the hope and reassurance to parents that their child can learn to talk and lipread, and that with these tools he or she will fit into hearing society as a "normal" person would. How many deaf persons wish that this were true! They may wish also that it were that simple; but they know from personal experience, that it is not.

Oralism is not the easy way, parents are warned— and it certainly is not. They must stay away from signs, they are told. If they use signs or permit their deaf child to sign they will retard or ruin his speech development. The use of signs will become a "crutch"; the child will depend on them and neglect speech and speechreading, they are reminded. In other words, signing is bad for those who wish to develop speech.

This obsession against signing has scared parents of deaf children away from deaf adults who use sign language. Many parents have been told that those who use signs become clannish when they grow up and that many live in "deaf ghettos." Parents do not realize, often until it is too late, that such contacts with deaf adults could be beneficial and could help them make constructive contributions to their child's development. Frequently, the deaf adults they chance to see are the models for their children.

This attempt to make a "hearing" person out of a deaf child; to demand that the child talk, talk, talk and to forbid him or her the use of that natural means of communication, to refuse to permit him or her to relate to other members of the deaf community are seen by many deaf people as cruel, unrealistic and unfair. People who do this would never think of giving a blind child a pair of glasses and demanding that the child see, see, see. Nor would they be so hardhearted as to take away the crutches from a crippled child. Yet in their determination to make a deaf child "normal," these same people unconsciously deny the deaf child the right to be himself. They are, in effect, saying that it is wrong to be deaf.

Normal? What is a *normal* deaf person? Deaf people have often asked themselves that question. Is a poor imitation of a hearing person a normal deaf person? Is pretending to understand, smiling and nodding at what is being said when one does not really comprehend, normal? Is rejecting the use of sign language because it is "the easy way out" and because hearing people do not use it and because it "classifies" you as deaf normal? Is not admitting one's disability and learning to cope with it the best you can normal? Why, then, do some people try to make an abnormal person out of a normal person who just happens to have a hearing disability? Why do they try to instill a sense of inferiority in a deaf person who initially sees life as a challenge? Why throw cruel, unnecessary stumbling blocks in the path of a deaf person or forbid him the right to use his natural means of communication? Is it not ironic that deaf people are rarely, if ever, asked what they believe is best for them? Wouldn't it be amusing if those who think they know what is best for deaf people could be deaf for a while, experience the frustration, and grope helplessly trying to understand what is being said? These are some of the questions deaf people have asked themselves. But, the overriding question remains: What is wrong with being deaf and trying to live with one's deafness?

THE CONTROVERSY

The controversy over the best way to educate deaf children in this country raged from the 18th Century into the 20th. Hundreds of articles appeared in print, salvos of criticism were fired back and forth, and claims and counterclaims were made as each camp tried to win over parents and supporters. While the pure oralist proclaimed that speech was the way, the combinist argued that it was necessary to fit the method to the child, not the child to the method. Research findings, statistics, and statements, some lifted out of context, were used, further confusing parents who were neither familiar with the terms used in the studies nor with the persons conducting them. Personal testimonies of carefully selected deaf adults were held up as evidence of the "better way."

The controversy split families, broke up marriages, and led to divorces. It embittered deaf children and adults alike, leaving lifelong scars on the lives of many. It ran deep. In Nebraska, a mother of a deaf man made him promise on her deathbed that he would never use signs. Although he had attended a prestigious oral school his speech remained unintelligible throughout his life. As a result of that promise, neither hearing nor deaf people could understand him, and he had to resort to a pad and pencil to carry on a conversation with both groups.

Deaf children who did not succeed in oral schools were labelled "oral failures" and sent to residential schools where they were exposed to the more flexible combined system. Administrators in residential schools complained that their schools were becoming "dumping grounds" for oral failures and that the lateness at which they received these students, usually when the students were in their teens, made it impossible to make up for the lost years.

Contrary to widely held beliefs, most deaf adults did not oppose the teaching of speech and speech-reading. National Association of the Deaf President James L. Smith stated in 1904: "We are friends and advocates of speech and speech-training, but not for all the deaf. In order that the deaf may get the highest measure of intellectual, social, and moral happiness in this world, an adaption and combination of methods is necessary." Smith's stand has been held by a majority of deaf leaders through the decades. Many of them who can talk and lipread, as well as those who cannot, stress the value of those skills. But, deaf adults also repeatedly express concern over the heavy emphasis placed on the teaching of articulation at the expense of an education. "What good is it to be able to talk if you have nothing to say?" is a popular refrain.

W. L. Hill, a deaf man who became a successful newspaper publisher, said: "My object in going to school was to obtain an education, not simply a means of communication with hearing people." Issac Goldberg said: ". . . what I am today I certainly do not owe to my ability to speak or read the lips." Goldberg was a product of an oral school, a chemist, and an inventor of perfumes.

Nevertheless, the oralist-dominated years that followed had a profound impact on the lives of deaf people, most of it negative. Parents who had been convinced that sign language was detrimental to the speech efforts of their deaf child would have nothing to do with deaf teachers. Many schools came under pressure to switch to the pure oral method. In some states, deaf teachers became extinct or an endangered species.

ATTEMPTS TO SUPPRESS SIGN LANGUAGE

As oralism took a strong grip on education of the deaf in the United States in the 1860s and onward, there were attempts to suppress the use of sign language. It came under a mounting barrage of criticism. In the eyes of oral advocates, sign language was the culprit for everything wrong in the education of the deaf. It was blamed for deaf children's lack of speech, for their poor grasp of the English language; it was accused of promoting clannishness among deaf persons. If anything were wrong with deaf people, sign language was rapped as the cause.

In order to concentrate on teaching speech and speechreading, oral educators tried to provide an un-contaminated pure oral atmosphere for their students. They solicited the cooperation of parents. They refused to hire deaf teachers, even their own products. Deaf children were told that using signs was bad and degrading. They were told that it would prevent them from growing up "normal" and that they would not be able to live in a hearing world if they relied on signs and did not learn to talk and lipread. Even in the purest oral atmosphere, nevertheless, deaf children continued to use signs. Suppression only succeeded in driving sign language out of sight, behind the desk or the teacher's back, under the table, into the bathroom. Those who were caught breaking the rules were scolded or punished. Rapping a child's hand with a ruler was one of the punishments; clapping a child's mouth with a chalky eraser was another. Children had their hands tied behind their back or placed in brown paper bags. Still others were made to sit on their hands to keep them from going astray and forming signs. Although this natural way of communicating by deaf people defied suppression, the attempt to suppress it created a stigma towards sign language and a negative, guilty attitude about its use.

As sign language became outlawed in an increasing number of schools, there was a growing concern among deaf leaders that the beauty of the American Sign Language as used by the masters of old would be lost. Those masters had a special delivery of their own, a poetic motion, a Victorian dignity, standing ramrod straight with their lips tightly shut as they graphically etched in the air spellbinding presentations of beauty. It was considered gross in those early days to mouth words; platform signers placed emphasis on signs. If fingerspelling could be avoided it was.

Except at the Ohio School for the Deaf, Gallaudet College, and possibly a few other places, sign language was never formally taught. Children picked it up from their peers. Teachers, new and veteran, learned it from their students or from other teachers. Under such circumstances there was little control over its originality, and signs underwent many changes. William H. Weeks of Connecticut, addressing the National Association of the Deaf convention in 1889 expressed concern about this: "The sign language is the grandest means yet devised for rapidity and clearness of communication with the deaf. We must hold fast to the original purity and strength of our signs. There is a tendency to invent new signs, some of which mean nothing. Many of the good old signs have been chopped and clipped so that they have lost much of their original force."

Dr. James L. Smith, a teacher at the Minnesota School for the Deaf, echoed Week's concerns at the 1904 National Association of the Deaf convention: "The enemies of sign language are not confined to those who decry it and call for its abolition entirely. Its most dangerous enemies are in the camp of its friends, in the persons of those who maltreat it and abuse it by misuse. The sign language, properly used, is a language of grace, beauty, power. But through careless or ignorant use it may become ungraceful, repulsive, difficult to comprehend."

In the early 1900s George W. Veditz expressed concern that "'A new race of pharaohs that knew not Joseph' are taking over the land and many of our American Schools. They do not understand signs for they cannot sign. They proclaim that signs are worthless and of no help to the deaf. Enemies of sign language—they are enemies of the true welfare of the deaf."

THE DEAF: "BY THEIR FRUITS YE SHALL KNOW THEM"

When the New York School for the Deaf came under pressure to abandon sign language in favor of the pure oral method in the instruction of deaf children, Principal Enoch H. Currier decided to solicit the opinions of deaf leaders of the day. Here are some excerpts from some of the letters he received. The letters were published in a booklet, **The Deaf: "By Their Fruits Ye Shall Know Them."**

"It is hard to conceive that there are minds and hearts so small and shriveled that they would say to the deaf, 'You are to acquire knowledge and understanding by watching the motion of the lips or not at all.' The deaf, as well as the hearing, are entitled to learn all they can by such methods as are most expeditious."—J.C. Howard

"... I feel that it is my right to come by knowledge in whatever way God has given me, since it was His good will that I should not hear. I do not recognize the right of any human being to deprive me of the means of communication that God has left to me."—J.C. Howard

"I have met many deaf people—some educated by the oral method and some by the combined method, where signs are used. In every case those who have been educated by means of signs are the more intelligent, more independent, self-reliant, and have an air of being capable, competent and unafraid. They are happier and experience more real joy in life."—A.R. Spear

"In attempting to abolish signs as used as aids in educating the deaf, the unfortunate children are not only being deprived of their birthright, but a means of education is being taken from them."—A.R. Spear

"From the standpoint of a totally deaf person, proficient in speech and lip-reading, and with forty years' experience in the art, I can only say that lip-reading at its best is a matter of skillful guess work, and a sorry mess we sometimes make of it."—A.R. Spear

"The deaf do not object to speech and lip-reading. They know it is a great advantage to those who can attain to a working proficiency. The combined schools provide this as well as oral schools, and at the same time educate those who cannot profit to any great extent by pure oral methods. This is so apparent it seems a waste of time to state it."— G.M. Teegarden

"I know the value of speech. I can speak well and read the lips well. But I plead for broadness as against narrowness. I plead for the child rather than for the method itself."—G.M. Teegarden

"You cannot eliminate the sign language. It is the natural language of the deaf. You may suppress its use to an extent, but in doing so you close an avenue to the mind and soul of the deaf-mute, and in so doing add to his losses."—G.M. Teegarden

"Nature hates force. Just as the flowing stream seeks the easiest path, so the mind seeks the way of least resistance. The sign-language offers to the deaf a broad and smooth avenue for the inflow and outflow of thought, and there is no other avenue for them like unto it."—G.M. Teegarden

"Under the best of circumstances, both the young and the adult deaf are heavily handicapped, and, in their instruction, no *method* which will aid in the smallest degree, to give them knowledge and power, should be excluded from the curriculum."—Alice C. Jennings

"It is a lamentable fact that, in matters relating to the deaf, their education and well-being, few if any take the trouble to get the opinion of the very people most concerned—the deaf themselves."—John H. Keiser

"If you try to suppress signs you will teach deceit, for the deaf will always use it on the sly. To deprive a deaf-mute of the sign language is like clipping a bird of its wings."—F. Maginn

These concerns led to the formation of a morion picture committee of the National Association of the Deaf during Veditz' administration. The sum of $5,000, a large sum in those days, was raised in short order, and filming of the old masters of sign began. The NAD recorded for posterity presentations in sign language by Edward Miner Gallaudet, John Hotchkiss, Edward Allen Fay, George W. Veditz, Robert McGregor, and other old masters. These films have been videotaped and are available for viewing at the Edward Miner Gallaudet Memorial Library at Gallaudet College.

With sign language under fire, it was obviously not a time when people sought the advice and opinions of deaf people. The education and welfare of the deaf was largely in the hands of hearing persons. It was rare indeed to find a deaf person serving on a school board or in an advisory capacity to a program that affected the welfare of the deaf. Few school administrators took counsel of deaf people, but one who did was Principal Enoch H. Currier of the New York School for the Deaf (Fanwood). When pressure was brought to bear on the Board of Directors of the school to switch to the pure oral method in 1912, Currier decided to seek the opinions of the leading deaf persons of the day. He received so many responses to his inquiry that he decided to publish them in a booklet entitled: *The Deaf: "By their fruits ye shall know them."* Those who responded to the invitation included professionals, businessmen, educators, members of the clergy, and a number of products of oral schools. Excerpts of some of their responses are printed elsewhere to give a feeling for the sentiments of the times. NYSD remained a combined method school.

On the other side of the coin, some oral products succeeded remarkably well. Mabel Hubbard Bell, the wife of Alexander Graham Bell, was deafened at the age of five years by scarlet fever. She attended Clarke School for the Deaf in Northampton, a school her father, Gardiner G. Hubbard, had helped to start. Mabel Bell was a skilled lipreader.

Latham Breunig, a 1935 graduate of the Clarke School for the Deaf, also deafened at the age of five years, earned a doctorate at Johns Hopkins University and became a statistician for the Eli Lilly Co. in Indianapolis. Breunig was the first chairman of the Oral Deaf Adult

Section when it was organized within the Alexander Graham Bell Association, and he was the first deaf person to become president of that Association.

James C. Marsters was born deaf. He got his elementary education in a public school and attended the Wright Oral School in New York. He earned his BS degree at Union College in New York and attended Columbia University in New York City. Marsters earned his doctor of dental science (DDS) at the New York University College of Dentistry and later an MS at the University of Southern California. Marsters is a self-employed orthodontist in Pasadena, California. He has lectured in orthodontistry at USC. He holds a pilot's license and is active in an organization promoting telecommunications for the deaf.

Richard E. Thompson is another successful Clarke School graduate. Born deaf, Thompson earned an AB degree from Harvard *cum laude* in 1952 and a masters and a PhD in clinical psychology from Boston University. He was a member of the first National Advisory Committee for Education of the Deaf He is a member of the Beverly School board. He was co-director of Psycho-Social Services for the Deaf at Newton Center before becoming director of the Massachusetts Office of Deafness. Now a skilled signer, he is very active in organizations of the deaf.

Barbara Ann Brauer was born deaf. She attended a residential school for deaf children in Michigan until the sixth grade when she was enrolled in the public school system. She earned her master's at Columbia University and a doctorate in clinical psychology at New York University. She is currently director of Mental Health Research in the Division of Research at Gallaudet College.

AMERICAN SIGN LANGUAGE COMES OUT OF THE CLOSET

And so it went through the decades until the 1960s What took sign language so long to become acceptable again? Ignorance. Insensitivity. Cruelty. Pride. Well-meaning but over-zealous and misguided intentions.

Slowly more and more people were beginning to realize that limiting a deaf child to a totally oral program did not guarantee success in speech and speech-reading skills. Researchers were beginning to find evidence that early use of sign language did not retard a deaf child's development of speech as many had thought it did. Other studies of deaf children of deaf parents who used sign language with their children showed that these children generally fared better academically, socially, and in the acquisition of written Language than did those deaf children of hearing parents who did not use sign language.

The exposure of deaf people on television, a changing national mood towards disabled Americans and the increasing articulateness and visibility of deaf leaders, weather factors. Another reason for sign language's acceptance was a man named Bill Stokoe.

In the mid-1950s Dr. William C. Stokoe, Jr joined the Gallaudet College faculty as chairman of the English Department. He soon became fascinated by the language of signs, the leading means of communicator used on campus. When he proposed a study of sign language, however, his colleagues surprisingly stowed little interest. Some even thought that he was

Silent Homage

(A Tribute to Interpreters)
The moving lips speak voicelessly-but hark:
The winging words fly from your fluttering hands;
And each, who dwells in silence, understands
How Dawn, the rosy-fingered, burns the dark
From shadow-worlds wherein the teeming brain
Lay, like a captive, in a dungeon-cell;
Your magic bursts the iron citadel,
And breaks the lock, and brings the light again!

Dear friend, how empty, vain and commonplace
Must seem this gratitude we offer you;
Yet now we render homage, as your due,
Remembering your patience, love and grace—
With twining fingers as you blithely go,
Daily, to fell our Walls of Jericho

—Loy E. Golladay

crazy to think of such an undertaking. Even deaf colleagues were indifferent. But, Stokoe persisted. In 1957 he started the Linguistics Research Program, an after-hours and summer research project. With two deaf assistants, Carl Croneberg and Dorothy Caster-line, Stokoe began filming individuals giving presentations in sign language. Few of the participants understood what he was trying to do or the significance of his work, and most who took part in the experiments did so to humor him.

Next Stokoe and his team spent thousands of hours carefully studying the signs captured on film. From these studies he noted familiar patterns emerging. He identified points of contrast, morphemes, and syntactical patterns, those necessary ingredients of a language. He was the first linguist to subject sign language to the tests of a real language, and he found that it withstood them all. When he published his initial findings in 1960, however, few people got excited or paid much attention. He was nearly alone in his belief that sign language, instead of being a collection of grotesque gestures, as many thought it was, was indeed a language in its own right.

In 1965 Stokoe, Casterline, and Croneberg published the results of their work in *A Dictionary of American Sign Language on Linguistic Principles* In this book they presented signs of American Sign Language in symbols based on linguistic principles. (A revised edition, *Sign Language Structure,* followed in 1978.)

Stokoe's work, however, caught the attention and interest of other linguists in the United States and abroad. He had made sign language a legitimate and academically acceptable research topic. Other hearing linguists began studying it. A few deaf people also became interested in linguistics because of this work, entered degree programs in linguistics and began their own research related to American Sign Language. These studies overflowed into other academic disciplines—anthropology, sociology, psychology. In 1973 James Woodward completed his dissertation at Georgetown University on American Sign Language and became the first linguist to earn a doctorate in that subject.

These researchers found that American Sign Language, like other languages, undergoes change. They discovered that, contrary to popular belief, it has its own grammatical structure and that it can and does convey abstract concepts. Just because American Sign Language appears ungrammatical when it is translated word for word into English does not make it ungrammatical. Harry Markowicz, who studied both American Sign Language and French Sign Language and who has written many articles on the subject, explained that other spoken languages with different word orders from English also appear ungrammatical in word for word translations in English. Much of this research has found its way into print and has heightened interest in American Sign Language.

Stokoe defines American Sign Language as both a native and a natural language. A native language is the first language an individual learns to use for normal communication. It is believed that every human is born with a language capacity. An individual's native language depends on the language those around him are using and on his ability to receive all the signals of that language. ASL is usually the native language of those deaf and hearing children born of deaf parents in a home where sign language is the language used. In households where both ASL and English are used, many of these children grow up with two or more native languages equally exercising their native language capacity. These bilingual children are often intellectually advanced and academically superior to other children.

Stokoe describes a natural language as the language people of the world use in their everyday activities among themselves as well as for other purposes. A natural language is developed by its users, and it evolves over a period of time. He estimates that American Sign Language is the natural language of some 200,000 to 400,000 deaf Americans and deaf Canadians.

The discovery of American Sign Language as a true language has led to the identification of deaf culture as a rich, untapped field of study. Observed Carol Padden, a deaf linguistics student: "The culture of deaf people has not yet been studied in much depth. One reason is that, until recently, it was rare to describe deaf people as having a *culture. . . "*

American Sign Language began to increase in popularity, Colleges, universities, high schools, private and public organizations, and agencies began offering courses in ASL. Deaf people suddenly found themselves in demand as teachers of their language. This interest and acceptance of sign language caught many deaf old timers by surprise. It has influenced the attitudes of deaf persons towards themselves, their language, their culture and made them take a closer look at their rights as American citizens.

In 1980 friends and colleagues of William C. Stokoe got together and secretly prepared a collection of essays his honor. The book, Sign *Language and he Deaf Community: Essays in Honor of William* C. *Stokoe,* was published by the National Association of the Deaf and presented to a surprised Stokoe at the NAD Centennial Convention. Royalties from the sale of the book will go into the William C. Stokoe Scholarship Fund To encourage continued research in the area of sign language.

Meanwhile, Bill Stokoe has found mastering sign language himself a tough subject. He is, as a colleague tactfully put it, "not a fluent signer." He continues to work on *his* sign language.

SIGN LANGUAGE BOOKS

There appeared at the Convention of American Instructors of the Deaf meeting in Salem, Oregon, in the summer of 1961, a commercial artist from Winneconne, Wisconsin, named David Watson. Watson was from a deaf family—deaf parents, a deaf brother, and three deaf sisters. He had with him some sketches of animated signs which he had been preparing for a book. He wanted to know what the teachers at the convention thought of the drawings. To his surprise and delight everyone who saw them liked the drawings and encouraged him to complete his project. Inspired, Watson returned home to his drawing board and set to work. *Talk With Your Hands* was completed three years later. It was an instant success and within nine months the first run of 10,000 copies was sold out. His drawings appeared in two colors and showed the movement of signs. Wrote one customer: "Your book breathes." Watson has since produced a second volume and is at work on a third.

In 1963 Lottie Riekehof's *Talk to the Deaf,* L.M. Guillory's *Expressive and Receptive Fingerspelling for Hearing Adults* and Roger M. Falberg's *The Language of Silence* appeared. A year later Louie Fant's *Say It With Hands* rolled off the press. Much earlier—in 1909— J. Schuyler Long had produced *The Sign Language: A Manual of Signs* but, not since John W. Michael's *Handbook of Sign Language of the Deaf* which was printed in 1923 had there appeared a new book on sign language. These books opened the floodgate of many more sign language books that would appear during this decade and the next—more books on the subject than the country had ever seen. The list included hymnals, religious signs, flash cards, sign language games, manuals for deaf-blind children, curriculum guides for teaching interpreters. *A Basic Course in Manual Communication* prepared by Terrence J. O'Rourke and published by the National Association of the Deaf appeared in 1970. It has sold almost one-half million copies since its release. By the end of the 1970s some 40 sign language-related books were on the market. Riekehof published a second book *The Joy of Signing,* and Fant has since published three more books *Ameslan: An Introduction to American Sign Language* (1972), *Sign Language* (1977) and *Intermediate Sign Language* (1980).

In 1980 T.J. Publishers brought out a package of materials for teaching American Sign Language. Written by Charlotte Baker and Dennis Cokely, it included a series of three student textbooks, two teacher's resource books on curriculum, methods and evaluation, and grammar and culture. A series of videotapes were also prepared to accompany the texts.

A Basic Course in American Sign Language by Tom Humphries, Carol Padden and Terrence J. O'Rourke also appeared that year.

THE NAD COMMUNICATIVE SKILLS PROGRAM

The Rehabilitative Services Administration of the U.S. Department of Health, Education, and Welfare awarded a grant to the National Association of the Deaf in 1967 to begin a series of pilot sign language classes in the United States. Terrence J. O'Rourke, a deaf teacher of the deaf, was hired as director of this new Communicative Skills Program. Through this program thousands and thousands of persons have been introduced to sign language.

In 1972 the Graduate School at New York University began accepting American Sign Language as satisfying a language requirement. By the end of that year 38 other colleges were offering credit courses in manual communication.

In the 1970s the Communicative Skills Program began to focus more on improving the quality of the' courses offered, and on assisting colleges, universities, and government agencies to begin sign language training programs of their own. In 1975 CSP formed the Sign Instructors Guidance Network (SIGN), a professional organization of sign language instructors, with evaluation and certification responsibilities. In 1977, CSP organized the first National Symposium on Sign Language Research and Teaching in Chicago. A second symposium was held in San Diego, California, in 1978 and a third in Boston in 1980.

Terrence J. O'Rourke left the program in 1978 to start his own publishing business. He was succeeded by S. Melvin Carter, Jr. That year CSP added a program for training sign language instructors and doing curriculum development in the teaching of American Sign Language. Ella Lentz was hired as coordinator and assistant director of CSP. Through this program she works with sign language instructors in the ten Rehabilitation Services Administration regions, assisting them in upgrading their programs.

Edna Adler, a deaf consultant in the Office of Deafness and Communicative Disorders, Social Rehabilitation Services, Department of Health and Human Services, believes that this program "more than anything else helped remove the stigma of using sign language."

TOTAL COMMUNICATION ARRIVES

In the early 1960s, Dorothy Shifflett, a teacher with the Anaheim Union High School District in California and the mother of a deaf daughter, became disillusioned with the lack of progress her daughter was making through the oral approach. After contacts with deaf adults in the community, she switched to the combined system and began using a multi-approach to teaching deaf children in her school. She was influential in persuading teachers, parents, deaf and hearing children, and those who worked with deaf children to take classes in sign language. Deaf children were exposed to speech, speechreading, and auditory training as well as fingerspelling and signs. They were integrated with hearing children in physical education classes, during recess, and at lunch. Some attended classes for hearing children, including classes in Spanish and in band! One deaf boy was even included in the school's marching band. This approach did away with communication reservations, provided increased input to the deaf child, and stimulated his learning.

Mrs. Shifflett called her approach "The Total Approach." Although it was not the first time that deaf and hearing children had been integrated in a regular public school program and been taught sign language, it was a philosophy whose time had come. Dorothy Shifflett hired Herb Larson, a deaf teacher; he became one of the first deaf teachers to teach in the public school system outside a residential school in California.

In the fall of 1968 Roy Holcomb became the first area supervisor of the program for deaf students at the James Madison Elementary School. This school, with an enrollment of 800 hearing students, was part of the Santa Ana Unified School District in California. The program for deaf children was the oldest program of its kind in Orange County. The program's first teacher was Kathryn Fitzgerald, a relative of Edith Fitzgerald, inventor of the Fitzgerald Key. In 1968, the program consisted of six classes serving 34 deaf children from three to 12 years old.

Holcomb, a Texas School for the Deaf, Gallaudet College and California State University, Northridge product, and his teachers were aware that good communication was the key to a deaf child's successful learning process. They knew that once a child fell behind academically in his early years, he seldom, if ever, caught up. They wanted to provide each student with as much information as possible during these early formative years. They were interested in providing each student with a barrier-free communication environment and not in what they said were "theories as to what might be better for him in later life." They were interested in "real and genuine communication." They used the total approach at all levels at the school.

A year later Holcomb began using the term, "Total Communication." He widely publicized this system, and as other educators learned about it, they began adopting it and Holcomb became known as the "Father of Total Communication."

Roy Holcomb, who wears a hearing aid although he has a 90-decibel hearing loss, was one of the founders of the International Association of Parents of the Deaf and the author of *Hazards of Deafness.* (He once received a letter from the California State Credentials Department warning him that his job might be in jeopardy because of his deafness.) He was in demand as a speaker and was invited to serve on the advisory boards of at least six colleges that had programs for hearing impaired students. He is the recipient of numerous honors including the Dan T. Cloud Award (his wife, Marjorie, was also a recipient) given annually by the Center on Deafness at California State University at Northridge. Gallaudet College awarded him an honorary Doctor of Laws degree. Eventually he left Santa Ana to become director of the Margaret S. Sterck School for the Deaf in Delaware.

The Maryland School for the Deaf was probably the first residential school to adopt officially the Total Communication philosophy and, under the leadership of Superintendent David Denton, became one of its strongest advocates. Margaret S. Kent, principal of MSD, defined Total Communication as the "right of every deaf child to learn to use all forms of communication so that he may have full opportunity to develop language competence at the earliest possible age." She and her colleagues at the Maryland School saw it as including "the full spectrum of language modes: child-devised gestures, formal sign language, speech, speechreading, fingerspelling, reading, and writing."

As it became increasingly used, Total Communication underwent modification, changes, and refinement In 1976 an official definition of Total Communication was agreed on by members of the Conference of Executives of American Schools for the Deaf. The CEASD version read: "Total Communication is a philosophy requiring the incorporation of appropriate aural, manual, and oral modes of communication m order to insure effective communication with and among hearing impaired persons."

The pendulum was swinging back toward sign language. By 1976 two-thirds of the schools for the deaf in this country reported that they used Total Communication although many teachers in these schools could not sign well and made little or no effort to learn.

MANUALLY CODED ENGLISH SYSTEMS

The search to find a better way to teach English to deaf children has long eluded educators of the deaf. Special systems have been devised to assist in this process; they include the Barry Five Slate System, Wing's Symbols, and the Fitzgerald Key. (Both Wing and Fitzgerald were deaf.) Grammar textbooks used in public schools have been used and other teachers have had their own systems. English still remains a very difficult language for deaf students to master.

One spring day in 1962, David Anthony was reading a story about Basic English in *Life* magazine. The article told about a system created in the 1920s and 1930s by Charles K. Ogden, and Ivor A. Richards of Cambridge University. They had developed a list of 850 basic English words and rules for their use in an attempt to simplify English and make it easier for others to learn.

Born deaf and the son of deaf parents, Anthony knew first-hand the difficulties deaf children encounter in acquiring a working command of English. He was then a teacher of mentally retarded deaf children and adults at the Deaf Research Project at Lapeer State Home and Training School in Lapeer, Michigan.

Anthony, a graduate of Gallaudet College, saw weaknesses in the two traditional methods of teaching deaf children then in use. American Sign Language has a different grammatical structure and does not follow English syntax or word order. Speech and speechreading, on the other hand, were no better. While following the spoken English word order, lip-reading involved too much guesswork; at best, only about 40 percent of the spoken words are visible on the lips. Anthony knew, as did other educators, that a hearing child has a decided advantage in acquiring English. He is acoustically bombarded with words on a daily basis. He hears them on radio, television, in conversation with others, and at the dinner table. Deaf children, on the other hand, are shut off from such valuable, yet effortless, learning sources. Every single English word they learn has to be learned with an effort. Since deaf children cannot hear spoken English, Anthony wanted to find a way for them to see it as it is spoken. He thought that this Basic English list might be used to help his children. He realized that he had another problem: many of those words on the list had no signs. An idea was beginning to form in his mind.

David Anthony returned to Lapeer and discussed his idea with his colleagues there. They thought it had possibilities. The more he thought about it and discussed it the more sense it made. He proposed a system called Signing Essential English with the acronym

SEE in keeping with his philosophy that to learn English deaf children must *see* it. This new sign system, developed largely by the inventiveness of his pupils, was the theme of his master's thesis at Eastern Michigan University where he was completing work on his degree in English.

In developing SEE, Anthony decided to use as little fingerspelling as possible. Every English word would have a distinct sign—even parts of a word (morphemes) would have a sign—and these signs would follow the spoken English word order. He developed signs for morphemes—those small units of meaning for words, prefixes (re-, com-, anti-, etc.), roots (-sist, -vali-, etc.), and suffixes (-ed, -ing, -ment, -ness, etc.)—so that it was possible to distinguish among, for example, *play, plays, playing, played, player,* etc. In SEE, a single word could have more than one sign. Take *boyishly,* for example. That word would be broken down into the morphemes: "boy," "ish, " and "ly," and three different signs would be used in sequence. To deaf adults accustomed to American Sign Language who would normally fingerspell that word or use the signs "idea same" and "boy," Anthony's approach looked awkward and silly. Many felt that he was messing up sign language. But Anthony believed that if deaf children were to learn the term "boyishly," they would have to see it and that "idea same boy" was not the way the word was spoken or written Breaking a word up into signs made it easier to understand than did fingerspelling it. Further, Anthony explained, "idea same boy" takes three signs to render, as does "boy" "ish," "ly."

SEE also uses the same sign for a word with different meanings. So, regardless of whether you run out of gas, run for election, or just plain run, the same sign is used for all three different versions. Anthony believes that a deaf child can figure out which meaning of the word is being used from the context of the sentence.

The scene next shifts to California where Anthony joined the teaching staff of the Brookhurst Junior High School in Anaheim. There a core group was formed to further develop Anthony's ideas. On Anthony's recommendation the group changed the name of his system to Seeing Essential English to play down the emphasis on signing so that the system would appeal more to parents. The members of this core group, besides Anthony, included Gerilee Gustason, Donna Pfetzing, Esther Zawolkow, and Dennis Wampler, among others. Gustason was deaf, having lost her hearing at the age of five. Pfetzing was the mother of a deaf daughter, a rubella baby, and a disillusioned oral proponent. Zawolkow was the daughter of deaf parents; Wampler was the son of deaf parents. Like Anthony, Gustason and Wampler were teachers. Pfetzing and Zawolkow were interpreters at Anthony's school. This group solicited reaction and input from many other deaf and hearing adults, parents, teachers, and interested persons. They began using the new system at their respective schools, refining it and adding to it. All of them were convinced that they were on the right track toward developing a system that would provide deaf children with a better way to develop better skills in written English.

About this time the members of the group began to disagree on some basic principles. Anthony believed that whenever necessary a new sign should be created. He also believed that each part of a word should have its own consistent sign. The others favored retaining as many traditional signs as possible. They also felt that excessive breaking up of words with signs was not the way to go. This disagreement led to a split, and two other visual English systems emerged.

Dennis Wampler felt that the signs should be presented in the symbols Stokoe had developed as opposed to descriptions or drawings of the signs. At the Starr King School in Sacramento, he developed the Linguistics of Visual English (L.O.V.E.) system. He also believed that a word must be signed the same way regardless of meaning, and he attempted to relate a sign to speech, sound, and spelling. His system was published but little more has been heard of it since then.

The third group involved Gustason, Pfetzing, Zawolkow. They called their system Signing Exact English or SEE II.

All three groups retained the same basic objective: to ease the acquisition of English by deaf children. All established principles to govern their systems and attempted to retain or modify existing signs which were unambigious. All three adhered to the sound/ spelling/ meaning criteria which Anthony had initially developed. They do not see their systems as a replacement for American Sign Language.

These visual English systems began to introduce many more initialized signs into our sign language These initialized signs were formed by using the first letter of a word and a traditional sign, if one existed. Where no satisfactory sign existed, a new one was created. The use of initialized signs had been proposed earlier in the mid-1950s by Max N. Morsel, a mathematics teacher at the Missouri School for the Deaf, in a series of articles appearing in *The Silent Worker* entitled "Manually Speaking." Mossel proposed using the same sign and movement but changing the initialization. For example, the sign for "way" with the "r" letter became road, "s" became street, "p" became path, "l" became lane, and so on. His ideas did not catch on until the visual English systems began using them.

At about this time, Dr. Harry Bornstein, Barbara Kannapell and Lillian Hamilton were working on a series of Signed English books for preschool deaf children at Gallaudet College.

Meanwhile, other manually coded English sign systems emerged.

In 1971 Anthony produced the first *S.E.E. Manual.* It had approximately 3,000 signs. In 1980 *Seeing Essential English: Codebreaker* and *Seeing Essential English: Elementary Dictionary* appeared. Anthony is one of the co-authors of both books.

A manual on *Signing Exact English* by Gerilee Gustason, Donna Pfetzing and Esther Zawolkow first appeared in 1972. It has since gone through many printings and three editions. Within four months of the appearance of the 1980 edition all 15,000 copies were sold out.

The proponents of these visual English systems believe their approach appeals to a larger number of parents of deaf children because it is easier for English speaking adults to learn to use signs following the spoken pattern of English than it is for them to learn American Sign Language. When visual English first appeared many deaf adults who lacked good English skills saw it as a wonderful opportunity for deaf children and regretted that it had arrived too late for them. But, in recent years, as it has been adopted by an increasing number of schools, an increasing resistance and negative attitude towards it has grown. This could stem, in part from those who see visual English as a threat to American Sign Language, who do not understand it and who are concerned about it "tarnishing" the beauty of American Sign Language. Some visual English signs have already found their way into American Sign

Language. But, unlike American Sign Language, which linguists have identified as the natural language of deaf American people, visual English is an artificial language. Linguists who have studied languages for many years do not see an artificial language as a threat to a natural language, as lone as it is not imposed on people and communities.

AND INTEREST GROWS ...

This interest in sign language grew beyond some deaf old timers' wildest expectations. ASL became a popular language in the United States. (It has been erroneously reported as the third most wildely used language in the country but actually it ranks lower than that.) Dr. Ross Stuckless of the National Technical Institute for the Deaf reported that by the late 1970s more hearing than deaf people had learned it.

"The Sign Language Store" opened on Yoland Street in Northridge, California. Another store, "The I Love You Gift, Co," opened in Alexandria, Virginia. At these stores customers could buy wearing apparel, jewelry, school supplies, novelties, and miscellaneous other items with signs and fingerspelling or the I-Love-You symbol printed on them.

Posters and bumper stickers appeared in sign language or fingerspelling urging the public to "Stop Noise Pollution. Learn Sign Language," or "Let Your Fingers Do the Talkin'" or proclaiming "Total Communication—The right of every deaf child." Others advised: "I'm Not Ignoring You, I'm Deaf!" In response to the "Honk, if You Love Jesus" bumper sticker, another appeared with "Wave, if You Love Jesus."

"Keep Quiet," a crosswords cubes game with the manual alphabet on cubes, appeared on the market. Suzie L. Kirchner produced two books, *Play It By Sign* and *Signs for All Seasons: More Sign Language Games* which told how to play games in signs, pantomime, gestures, and fingerspelling. Pre-school readers, cookbooks, and song books in sign language and English came off the presses.

A song, "I Hear Your Hand," written by Mary Jane Rhodes, the mother of a deaf son, was signed on national television by Rita Corey. Deaf and hearing high school and college students and hearing interpreters formed sign-sing groups with such names as "Rock Gospel," "Deaf Awareness Troupe," "Singing Hands," "Breakthrough," "The Expressions," "Sing a Sign," "Vibrations," "Joyful Signs," and others and became popular local performing groups. Mitch Leigh's "The Impossible Dream," and Joe Brook's "You Light Up My Life," became two of the favorite songs used by deaf signers. The signed renditions of these songs touched the hearts of thousands.

Even chimpanzees and a gorilla got into the act. In 1966, Drs. R. Allen and Beatrice T. Gardner, a husband and wife research team at the University of Nevada, began teaching a young female chimp, named Washoe (signed "W" fanning the ear), sign language. The Gardners were interested in learning more about chimpanzees' behavior and capability to learn a human language. Since chimps do not possess the necessary vocal mechanisms to imitate human sound and since their hands closely resemble those of a human, the Gardners decided to experiment with signs. Washoe became the first chimp to converse with people in the language of signs. She learned 34 signs in 22 months and in four years knew 132.

Koko, the gorilla, learned enough signs to ask and respond to questions, to tell how she felt, and even to tell a lie. Francine Patterson, Koko's trainer, and a doctoral candidate at Stanford University at the time, became interested in the project when she learned about the Gardners' work with Washoe. Koko eventually developed a working vocabulary of 375 signs although she was recorded using as many as-645. Koko was pictured on the cover—she took the picture herself—of the October 1978 issue of *National Geographic*. The magazine printed a story of Patterson and her work with Koko entitled, "Conversations With a Gorilla." This interest in teaching chimps and apes sign language, of course, led to some wisecracks with oral-manual overtones. One went: "Which would you prefer: to be able to talk like a parrot or sign like a monkey?" In the hallway of a pure oral school was hung a picture of Washoe signing; under the picture was a handwritten note: "Do you want to be like her?"

The I-Love-You symbol which dates as far back as 1905 was resurrected and became universally popular. The king and queen of Sweden used it when visiting a school for deaf children recently. President Gerald Ford learned it when he was visited at the White House by Miss 1972 Deaf America, Ann Billington Bahl, and Miss 1974 Deaf America, Pam Young. While running for president, Jimmy Carter learned it on the campaign trail in Kansas City, Missouri, when he met a group of deaf people at one of his rallies. A picture of him using the symbol appeared in the national press. Following his election, *Time* magazine printed a color picture of him using the symbol during his inauguration walk down Pennsylvania Avenue in response to greetings from a crowd of deaf well-wishers. (Vice President Walter Mondale, following in an open car, unfamiliar with the symbol, but gamely trying to respond to the same group, was seen innocently waving an obscene gesture!)

Sign language classes spread. Some congressmen took classes at Gallaudet College; others hired teachers for themselves and their staffs. During the Carter administration, members of the White House security staff learned sign language. Deaf tourists to the White House were surprised to be asked in sign language if they had any questions. More churches began offering interpreted services. Government agencies, private industry, museums, and dinner theaters began offering interpreter services or sign language classes. Many police and fire departments trained their firefighters in basic signs so they could deal effectively with deaf persons in emergencies. The U.S. Park Service added interpreters to some of their regional historical tour sites and hired deaf guides. Some television networks began brief interpreted news programs for their deaf viewers and a few others employed deaf newscasters.

> Political candidates began including interpreters with their television ads. Ex-Lax Pharmaceutical Company became one of the first to include an interpreter with their national television commercial. Among those who saw it was Alan Coren, editor of the British humor weekly *Punch,* who commented: "Just the other night in Boston, we saw an Ex-Lax ad for the deaf on the telly. Ah, thank God for America, where the deaf get constipated, too."

Deaf customers around the country were pleased to note the increase in number of business establishments that had a person who could sign. Store clerks at a Washington, D.C., area store began wearing "I Sign" buttons. Fifteen Sears stores in Orange County, California, hired Santa Clauses who could sign for the benefit of deaf children. Macy's in New York City provided interpreters for its Puppet Theatre. Pan Am Airlines accepted sign language as meeting a foreign language requirement in their stewardess training program, and many stewardesses on that airline began using signs to serve their deaf passengers better.

Participants attending the National Association of the Deaf convention at the Olympic Hotel in Seattle, Washington, in 1974 were greeted with cheerful "Good morning" signs, or asked if they would like some coffee by waitresses using signs in the hotel restaurant. Larry Peterson had taught some 40 hotel employees basic signs prior to the convention.

So many people were using simultaneous communication that at times deaf people could not tell if the stranger signing and mouthing words was a deaf or hearing person. Perhaps the biggest surprise of all was the announcement that both oral and manual interpreters would be provided at the Alexander Graham Bell Association convention being held in St. Louis in the summer of 1978.

Community Theatres of the deaf using deaf and hearing actors became popular in the late 1970s. By 1980 there were over 50 such theatrical groups around the country.

In 1974, "Sign Me Alice," was written by Gilbert Eastman, a deaf playwright. It was the first play of its kind. It was a delightfully funny play in sign language, a comedy spoofing sign language and the various sign systems of the day. George Detmold called it "the most popular play ever shown at Gallaudet; it had the longest run, the largest audience, the greatest critical acclaim."

"Tales from a Club Room," another original play, premiered at the National Association of the Deaf centennial convention in Cincinnati, Ohio, in 1980. Written by Eugene Bergman and Bernard Bragg, it was performed with heavy emphasis on American Sign Language.

But oralism was not without its influence. Times had changed. As more and more people learned more about American Sign Language many teachers of deaf children and deaf adults realized that what they had been using in everyday conversation was not pure ASL, as they had thought, but a combination of ASL and English. Some called it "Pidgin Signed English" and others, "Manual English." Signing in an English context, of course, was nothing new. It was the labels that changed. Signing in an English context, in the 1940s for example was referred to as using the "correct language of signs" and called "Straight English." G. Dewey Coats who coined the term, "Manual English" in 1948, called its users "the hallmark of the better educated deaf person."

There remained, of course, those who preferred "pure" American Sign Language. They believed that, since it was their natural language, they had the right to use ASL at all times. They believed that deaf children should be taught ASL before attempts were made to teach them English, their second language. They believed that deaf children should be introduced to deaf culture as early as possible. Said one ASL proponent: "ASL is very much a part of a deaf person. If you want to change ASL or take ASL away from that person, you are trying to take his or her identity away." Some ASL militants even went as far as to call post-lingual deaf persons who spoke well and used sign simultaneously, "hearing deaf persons."

Today an increasing number of deaf persons sign, fingerspell, and speak or mouth words simultaneously when talking in mixed crowds. Maintaining tightly closed lips is no longer in vogue. The old sign language masters would have winced at such a sight.

Deaf Poets' Society

SUBVERTING THE HEARING PARADIGM

WRITTEN BY

SUSAN BURCH

Hearing people commonly understand deafness as the inability to perceive sound. They see deafness as a communicative as well as a physical disability. But in the past few decades the Deaf community has sought actively to transform these narrow views, both within the Deaf community and "outside" in the hearing world. At the core of this transformation is the use of American Sign Language (ASL), not only as a means of communication among the deaf but also as a means of communication with the hearing world. ASL is, however, a language foreign to most of the hearing world. How, then, can this language bring the two worlds together? ASL poetry can help create a dialogue between the Deaf and hearing communities by illustrating the complexity and value of Deaf culture and of its means of communication. The work of Bernard Bragg, Clayton Valli, and the Flying Words Project will serve as examples.

Poetry has been traditionally an auditory art form. Rhyme, alliteration, and meter have always been meant for the appreciation of the ear, if only the internal ear. But poems never have been simply words. They are extensions of the self, the exploration of thoughts, moods, and feelings, even whole philosophies and cultures. Poetry demands a heightened sense of language and an appreciation of the psychological universe behind its linguistic structure. Assessing deaf poetry, therefore, can help the viewer understand not only one mode of communication between the Deaf and hearing communities, but also the entire world of the Deaf community—how the deaf want to be perceived and how they perceive themselves.

At the same time and by its very nature, ASL poetry subverts both the hearing and written paradigms normally associated with poetry. Signers and viewers of ASL poetry become the majority; the hearing audience become the minority. The discomfiture of this position, unusual in itself for the hearing, is intensified by the non-written and non-oral nature of ASL poetry and by the use of a language most hearing do not understand. This reversal of roles and this new kind of poetry become powerful challenges to old traditions and misconceptions, to normal concepts of poetry, and to the role of audience. Poetry is no longer abstract; in ASL it is a physical presence that cannot be avoided.

For the sake of efficiency and clarity, *deaf* will refer only to the audiological condition and to people who have this condition; uppercase *Deaf* will be used when referring to a particular group of people who use American Sign Language as their mode of communication, who are pre-lingually deaf, and whose identity is tied to cultural aspects of deafness—certain deaf associations, clubs, institutes, and so forth.

ASL is perhaps the most defining and unifying aspect of Deaf culture, and its history is reflective of the relationship between the Deaf and hearing worlds. The establishment in 1817 of the first permanent school for the Deaf, The American School for the Deaf, in Connecticut, began a tradition of sign-language-based education, a tradition that continued through most of the century. Schools became the centers of Deaf culture, the place where deaf children could meet, communicate in their natural language, and discover a culture that valued their experience.[1] By the latter half of the nineteenth century, however, hearing educators of the deaf from around the world voted to disregard sign language as a communication method and to focus on speech pathology—on oralism. In the U.S., heated debates raged over the correct course of deaf education because of this philosophy of "hearing knows best." The outcome of these debates permanently affected the culture, education, and identity of deaf people.[2] For nearly a century, deaf students would be taught almost exclusively by hearing teachers and exclusively by the oral method. Their marginalization was symbolized by a legacy of hearing presidents at the exclusively deaf liberal arts college, Gallaudet University.

The Deaf community in the first half of this century—subsumed by a hearing society and with its culture and language unnamed and unrecognized—displayed coherence and self-awareness in its battle to maintain Deaf cultural artifacts, particularly sign language. Deaf people petitioned school administrators and politicians, organized groups and campaigns, and began a successful grass-roots organization in order to mobilize against this infringement upon their cultural identity. By the 1940s and 1950s, they enjoyed tangible results, as schools for the deaf began to reinstate sign-language classes. The 1960s publications of Dr. William Stokoe's linguistic research on ASL, which proved the legitimacy of ASL as a language, encouraged its greater acceptance by educational specialists and by general society.[3] In 1988, Gallaudet students rallied for a deaf president, demonstrating their ability proactively to assert their identity and values and to insist upon a reinterpretation of Deaf-hearing relations.[4]

Deaf Americans as a whole now increasingly demand that others see them *not* as inferior, or even disabled, but simply as a linguistic minority.[5] The public acceptance of ASL thus snowballs in importance, because it forces the hearing community to acknowledge the identity of the Deaf community and its sense of self.[6] Deaf poetry directly confronts the issues—the perception of Deafness as a physical disability and as a barrier to communication—that still separate Deaf from mainstream society. ASL poetry represents an effort to reinterpret the meaning of Deafness and to reevaluate the relationship between the hearing and Deaf worlds.

There are two general movements in Deaf poetry. One adheres to the more traditional forms of both contemporary and classical written styles.[7] The other follows an older form in the

Deaf community—the equivalent of an oral tradition in the hearing community. The latter, called performance poetry or ASL poetry, is the focus of this paper. Like all poetry, ASL performance poems incorporate technical and structural facets, such as rhyme and meter, plays on words, similes, and alliteration, but they are interpreted into a visual dimension: "[an] alliteration of handshape, [a] rhyme of movement, [a] meter of sign, [a] rhythm of expression (articulation- enunciation-delivery), [and a] tone of non-manuals (emoting-inflecting)."[8] In addition, ASL makes use of poetic devices: "[s]ymbolic use of space and of directionality, [c]ertain handshapes that echo the actual image (like onomatopoeic sounds), [and] [i]ronic contrast between facial expression and what the hands are 'saying.'"[9] Although it exploits aspects of drama and mime, ASL poetry is not simply another art form:

> ASL poetry is a most unusual art form involving hand movement and hand shape in an exacting and flowing manner to convey the mood and emotion of the piece. It is a condensed sign technique that focuses on sign simplicity and economy of movement. It cannot be appreciated written down on paper—rather it must be seen as a "visual-spacial" poetry.[10]

On the artistic and academic level, performance poetry converts traditional poetic structures into performance structures while exploiting nontraditional uses of poetic language. For example, traditional poetic structures like rhyme schemes are achieved by the repetition of particular path movements of the hand (contour path rhyme), by repeating particular hand configurations (handshake rhyme), and by nonmanual signals (eyebrows, eye gaze, cheeks, mouth movement, head shift/body shift). By weaving similar handshapes into lines of poetry, Deaf poets create visual alliteration, and they can use contour paths of motion to create a sense of assonance.[11] Likewise, the intentional sculpting of certain handshapes that mirror the actual image creates a visual onomatopoeia. The elasticity of ASL and its inherent visual character extend creativity and expressions of plays on words by literally placing them in a new dimension—space. Meanings, images, and words literally become less flat, more active and expressive. By playing on signs that share similar configurations or spatial flow, ASL poets alter phonetic nuances into visual ones, one-dimensional words into three-dimensional shape.[12] The motion and pacing of poetry—rhythm—play out in the varied stress of syllables in English poems; ASL works use lexical signs, consisting of varied hold and movement segments that can produce syllabic meters.[13] Moreover, many ASL poets extend poetic boundaries by using a visual vernacular. The performer not only signs but also embodies various images and elements of the poem. In this way, the poet's body and the space between performer and audience become an intimate part of the text.[14]

The full physical experience of the performer—and frequently of the audience—also plays an important role in understanding the changing Deaf-hearing relationship. This physical interaction with and embodiment of the poem still require translation because they are not as overt as mime, which is disassociated altogether from language. However, the physicality of the poem adds new levels of poetic and linguistic meaning and creates an implicit political discourse between the Deaf and hearing worlds. By creating and performing ASL in their poetry, Deaf artists change the traditional Deaf-hearing relationship by asserting the identity of Deafness and Deaf culture as equal to—yet different from—that of the hearing world and its mode of communication. Deaf poetry forces the hearing community to reevaluate the view of ASL as an inferior form of English, incapable of complex concepts. It also creates a middle ground for interpretation and gives access to the Deaf community.

Visually, then, ASL poetry works as a potential bridge between languages—ASL and English—as well as between peoples—Deaf and hearing. In a world consumed with multimedia presentations and in their need to express themselves in clearer and more complex ways, contemporary poets increasingly focus on symbolic images.[15] In the audience this focus on the visual turns to the voyeuristic as we seek to look through the eyes of poets to understand the images.[16] Like other languages, ASL was constructed to satisfy the needs of the perceiver. It is thus visually oriented and requires eye contact.[17] That intimate bond, the eye-to-eye nature of the language, creates a different interaction between hearing and Deaf people. Literally faced with Deafness, audiences of ASL poetry (often the hearing) are drawn into the poems and become participants in the poetry of motion. Because the audience is present with the poet-performer, its responses—facial expressions, gestures, and the like—frame the meaning of every poem's interpretation. Both the poetic reinterpretation of space and the movements between the poet and the audience draw the spectator into the performance. The physicality of performance and the necessary physical proximity of performer and spectator establish a heightened sense of intimacy. Direct eye contact seals this connection, for the audience literally cannot close its eyes to such a reading of an ASL poem. Focused on the performer, locked into her or his gaze, the viewer simultaneously can watch the performance and see through the poet's eyes. The physical recognition of this experience joins the mind and body in a way that subverts the abstraction of written poetry and its interpretation and makes the poem a shared experience, the most intimate form of communication.

While ASL relies on visual imagery, arguably the most universal mode of communication, access to the meaning of ASL performance poems remains a significant issue. The extent to which non-signing audiences can comprehend the multifaceted meaning and various levels of poetry often depends directly on the use of sign-language interpreters who simultaneously "voice" the signed poem. The varying need for such interpreters is symbolic of the heterogeneity of the ASL poetic community and of the diversity and complexity of Deaf-hearing relations. No matter how the deaf poet prefers to communicate with his or her audience, the spectators participate in the execution of an ASL poem: they become part of the poetic text, responding to the visual reading in visible, physical ways. Consequently, ASL poems change in meaning and nuance with every "reading" or performance. And, once the poem is finished, it becomes ephemeral—there is no written form. Thus the audience must rely, as most deaf people do, on its memory and discussion of the performance. They must retain in their mind's eye the essential image of the poem.

ASL poetry, like the Deaf community, cannot be reduced to a homogeneous category. Acclaimed ASL poets Bernard Bragg, Clayton Valli, and The Flying Words Project (composed of hearing interpreter/poet Kenny Lerner and Deaf poet Peter Cook) each represent distinct responses to the role and meaning of the audience in their works. Bragg primarily offers signed interpretations of classic ("hearing") written poetry as well as of his own poetry.[18] Bragg's ASL works reflect a deep commitment to traditional poetic norms. For example, his experimentation with hand shapes and ASL forms creates visual parallels to alliteration and onomatopoeia. Moreover, many of his works are recorded on paper, and he offers spoken or closed-captioned translations of his performances. As the title of his book, *Meeting Halfway in American Sign Language,* implies, Bragg writes ASL poetry to express his experiences as a deaf man, but he aims his message at a predominantly hearing audience. Therefore, *Meeting Halfway in American Sign Language* is coauthored by hearing teacher, researcher, and author Jack Olson. The goal of Bragg's work is to educate and to create common ground between hearing and Deaf people.[19]

In his own ASL poem "Culture," Bragg exemplifies these points. "Culture" is published in both written and signed format:

> Culture, deaf communication
> > Hearing people aside
> > Hearing mind aside
> > Listen with ears, no!
> > Listen with eyes, yes!
> Force you? Force me? No!
> > You and me
> Part of one culture

As is clear from the photographic frames picturing his signing of the poem (see illustrations), Bragg uses only two handshapes, *C* and *D* (perhaps to emphasize the ideas of deafness and culture).[20] Whereas hearing people create assonance or alliteration by using only words that start, for example, with the letters *a* or *d*, Bragg creates them by playing with signs. There are a multitude of signs that use the handshape for *C* and *D*. What makes them different words or concepts is the position of the hands. For example, the sign for *democracy* is the handshape *d,* but the hand is shaken at chest level off to the side of the body. The sign for *deaf* is still the handshape *d,* but the pointer finger moves from the ear down to the chin. Just because the handshape looks like the letter does not mean, however, that the word it represents begins with that letter. The sign for hearing people also begins with the handshape for *d,* but the palm side of the hand is facing the body and horizontal, while the pointer finger twirls in front of the lips. The symmetry of Bragg's handshapes and the location of signs to both his right and left side create visual alliteration and onomatopoeia while also symbolizing the message of his piece—the marriage between Deaf and hearing cultures. Likewise, throughout the piece Bragg looks at the audience, establishing with the viewer a direct eye contact that makes the two equals. The only moment he breaks eye contact is when he focuses on the signs *one culture,* which also forces the viewer to look at the concept (represented literally and symbolically in the sign).

Ultimately, however, Bragg's attempt to demonstrate the validity and potential of ASL as a means of communication between hearing and Deaf is restricted by his adherence to hearing norms of poetry. His poetry does not attempt to create ASL poetry, but instead focuses on proving that ASL can be adapted to the English language and its modes of communication. This attitude in many ways imprisons a language created and maintained to counter the limitation of the recorded, phonocentric word.

Clayton Valli, in stark contrast, creates and executes his poems in a more pure ASL form. His explicit intention is to celebrate Deaf culture, and he focuses on ASL as both the medium and symbol of his work.[21] Valli's works, for those who understand ASL, offer a creative and powerful expression of Deaf values and politics and demonstrate the subtle nuances of ASL.[22] Valli's themes rely heavily on Deaf issues—education, technology, and communication—and he consciously denies access to non-signers by refusing written or voiced translations of his poems.

Valli searches for no common ground between hearing and Deaf worlds. Indeed, his rigorous attention to technical aspects of ASL as well as to his overt political message epitomize his desire to undermine the hegemony of hearing perceptions of the Deaf community and of its language as lacking or disadvantaged.[23] By forcing his audience to understand him in only a Deaf language (ASL), he compels all discourse to enter a realm dominated by a historically voiceless minority. Ironically, while Valli exploits ASL's visual qualities to a greater degree than does Bragg, Valli still confines himself to traditional poetic norms, emphasizing, for instance, line breaks through repeated movement, spatial locations, and hand configurations. Nonetheless, his works represent the most explicit attempt to alter Deaf-hearing communication.

Perhaps the most complex approach to the Deaf-hearing paradigm using the vehicle of ASL poetry can be found in the poetry of the Flying Words Project (FWP): Peter Cook is a Deaf performance poet and Kenny Lerner is a hearing poet-interpreter. They write their work together, although they are often geographically separated. They meet to combine work and brainstorm. Both are avid readers of Beat poetry and are particularly influenced by Allen Ginsberg. Their approach represents the most radical experimentation in the structure of ASL poetry. To express its goal of conveying clear images and concepts, FWP emphasizes visual imagery. Because the aim of FWP's poetry is clarity of thought and image, it does not focus on a "Deaf message" as do Valli's and (to a lesser extent) Bragg's poetry. Rather, FWP views ASL performance poetry as the natural extension, even the merger of hearing and Deaf poetic traditions.[24] Since the quest for clarity of meaning and the emphasis on image in poetry are fulfilled in ASL's inherent qualities, FWP uses Lerner's voice in performed poems only to complement specific signs rather than to translate the larger piece.[25] Although this spoken version affords greater access to a non-signing audience, Peter Cook's expressive body and face, plus his ability to sculpt space, remain the consistent and primary focus of the performance, allowing the natural asset of ASL—its image orientation—to transcend phonetics and speak for itself. Such an approach to language and to poetry changes the role of the audience. For FWP, the intention is not to polarize a performance into Deaf and hearing versions, but to "convey meanings in the most clear, accessible way for all members of the audience."[26]

Flying Words Project's poems focus primarily on universal, historical human experiences and emotions. They consequently offer a more complex and nuanced view of Deafness by not limiting their repertoire to Deaf-only topics. Even in their poem "I Am Ordered Now to Talk," FWP addresses the general experience of oppression through a direct and personal reflection on a painful encounter between the Deaf and hearing worlds. This poem deserves special attention for its interplay between the specific use and meaning of ASL poetry for self-expression and its impact on a predominantly hearing audience. "I Am Ordered Now to Talk" describes the lessons in speech pathology that Cook had to take when he was a young boy, then moves into his larger struggle for identity, expression, and understanding.

The presentation of "I Am Ordered Now to Talk" exploits several levels of poetic communication. A written form of the poem is dispersed among the audience before Cook and Lerner, in switched roles, perform. Lerner (the hearing interpreter) signs the poem while Cook (the deaf poet) uses his voice to read it. Standing side by side, Cook and Lerner force the audience to struggle to interpret Cook's voiced words, which are truncated and unclear. Simultaneously, the non-signing audience naturally searches the written page for a more accessible means to understanding the poem. Concurrently, Lerner signs the words and letters. In so doing, he demonstrates the clarity of ASL—the natural language for Deaf people. For example, the signed letters B and P have, visually, almost no similarity; however, phonetically, they are very similar and thus pose a barrier for Deaf people trying to read lips or learn pronunciation. Of particular interest is the execution of these lines in the poem: Lerner, leaving his location on the stage, moves and stands behind Cook, and, from there, signs the letters on alternate arms. Cook simultaneously pronounces the letters, but the most lucid distinction between the letters is the *visual* component: Lerner symbolically gives Cook a clear voice by adding his outstretched, signing arms to Cook's relatively still body. Cook rapid-fires a list of such letters, B and P among them, and his attempt literally to speak to the audience (on its terms) such letters and words beginning with them reiterates the point of language and natural expression: clarity of words is lost. However, the visual aspects of this poem—the pained facial expressions, Lerner's use of body shifts and spatial references for specific letters, and the visual asymmetry of Cook's closed body and Lerner's outstretched, communicating arms— convey the meaning with precision and power.

The audience is faced with a physical text on stage: two bodies. The audience is not limited to reading the physical text from left to right but is challenged to read the performances simultaneously, from head to foot and foot to head, audibly and visually, and to contrast the performers' use of space, face, body, and voice. And the written form, while adding meaning, cannot describe the pained expressions, the incomprehensible speech of Cook, the sharp execution of Lerner's signs, or the experiential meaning. Moreover, as non-signers search the page in front of them, they miss part of the poem before them, creating an anxiety not dissimilar from the frustration Deaf people feel when reading lips and functioning in a world hostile to their needs. Although the poem condemns strict oralism and hearing domination, it also speaks to being misunderstood, being unheard, being alone. It confronts the struggle for human communication, the need to make meaning, and the experience of life.

The issues involved in ASL poetry represent the greater issues facing the Deaf community: how it perceives its community and future and what new boundaries, or lack thereof, will exist between hearing and Deaf people. ASL performance poetry not only leads to a sense of greater cohesiveness among the Deaf community but also provides the medium in and through which hearing people must reassess the Deaf-hearing relationship. This type of performance poetry also creates an opportunity for the hearing to experience otherness. By being the minority during ASL performances, the hearing can literally see what the Deaf community daily faces: the difficulty of understanding and of being understood, the feeling of being considered dumb, the sense of being unheard and of being invisible.

Because ASL poetry defies the reduction of language to a linear and phonocentric model, it challenges everyone to push the linguistic envelope of expression and communication. "Words" are no longer that which is spoken and written; poetry becomes a language of motions in space and time. Through these challenges, ASL poetry creates a new arena in which both Deaf and hearing can explore meaning, expression, and understanding within their common world.

NOTES

1. The role of deaf teachers of the deaf cannot be understated in this matter. Since the vast majority deaf people have hearing parents, siblings, and children, access to Deaf culture frequently is limited or impossible. Deaf cultural transmission across the generations, therefore, habitually occurred from the interaction of deaf children and deaf adults.

2. Various works address the oral-manual debate. See John V. Van Cleve and Barry A. Crouch, *A Place of Their Own: Creating the Deaf Community in America* (Washington, D.C.: Gallaudet Univ. Press, 1989); and Richard Winefield, *Never the Twain Shall Meet: Bell, Gallaudet, and the Communications Debate* (Washington, D.C.: Gallaudet Univ. Press, 1987).

3. See William C. Stokoe, *Sign Language Structure: The First Linguistic Analysis of American Sign Language,* Studies in Linguistics Occasional Paper 8 (Buffalo, N.Y.: Univ. of Buffalo Press, 1960).

4. Scholarly works on Deaf cultural history continue to increase. For examples, see Jack R. Gannon, *Deaf Heritage: A Narrative History of Deaf America* (Silver Spring, Md.: National Association of the Deaf, 1981); John V. Van Cleve, ed., *Gallaudet Encyclopedia of Deaf People and Deafness,* 3 vols. (New York: McGraw-Hill, 1987); Susan Burch, "History Misinterpreted: American Deaf History, 1917–1953," (paper presented at the Deaf Studies IV Conference, Woburn, Mass., 1995). For a more general approach to Deaf culture, see Carol Padden and Tom Humphries, *Deaf in America: Voices from a Culture* (Cambridge, Mass.: Harvard Univ. Press, 1988), or Oliver Sacks, *Seeing Voices: A Journey into the World of the Deaf* (New York: HarperCollins, 1989).

5. For literary images of Deaf people, see Brian Grant, comp., *The Quiet Ear: Deafness in Literature* (Boston, Mass.: Faber and Faber, 1987). Excellent linguistic analyses of ASL can be found in Edward Klima and Ursula Bellugi, *The Signs of Language* (Cambridge, Mass.: Harvard Univ. Press, 1979) or their work, *Poetry and Song in a Language without Sound* (n.p., 1976).

6. This struggle is hardly over. It should be noted that the Modern Language Association still does not recognize ASL as a foreign language but categorizes it as an artificial language. Fortunately, that issue is currently being addressed.

7. For signed examples, see Bernard Bragg, *Creative Interpretation of Literature in Sign* (Rochester, N.Y.: National Technical Institute for the Deaf, 1986), video; Eric Malzkuhn, *The Jabberwock with Dramatic Interpretations* (Washington, D.C.: Maryland Secondary School for the Deaf, 1975), video. For written forms see Jill Jepson, ed., *No Walls of Stone: An Anthology of Literature by Deaf and Hard of Hearing Writers* (Washington, D.C.: Gallaudet Univ. Press, 1992); David Wright, *Nerve Ends* (London: Hodder and Stoughton, 1969); Robert Panara, *The Silent Muse: An Anthology of Prose and Poetry by the Deaf* (Toronto: Gallaudet College Alumni Assoc., 1960).

8. Bernard Bragg and Jack R. Olson, *Meeting Halfway in American Sign Language: A Common Ground for Effective Communication among Deaf and Hearing People* (Rochester, N.Y.: Deaf Life Press, 1994), 149.

9. Ibid.

10. Ibid., 133.

11. For examples, see Clayton Valli, "Poetics of American Sign Language Poetry" (Ph.D. diss., Union Institute Graduate School, New York, 1995), 37; and Bragg and Olson.

12. Flying Words Project, personal interview, 15 November, 1995. An excellent example of this is in Flying Word Project's poem, "Poetry Around the World."

13. Bragg and Olson, 27.

14. For examples, see Flying Words Project's poem, "Poetry" or Valli's "Lone Sturdy Tree."

15. Allen Ginsberg's poetry, with its emphasis on image and story, for example, continues to influence FWP poetry.

16. For example, in the FWP poem "Poetry," the audience watches Cook in front of them as he paints on an imaginary canvas. When Cook shifts his body, the perspective changes, and the audience then views the painting from the vantage point of the artist, experiencing the act of painting simultaneously with (or through) the painter.

17. It also satisfies the communicator's needs by presenting the most accessible, natural tool for expression—the body.

18. For example, Bragg offers a signed interpretation of Robert Frost's "Stopping by Woods on a Snowy Evening" in Bragg and Olson, 118–27.

19. For more information on Bragg, see Bernard Bragg, *Lessons in Laughter: The Autobiography of a Deaf Actor* (Washington, D.C.: Gallaudet Univ. Press, 1989).

20. Bragg and Olson, 145–48.

21. Clayton Valli offers an insightful critique of Deaf culture in his work ASL PAH!: *Deaf Students' Perspective on Their Language* (Burtonsville, Md.: Linstok Press, 1992), video.

22. Interpretations of Deaf values vary, but common factors include the use of sign language, participation in Deaf clubs, pride in Deaf history, support of Deaf institutes, appreciation of common experiences caused by being Deaf, and so forth.

23. For examples of his work, see Clayton Valli, *Poetry in Motion: Original Works in* ASL (Burtonsville, Md.: Sign Media, Inc., 1990), video series; ASL *Poetry: Selected Works of Clayton Valli* (San Diego, Calif.: DawnSign Press, 1995), video.

24. A focused discussion of this merger can be found in Jim Cohn, "The New Deaf Poetics: Visible Poetry," *Sign Language Studies* 52 (1986): 263–77.

25. Flying Words Project Performance, Hudson Valley Community College, N.Y., November, 1988; Flying Words Project Performance, Colorado College, Colorado Springs, Colo., 1990.

26. Kenny Lerner, personal interview, 15 November, 1995.

What Is Deaf Art?

WRITTEN BY

DE'VIA

Eight Deaf artists gathered for a four-day workshop immediately before the Deaf Way arts festival at Gallaudet University in May, 1989. At this workshop, led by Betty G. Miller and Paul Johnston, these artists produced the following manifesto, defining Deaf Culture Art, which they called De'VIA, short for Deaf View/Image Art

THE DE'VIA MANIFESTO
DEAF VIEW/IMAGE ART

De'VIA represents Deaf artists and perceptions based on their Deaf experiences. It uses formal art elements with the intention of expressing innate cultural or physical Deaf experience. These experiences may include Deaf metaphors, Deaf perspectives, and Deaf insight in relationship with the environment (both the natural world and Deaf cultural environment), spiritual and everyday life.

De'VIA can be identified by formal elements such as Deaf artists' possible tendency to use contrasting colors and values, intense colors, contrasting textures. It may also most often include a centralized focus, with exaggeration or emphasis on facial features, especially eyes, mouths, ears, and hands. Currently, Deaf artists tend to work in human scale with these exaggerations, and not exaggerate the space around these elements.

There is a difference between Deaf artists and De'VIA. Deaf artists are those who use art in any form, media, or subject matter, and who are held to the same artistic standards as other artists. De'VIA is created when the artist intends to express their Deaf experience through visual art. De'VIA may also be created by deafened or hearing artists, if the intention is to create work that is born of their Deaf experience (a possible example would be a hearing child of Deaf parents). It is clearly possible for Deaf artists not to work in the area of De'VIA.

While applied and decorative arts may also use the qualities of De'VIA (high contrast, centralized focus, exaggeration of specific features), this manifesto is specifically written to cover the traditional fields of visual fine arts (painting, sculpture, drawing, photography, printmaking) as well as alternative media when used as fine arts such as fiber arts, ceramics, neon, and collage.

Created in May, 1989, at The Deaf Way.

The signatories were: Dr. Betty G. Miller, painter; Dr. Paul Johnston, sculptor; Dr. Deborah M. Sonnenstrahl, art historian; Chuck Baird, painter; Guy Wonder, sculptor; Alex Wilhite, painter; Sandi Inches Vasnick, fiber artist; Nancy Creighton, fiber artist; and Lai-Yok Ho, video artist.

Dysconscious Audism

A THEORETICAL PREPOSITION

WRITTEN BY

GENIE GERTZ

DYSCONSCIOUS RACISM
AND DYSCONSCIOUS AUDISM

In Joyce King's work on dysconscious racism, she shares her interpretation of how her university students perceived the meaning of racial inequity. She claims that her students exhibited uncritical ways of thinking about racial inequity: they did not think of the underlying causes of racism and, more importantly, possible solutions to racism. To think critically is to explore, analyze, and evaluate thoroughly the conditions caused by racism. Why did a certain situation happen and how can it be improved or modified? Instead, her students accepted and perpetuated "certain culturally sanctioned assumptions, myths and beliefs." King discovered that students had "impaired consciousness" of what racism means due to their limited understanding and experience.[1]

King then defines dysconscious racism as a form of racism that implicitly accepts dominant white norms and privileges. She emphasizes that it is not the absence of consciousness but rather impaired consciousness that engendered this term. When challenged to think critically, we must question the ideology of racial inequity and be able to identify and criticize it objectively. The students did not recognize that structural inequity is linked to racial inequity as a form of exploitation. King's students were aware of the racial issues, racial inequity, and racial prejudice. However, they lacked the depth of ethical judgment connected to formulating some rationale for inequity. King realized that their thinking was impaired when analyzing racial ideology. King builds a framework for us to recognize dysconscious racism where an analysis can be developed of how clearly people understand the consciousness of minority groups.

Some Deaf people do experience an impaired consciousness the same way students experienced it in King's study. Some Deaf people, though they resist being assimilated into the dominant culture, still incorporate some antithetical values from the dominant culture. In this manner, these Deaf individuals experience an impaired consciousness: a phenomenon for which I coined the term "dysconscious audism." This is a new concept and I have created this phrase based on Joyce King's work on dysconscious racism.

With the term "dysconscious audism," I describe a phenomenon that is defined as a form of audism that tacitly accepts dominant hearing norms and privileges. It is not the absence of consciousness but an impaired consciousness or distorted way of thinking about Deaf consciousness. "Dysconscious audism" adheres to the ideology that hearing society, because it is dominant, is more appropriate than the Deaf society. Such Deaf people can be characterized as not having fully developed Deaf consciousness connected to the Deaf identity, and they may still feel the need to assimilate into the mainstream culture.

DR. RACHEL STONE AND THE CALIFORNIA SCHOOL FOR THE DEAF, RIVERSIDE: AUDISM AND DYSCONSCIOUS AUDISM

In the year 2000. California School for the Deaf, Riverside (CSDR) selected Dr. Rachel Stone as the superintendent.[2] She became the first Deaf and female to head the school. Less than two years after the appointment. Dr. Stone was dismissed, likely for her strong views of Deaf bilingualism and biculturalism on educating Deaf students. She also emphasized the importance of bilingualism for the students—with equal importance placed on both English and American Sign Language (ASL). Her priority was student success, as she saw no reason that the deaf could not receive quality education. Dr. Stone believed that effective pedagogical approaches specifically appropriate for Deaf students would make all the difference in their academic success, which up to this point had not been progressing sufficiently. Dr. Stone's desire for an effective bilingual-bicultural environment was simply oppressed by administrators, teachers, and parents who espoused traditional hearing centric education for the CSDR students and wanted to see that system remain status quo. Quite a few Deaf staff along with some hearing individuals did take a position in support of Dr. Stone and fought valiantly on her behalf. However, a sizable number of Deaf teachers, administrators, and parents who supported her philosophical stance stood helplessly in the ouster of Dr. Stone as CSDR Superintendent.[3]

The unwillingness to accept Dr. Stone's leadership and vision for a Deaf bilingualism and bicultural education at CSDR reveals the hidden power of oppression; namely, audism. It has a strong bearing on the hearing supremacy in educating deaf learners, even in a Deaf school setting like CSDR. While the term audism is not yet inserted in dictionaries, an in-depth treatise on audism can be obtained by reading Dirksen Bauman's article "Audism: Exploring the Metaphysics of Oppression."[4] His article will strive to further define the term as well. Some CSDR members were clearly audists in their overthrow of Dr. Stone. As for those Deaf administrators, teachers, and parents who took no action to aid Dr. Stone, even though they supported her goals for CSDR, why did they do nothing for her? The term dysconscious audism might provide some explanation for their lack of action in taking a strong stand for her and indirectly for themselves. This article will both introduce the concept of dysconscious audism, as well as present a theoretical proposition of it. Further examples will best illustrate the important features of dysconscious audism and its strong connection to audism.

DEAF EDUCATION AGENDA
CONTROLLED BY HEARING EDUCATORS

Now more than ever, I see so many issues at hand, especially with the larger society due to its lack of understanding about Deaf language, heritage, and culture. The true benefits of education escape most Deaf individuals because a large majority of hearing educators controls the "deaf education" agenda, which is laden with misconceptions.

To make matters worse, even as more effective means of educating Deaf individuals are demonstrated, Deaf language and culture are still not receiving widespread acceptance in classroom.[5]

Hearing educators' main focus is on the stigma that Deaf individuals need to be "fixed" to correct their hearing and speaking deficiencies. More often than not, this further perpetuates society's larger view of Deaf people as inferior and subhuman and who need to be "rehabilitated" into being like hearing individuals for the sole purpose of assimilating them into mainstream American society.[6]

Basically, this is a classic example of ethnocentrism. However, it does not mean that hearing educators who are comfortable subscribing to Deaf bilingualism/biculturalism cannot be our allies. At present, the system of educating deaf individuals is failing to meet their educational and societal needs. There is a very common pattern among Deaf individuals who are kept away from effective visual language and a rich cultural heritage. As a result, many of them proceed through school life without a sense of direction. To properly educate and motivate Deaf individuals in life, we must see that, first and foremost, they are treated as human beings and are empowered with a natural language and rich cultural heritage.

Let's look at the story of Dr. Stone's ouster at CSDR once again. Were CSDR Deaf people's perceptions of their experience shifting away from Deaf empowerment toward the hearing dominant majority? They might have unwittingly accepted the changing Values in the Deaf community to "please" the hearing world. Do Deaf people, generally speaking, experience the loss of their Deaf empowerment? Is the loss of their Deaf center creating Deaf individuals who view the Deaf world differently? Without Deaf empowerment, the Deaf consciousness is affected, becomes chaotic, and brings nothing in the world from Deaf people but a strange version of hearing people. The voice from Deaf-empowered individuals is critical to creating a just society of Deaf people.

DEAF CONSCIOUSNESS TOWARD AUDISM

In order to explore the impact of audism on the lives of Deaf individuals, I conducted an ethnographic study that included eight Deaf adults of Deaf parents who were selected for the study to validate the existence of oppression on Deaf people.[7] They shared their experiences as members of the Deaf community. They have had Deaf Culture, American Sign Language, and other features that made being Deaf a positive experience. At the same time, they faced the negative experiences of oppression. Oppression has continually and, in most cases, surreptitiously been interwoven into the lives of Deaf people, Including their own life encounters that are layered with audism.

The oppression of Deaf people appears to be omnipresent and everlasting. Some of the eight Deaf adults of Deaf parents experienced firsthand the prohibition of the use of sign language because they were told that sign language would ruin their chance for succeeding in American society. Some witnessed hearing people's devaluation of Deaf people's attempt to build up their Deaf identity. Some valued a strong Deaf identity to counteract their indoctrination about the superiority of hearing people's language, identity, education, and community/culture.[3] They expressed the awareness of hearing people who tried to recast Deaf people into the image of hearing people, but as lesser citizens in the hearing world. Some of them noted that hearing educators reported the deficiencies of Deaf learners in order to justify and validate themselves as worthy individuals or as acknowledged experts on the education of so-called helpless Deaf individuals. As a consequence, the hearing populace supported the hearing educators' plan of action in educating deaf children. Some saw that hearing people discredited Deaf people's yearning for their own community and culture. Even the history of Deaf community/culture had no meaning to such hearing people. All they wanted to do was erase Deaf Culture and history. In the name of their expertise on deafness, these hearing people felt obligated to eliminate deafness, by any means, as well as Deaf people whom they thought brought an embarrassment to the society.[8]

Below are the examples of situations as described by each to illustrate the different forms of oppression that are structural rather than individual, often happening in relationships between hearing and Deaf groups. Alan commented about the oralists from the Alexander Graham Bell Organization who tried to put a stop to sign language being promoted in public through an NBC television show. Bonnie encountered a hearing woman working at a school for the deaf who could not sign at all. The school for the deaf was ready to dismiss Bonnie because she took a position challenging to the nonsigning woman. Carl related the frustrations of his father, who was a top-notch printer but never received a bonus for his excellence at work while his hearing counterparts who showed less commitment to work received the bonuses. When Felicia was a young girl, she saw her deaf classmates beaming with pride for being rewarded for good speech while she was slapped by her teachers for signing. As an adult, Felicia looked back to that scene and cringed at the overemphasis on speech and underemphasis on real education. Edward reported that there were no history books on Deaf people when he was growing up. Debbie made a choice to attend a regular university with the provision of support services to Deaf students. At one time, she wanted to drop out of the university due to her frustration over dealing with incompetent interpreters who made her feel more isolated from her professors and fellow classmates by interfering with direct communication. As a native signer of ASL, Glenn found SimCom (an abbreviated term of Simultaneous Communication, which refers to the simultaneous use of signing and speaking) to be an obstacle to him in terms of undermining his comprehension of what was being said. Yet SimCom continued on no matter how many Deaf individuals held it to be an abomination. Helen mentioned a hearing-oriented media report that glowed with praise for former Miss America Heather Whitestone's decision to gel a cochlear implant. In that case, Helen argued, the media had no clue as to why the Deaf world did not applaud Whitestone in the way the hearing world did.

The thoughts and feelings as expressed by the eight Deaf persons in the above paragraph necessitate the attention to the term audism. These stories confirmed the existence of a deep-layered shroud of audism. Because of the prevalence of audist practices, both conscious and unconscious. Deaf people are oppressed in many ways. See Figure 1 for effects of audism on Deaf individuals. Presently, there is still a sizable group of Deaf people who would be categorized as "dysconscious audists" because they haven't developed their own Deaf consciousness and identity to the fullest. Generally their Deaf consciousness is distorted to varying degrees. Dysconscious audistic Deaf people unwillingly help to continue the kind of victimized thinking that they are responsible for their failure. Such thinking enables hearing people to continue pathologizing Deaf people.

Figure 1. Effects of audism on the Deaf individual.

The marked difference between "unconscious" and "dysconscious" when used with the word audism is that the word unconscious implies that the person is completely unaware whereas the word dysconscious implies that the person does have an inkling of his or her consciousness but does not yet realize it is impaired. Some Deaf individuals choose to do nothing about it or to take a "so be it" attitude. In this manner, it is not that they are completely unaware of the issues; it's just their decision on how to live with them.

With the "dysconscious audism" framework in mind, the weakening of Deaf identity associates with the lack of Deaf consciousness within the present context and the impact of hegemonic forces. Hearing people's obsession over the cure of deafness contributes significantly to the weakening of Deaf people's identity. When the Deaf person's identity is distorted, they cannot fully understand their own behavior. A large number of Deaf individuals are not even aware that they possess, to varying degrees, these kinds of audistic behaviors and attitudes. The critical features of dysconscious audism are the following:

- Dysconscious audism disempowers Deaf people from becoming liberated.
- Dysconscious audism disables Deaf people from expressing Deaf cultural pride.
- Dysconscious audism intimidates Deaf people and limits their promotion of the Deaf perspective.
- Dysconscious audism hinders Deaf people from attaining quality education.
- Dysconscious audism denies Deaf people full acceptance of ASL.
- Dysconscious audism weakens Deaf people in the development of their Deaf identity.

Upon the Formation of a Visual Variety of the Human Race

WRITTEN BY

BENJAMIN BAHAN

In New York City, a father and daughter sat in a café people-watching out the window and drinking coffee.

"Look across the street," signed the father.

His daughter quickly scoped the busy street packed with people hustling to and fro before quizzically looking back at her dad.

"One of them is deaf ... which one is it?" he asked.

She looked back and scanned the crowd. She noticed one man's eyes glancing from side to side. "The one with the brown overcoat," she guessed.

"I agree. Let's watch and see," he suggested.

The man in the brown overcoat was about to cross the street, but sensed the sudden shift in the crowd of people around him as they simultaneously looked in the same direction. He decided he too should check in that direction and saw sirens and flashing lights accompanying a speeding ambulance. After the commotion subsided, he crossed the street and continued walking past the café. The father waved his hands in the man's periphery. In the middle of a bustling city, the man in the brown overcoat noticed a flutter of hands through the window and quickly turned to see the father and his daughter.

"You deaf?" signed the father.

The man was astounded and asked, "How did you know?"

PEOPLE OF THE EYE

The characters in this short story are unique in that they inhabit a highly visual world. They use a visual language to communicate and have developed a visual system of adaptation to orient them in the world that defines their way of being. This is not an unusual story. Episodes like this have been shared and reported all over the world. The claim that deaf people are highly visual and tactile is not a new concept. It has been stated time and time again in various sources—both in writing and through the air ("orally"). The most notable statement came from George Veditz, who eloquently commented at the National Association

227

of the Deaf convention in Colorado in 1910, "... [Deaf people] are first, last and of all time the people of the eye."

The strongest support for the notion put forward by Veditz (and others) is the emergence of a visual-gestural language. Since the dawn of time, whenever and wherever there were deaf people on earth, a visual communication system (using gestures, mime, and home signs) would be developed to convey thoughts, feelings, desires, and ideas. Although there is no written record of this phenomenon from ancient times, one of the earliest recorded observations of deaf people using gestures and signs is found in Plato's *Cratylus*. In ensuing dialogue between Socrates, Hermogenes, and Cratylus on issues of names and language, Socrates made an observation in reference to deaf people using gestures/signs in Athens around 400 to 350 BCE:

> "Suppose that we had no voice or tongue, and wanted to communicate with one another. Should we not, like the deaf and dumb, make signs with the hands and head and the rest of the body?"

Observations of deaf people creating visual-gestural communication do not only occur in major metropolitan areas but also in isolated places around the globe from the jungles of the Amazon to the many islands scattered all over the world's oceans. In essence this discussion highlights what Veditz also said a few years later in 1913, "As long as we have deaf people on earth, we will have signs."

The desire and drive to create signs is deeply rooted in our fundamental human need for communication. The truth is "we cannot be truly human apart from communication ... to impede communication is to reduce people to the status of things." Deaf people, being of a human variety, have refused to be reduced to the status of things and found ways to communicate visually and developed visual languages. That is the essence of their being. All other things are constructed around this, channeled through and by vision.

The roots in visual-gestural languages have pushed the boundary of vision far beyond other human groups known. This paper will draw from various bodies of research and observations to further demonstrate the significance of "vision" to the Deaf world.

THE USE OF EYES IN LANGUAGE AND CULTURE

Before looking at the role that vision and the use of eyes play in the language and culture of deaf people we need to realize two things: (1) there are people who are not deaf but are highly visual in the way they think, behave and express themselves, and (2) unlike the ears, human eyes have communicative functions, which play a role in sending and receiving information. Almost all humans are able to display this duality. The size of pupils sends information on whether one is scared, interested, and so on. Droopy eyes send the signal of drowsiness. However, among signing deaf people, the role vision and the use of eyes expands exponentially. We must bear in mind that when using signed languages signers manifest many different kinesthetic features that are depicted visually: the body, head, hands, arms, facial expressions, and the physical space surrounding the signer and his/her eyes. The focus here will be on the role the eyes and vision have in linguistic and discourse exchanges and ways they are extended to other cultural and literary functions.

Various Eye Behaviors in Language

When signing, the signer's eyes are always moving in saccadic manner—rapid eye movements to and from fixation points—to signal various linguistic information in different layers. The eye movement may occur over a single word to convey specific meaning, appear in sentences to indicate the spatial position of the object, signal constituent boundaries, bring the addressee in and out of a story world, and/or play a role in turn-taking. All saccadic movement happens in one brief exchange.

At the lexical level, the eye gaze may shift to correlate with the manual portion of a sign and convey additional meaning to the word. Sentence 1 shows an example of this co-occurrence with an adjective. In this sentence the signer looks at the addressee, then quickly shifts his gaze to the hands where the shortness of the cute boy is conveyed, and then shifts his gaze back to the addressee.

Sentence 1

> *gaze down*
> BOY CUTE SHORT.

Translation: The boy is short and cute.
(Note: No eye gaze transcription over a sign means the signer is looking at the addressee).

At the syntactic level, the eyes play a critical role in relations to syntactic constituents, such as noun phrases and verb phrases in simple sentences. They have different functions depending on where in the sentence the eyes are being used. In noun phrases, the eyes can have function to convey the location and distance of an entity. Eye gaze frequently accompanies the indexical sign that expresses definite determiners in ASL. The eye gaze to the same location in space where the finger points: the location in space associated with the referent that is being referred back to, as seen in sentence 2.

Sentence 2

> *gaze left*
> IX-left MAN WANT BUY YOUR CAR

Translation: The man (over there) wants to buy your car.

Indefinite reference in American Sign Language (ASL) is associated with a broader region in space than just a single point. So, for example the indefinite determiner, SOMETHING/ONE is articulated by an upward pointing index finger moving in quick circles within a small region in space. The eye gaze that accompanies the indefinite determiner is also more diffused within that region of space. So, sentence 3 illustrates the distinction in that the definiteness/indefiniteness of the noun is reflected in the different types of eye gaze used.

Sentence 3

diffused gaze
SOMEONE MAN WANT BUY YOUR CAR
Translation: A man wants to buy your car.

In the verb phrase, the eyes used in transitive constructions serve as nonmanual markers of syntactic object agreement. In sentence 4, the direction of the eye gaze (to the left) marks the location associated with the object and augments the sentence by functioning as a nonmanual object agreement marker as it spreads across the verb phrase.

Sentence 4

gaze left
JOHN LOVE MARY.
Translation: John loves Mary.

When engaging in discourse, the listener usually fixes and maintains his gaze on the signer's face, particularly the eyes, thus creating a conversational partnership in regulating different discourse functions. As previously mentioned, the signer's eyes are constantly moving in a saccadic manner to convey various linguistic purposes. This eye movement continues throughout the exchange. The signer gazes away from the addressee (– gaze) for various linguistic and discourse-related reasons and gazes back to the addressee (+ gaze) to check on him/her, to keep him/her involved, and/or to give a turn. This "checking mechanism" often happens at points that are identified as constituent boundaries or lines. In a situation where the addressee wants to initiate a turn, he will place his hands in the signer's visual field, wait until the signer is gazing at him (+ gaze), and then start signing. In a heated exchange, the signer can maintain his role by minimizing the number of times he performs + gaze. By doing this he minimizes the chances of being interrupted.

The dynamics of a classroom involves more complex turn-taking strategies where the teacher usually assumes the role of a regulator. In the case of signing classrooms, this equation has been observed: the more fluent the teacher is with visual communication signals, the more fluid classroom discourse will be. These teachers maintain a clear distinction between two forms of gazes: individual gaze (I-gaze) and group gaze (G-gaze). In a classroom, the two different gazes serve different functions, for instance, when the teacher wants to address a particular student he employs the I-gaze at that student, by keeping his eyes transfixed to that student (with allowance for saccadic linguistic markers), and maintains mutual eye contact while engaging in questions and answers. When the teacher wants to talk to the class as a whole his gaze is less transfixed and more diffused as he addresses the whole group. The teacher will also sweep his gaze and head around the group to address all of the students. Handling this distinction between the two types of classroom eye gaze has been problematic for nonfluent signing teachers and has caused misunderstandings between the teacher and student. For example, a teacher used an I-gaze at one particular student when he was actually addressing the whole class. Signing "Please pay attention when I am talking," with the eye gaze at one particular student will likely result in the student responding "I have been paying attention; why are you picking on me?"

While telling a story, a signer typically does not relinquish his/her turn to the audience. Instead the expectation is that the storyteller maintains his/her turn until the story is completed. Thus, the role of eye gaze, while still vital to engaging the listener/audience, takes a somewhat different form. In addition to the constant saccadic shifts that fall within the categories described above (e.g., using eye gaze for lexical and syntactic purposes), the teller uses eye gaze in constructed action/dialogue, to present information from the point of view of a character in the story. This type of eye gaze serves a major function in storytelling. The teller assumes various characters' gazes while signing his/her actions and incorporates reciprocal gazes to clearly represent dialogues between two or more characters in a story. At a more global level, the teller brings the story world up right before the addressees' eyes, and eye gaze serves to modulate between the narrator's perspective, the story world and the more "direct" depiction of events through the eyes of a character. In addition closer scrutiny allows one to see that the teller's rhythmic gaze from the story world to the audience serves as a device for demarcating narrative units in a formulaic sense.

There are eye behaviors, other than gaze directions or saccadic movements, which play additional roles in the language that is worth mentioning here. While accompanying various spatial-related signs the aperture of the eyelids can also convey a sense of nearness or farness. When the eyelids widens in association with a lexical item it conveys closeness, whereas the squinting of the eyelids convey distance. Another behavior includes the way the closure of the eyes with a word conveys an emphasis; this has been identified as emphatic eye closure.

Another type eye behavior involves eye blinks in sentences. If one looks at the site where eye blinks occur with regularity one will find signers blink their eyes in constituent boundaries that are between the noun phrases and verb phrases and at the end of sentences as shown in sentence 5.

Sentence 5

	Blink		Blink	
LAST NIGHT JOHN		VISIT MARY		.

Translation: Last night John visited Mary.

The proposition that the role of eyes used for signaling communicative function among signing deaf people is expanded exponentially is thus confirmed. The essence of what may appear as simple eye-gazing behavior is in fact part of a complex multilayered linguistic system in ASL. That is, the signer's eyes are always moving in a saccadic manner to signal various linguistic information in different layers from a single word to interactions with a large group.

VISUAL LANGUAGE AND THE BRAIN

Oliver Sacks, a renowned neurologist and author, was astounded at the complexity and multi-layered role that eyes play in conjunction with sign production. He commented, "One can have a dozen, or a dozen and a half, grammatical modifications, done simultaneously, one on top of the other, and when this came home to me, the neurologist in me was aroused. I thought: "that's impossible. How the hell can the brain analyze eighteen simultaneous visual patterns?" I was filled with a sort of neurological awe. The answer to this, briefly, is that the normal brain can't make such visual analysis, but it can learn to do so."

There are a number of neurological studies examining the interactive function of signed language, vision and the brain that support Sacks' observation. In this essay the focus is on three research areas that portray this learned visual way of being: (1) peripheral vision, (2) spatial processing tasks, and (3) rapidly presented visual information tasks.

Since the 1980s several studies have looked at peripheral vision and deaf people through electroencephalograms (EEGs) and functional magnetic resonance imaging (fMRI) tests. The results have consistently shown that signers have superior attention to the peripheral visual space. This scientific proof gave legitimacy to what has been known in the Deaf community for a long time. The story in the beginning of this essay showed how the man in the brown overcoat was able to use his peripheral vision to "navigate" his way in the world of sound. This attention to the periphery develops at a very early age in children. One personal observation concerns my daughter when she was three and a half. She was engaged in a conversation with an adult seated across from her at the dining room table. I was seated to her right (in her periphery). They were going over the names of her classmates in preschool. I supplied a name sign hoping to clarify and help out the adult. My daughter quickly looked away from the adult and corrected the way I produced that particular classmate's name. I was astonished that at age three and a half, she was able to recognize the name sign error I made out of her peripheral line of vision. Her facility using peripheral vision is further evidence in support of the claim that signers have superior attention in this area.

Several spatial processing tasks were also done comparing native signers of ASL with non-signers. The tasks required subjects to recall, compare and identify various mental and visual images. They include being able to quickly identify, generate and transform mental and mirror images. Tests include spatial cognition tasks in nonverbal IQ tests such as block designs, a subtest of the Wechsler Intelligence Scale for Children, and recognition and matching an array of six faces oriented and shadowed differently with the target face. These spatial processing tasks show that native signers of ASL performed better than nonsigners.

Another task focused on the ability of deaf people to recognize rapidly presented visual information. Researchers created a videotaped test of invented Chinese characters written in the air with tiny light bulbs attached to a hand. The videotape was shown to a group of deaf and hearing Chinese first graders. The tasks required students to maintain in memory the path traced rapidly, analysis into component strokes, and finally reproduce on paper. The Deaf signing first graders significantly outperformed their hearing counterparts.

The perception tasks discussed above do not require knowledge or use of signed languages. However, comparative results show that the native signers had a consistent advantage when performing the tasks. These studies reinforce the notion that signing deaf people make better use of vision.

In Culture and Literature

The visual way of being in the world discussed thus far is carried over into the cultural lives, values, consciousness, social spaces, and literatures of signers. Recall the story in the beginning of this essay, where the father and daughter were able to identify the man in the brown overcoat as deaf out of thousands of people on the bustling city street. They noticed the subtleties that only members of this culture (those who share the visual experience) can see. The first visual cue was the way the man in the brown overcoat was orienting himself in the streets of New York City by executing saccadic eye and head movements. The father and daughter knew from observing the synchrony of these movements that there was something uniquely familiar about this man; something that is visable only to deaf people. This man had what is known in the community as "deaf eyes." The daughter's guess that the man in the brown overcoat was "the" deaf man was confirmed by observing how he read the world.

VISUAL-CULTURAL ADAPTATIONS

There are different sets of learned behaviors and adaptive systems that are passed on with respect to "reading the world." One learns to engage in observing, looking, and eventually seeing that sound has ways of bouncing off visual cues. I remember my father's advice as I was growing up. He would sign, "Observe others around you; if you notice them looking in one direction, something is happening over there. This is not limited to people walking, but also driving. If cars in front of you slow down or stop at an intersection when the light is green, do not attempt to pass without checking around you because this is a telltale sign of an oncoming ambulance or police in the intersection." My father also noted that pets and/or other animals are able to broadcast auditory cues. My wife and I are able to "hear" our kids coming down the stairs or playing upstairs when they are supposed to be in bed by noticing our pets (cats and dog) perk up from their sleep and glance at the space behind us. When I walk my dog in the woods I often "hear" things by noticing her glances in particular directions. Another "visual rule" my father hammered into me as a child was the necessity of looking back every time you leave a room or place. "You never know if someone may need your attention, so it is a courtesy to look behind you to check with others before you leave." I also learned the significance of periphery as an integral part of reading the world. The man in the overcoat used it to respond to the father through the café window just as my three and a half–year-old daughter used it to correct me when I incorrectly produced her friend's name sign.

When we look at social spaces we see that the proxemics or social distance between interlocutors is at a distance that is comfortable for the eyes. When more than two people are involved, the spacing arrangement between signers becomes triangular. When additional signers join the conversation the circle becomes larger, and always maintains visual sight lines of one another. At conferences or sporting events it is common to see many circles forming throughout the lobby and people maintaining appropriate visual proxemics.

When participating and/or joining a circle, signers need to be in synchrony with each other's body rhythms. Listeners need to be in sync with the signer's pace of signs, body and saccadic movements in order to take a turn. To join a conversation already underway, the newcomer needs to be in sync with the established interlocutors. When deftly done it appears as if the person was part of the initial conversation.

There appears to be symbiosis between native members of the signing community. Whenever native signers go to a location for the first time, whether it is a national or international site, they meet new people and hang out with new friends. Invariably these new friends are also native signers. It is remarkable that without actively seeking them out they naturally connect with other native signers. There is clearly a rapport, a synchronicity, and a subjective way of being that binds them. Having grown up in visual environments they learn to use the eyes and body for various functions related to language, discourse, and culture. When they meet someone else who has acquired and emits this ways of being, synchronicity happens and a connection results.

Another related area is how signers naturally create or modify their habitat as exemplified by the phrase "this is a deaf house." This comment indicates that the particular house has earned the "seal of approval" for the way it is structured for vision. The floor plan of a "deaf house" is usually open, has fewer walls and many windows in the common area. Additionally the line of sight to the second floor is not obstructed, and there are visual extensions of auditory signals such as flashing doorbell lights and phone and baby-cry signals. Some homes also have strategically placed lights to maximize vision at night and mirrors to allow for visual access in other parts of the house that are obstructed. The significant features of this type of habitat, a "deaf house," create minimal visual obstructions and enhance visual communication pathways.

Bird of a Different Feather

WRITTEN BY

SAM SUPALLA AND BEN BAHAN JUINE

Once upon a time in a land far away high up in a mountain airy Papa Eagle was sitting comfortably reading the sports page. As his scanned the scores his wife ran into the room.

"Honey" she screamed.

"What is it? What's wrong?" he said.

"It's happening."

Papa Eagle was thrilled with this news and leaped up out of his chair rushing into the other room.

He and Mama gazed at the four eggs lying there.

"Do you really think it's time?" he asked.

"Oh I know it is" said Mama Eagle.

And sure enough just at that moment the first egg began to rock. As Mama and Papa Eagle looked on a baby eaglet cracked out of the eggshell. It had a curved beak and big blinking eyes.

"Isn't it adorable?" she said as she and Papa hugged each other.

Then suddenly the second egg began to rock back and forth just as the first one had. Out popped another eaglet also with a curved beak and big squinting eyes. Then out of the third egg popped another eaglet with its perfectly curved beak. They turned expectantly to the fourth egg but it just lay there motionless.

Just when Papa and Mama thought something was dreadfully wrong the fourth egg began to move. With a sigh of relief they watched what happened next. The egg cracked and out popped an eaglet but their excitement quickly turned into shock as they could see that this eaglet had a straight beak. The fourth hatchling stood there blinking as Papa and Mama looked at each other stunned.

"Something is wrong" they cried and immediately summoned the doctor.

The doctor, a very imposing eagle with his bag under his wing flew over to Papa and Mama Eagle's next. After giving the first three eaglets a clean bill of health he turned to the fourth.

"This is the one" they told him.

"Let me take a look."

With a stethoscope he examined the eaglet's straight beak. At long last the doctor was ready to give his diagnosis. Mama and Papa Eagle anxiously waited.

"I'm afraid I must inform you that this eaglet has a birth defect. He has a straight beak."

"No" cried the parents. "It can't be true."

"I'm afraid it is."

"But what shall we do?"

"Well I'm afraid the eaglet is too young and too small to undergo treatment now. Bring him to my office in six months' time. I'll do a more thorough evaluation then. Then we can plan a course of treatment."

The doctor waved god bye and flew away.

Mama Eagle was inconsolable. In her grief she turned on her husband.

"It's your fault. Your side of the family has lousy genes."

"My side? Your family has had lousy beaks for generations. What are you talking about?"

Mama and Papa soon calmed down and collected themselves but privately they remained distraught and angry.

"This is a nightmare" they thought.

"But we have to remain positive. At least we have three normal hatchlings. This fourth one isn't but we just have to stay optimistic."

They put their eaglets to bed.

As they lay in bed Mama Eagle picked up the Enquirer. AN article caught her eye.

"Look at this" she said waking her husband.

"What is it?" he said.

"There's a preacher who can perform miraculous changes" she cried.

"Do you think we should bring Straight Beak to him?"

"It might be worth trying but the doctor said that we should wait six months."

"Why wait six months? Let's take him right away."

They decided to go and made all the preparations to take a long train ride to get to the church.

It was a huge edifice with a large steeple and cross. They took their place in the long line of preachers waiting for their moment with the healer. The line was so long it snaked all the way out of the church. The line moved slowly and once they got into the church they could see hundreds of creatures wailing and praying in their seats. Finally they stood before the preacher.

He was a stern looking bald eagle with a glaring white collar. He took one look at Straight Beak and began speaking in a different tongue to God. He concluded his prayer by laying his hands on the straight beak holding it shut. It looked as if he were trying to bend the beak into an eagle-like beak. When he let go the beak was still straight and the entire congregation was caught up in the religious fervor.

The preacher turned to the parents.

"You must have faith" he told them.

He handed them a Bible telling them which scriptures to read in order for Straight Beak to be healed.

The eagles took Straight Beak home and did as the healer said: reading the Bible and praying frequently.

Nothing happened. The beak was still straight.

Exasperated the parents then learned that a Native American medicine man lived nearby. They took Straight Beak to see him. This medicine man was known for his potions. Straight Beak sat under the hot sun by a blazing fire where he observed the medicine man making his potion. He mixed in the tongue of a lizard, the rattle of a snake and the exotic herbs and flowers that he had collected. That mixture sat boiling all day long while Straight Beak sat in the hot sun.

Around the fire the medicine man performed a ritual dance. At midafternoon he gave a cup of the potion to Straight Beak. It was clear from the expression on Straight Beak's face that he liquid was most vile-tasting and repugnant concoction. Everyone looked at him with anticipation expecting a cure to manifest itself, but nothing happened. The beak was still straight.

Not to be defeated the medicine man said to Mama and Papa Eagle

"Bring this potion home and feed it to him three times a day."

They followed his instructions and Straight Beak swallowed the awful tasting stuff every day for six months but to no avail.

They took him back to the doctor who after giving Straight Beak another examination shook his head and declared

"There's only one option left. I recommend surgery."

"Surgery? How much will that cost?"

The doctor quoted them an outrageous sum.

"We can't possibly afford that" they cried.

They got a second opinion from a different doctor only to be told the same thing. Surgery was required and it would be just as expensive. They went to every doctor they could find and were told the same thing each time.

Exasperated they decided to try one more doctor: an Era nose and throat specialist or ENT. He hooked Straight Beak up to some elaborate equipment and inserted a glass tube in his mouth. Wires connected his beak to a huge machine. The doctor fiddled with the knobs on the machine and its meters bounced back and forth.

Each side of his beak was stimulated. Straight Beak raised either his left or right wing. Finally the tests were completed.

The ENT said "I'm afraid he's 100% straight beaked. The only alternative is surgery."

"But it's too expensive. We simply can't afford it."

"Now, there is one alternative" the doctor replied. "There's a special school for the beak impaired. The school's mission is to train a defective bird like Straight Beak and turn him into an eagle. Upon graduation he will be able to take his rightful place as a contributing member of eagle society."

Mama and Papa Eagle were thrilled at this option. The doctor gave them all the information about the school. Mama Eagle immediately made plans to take Straight Beak to the new school.

It was a long journey and when they got there they were escorted to the principal's office. The principal was a stern-looking bald eagle. His desk was large and spotless. Mama Eagle and Straight Beak sat across from her. They gaped at the credentials displayed on her wall: a PhD in beakology and an honorary award from the AG Beak Association. Mama Eagle was very impressed.

What is your school's philosophy?" she asked.

"We believe these birds with beak disorders can live in the eagle world. They need to be trained to think like eagles. With intensive practice they will internalize the training and become integrated into eagle society."

Mama Eagle liked what she heard and decided to enroll Straight Beak at the school.

They were escorted to a classroom where a teacher was beginning her lesson. The class was full of oddly assorted birds of all different colors. Straight Beak was asked to take a seat. After getting the student's attention the teacher led them in rubbing their beaks in a downward motion helping Straight Beak who wasn't quite getting it.

Mama Eagle standing in the corner observing asked the principal "What is this technique for?"

"You see while they are still young their break tissue is flexible enough that we can bend its shape with proper exercise. We can't miss out on this critical period to alter the shape. With enough exercise the straight beak will become curved as they grow older."

"That makes so much sense" said Mama Eagle.

She was very impressed with the lesson and quietly left the classroom while the young students continued their beak rubbing. Straight Beak was so engrossed in the lesson that it took him a while to realize that Mama had left. He soon realized that he was to live at the school continuing his beak rubbing and learning the wing extension.

The principle behind wing extension was the same as that of beak rubbing. At this young age the youngsters were flexible enough that their tissues could be reshaped from defective to normal. Someday they would soar like eagles with outstretched wings and perfectly curved beaks.

Straight Beak took to his studies and was a model student. When he was ready he entered high school. His teacher passed out a form for all the students to complete.

"I want you to write down your goals. What sort of employment would you like when you grow up?" she asked.

As the students finished their work they handed their papers in to the teacher. As she began reading each paper in turn she got more and more furious. Her dismay with their answers became more than she could possible stand.

Boiling mad she leapt up and cried "You all put down such menial jobs." She turned to one student. "You want to be a musician? You are an eagle. Don't you understand? We eagles never sing. We're too good for that. Singing is for the lower classes. That is not you."

"And you" she said turning to the next student. "You want to collect berries. Berries? That career is forbidden. Your goal must be to hunt. You are all eagles. Do you understand me? You are not birds."

"I am an eagle" each bird said.

"Then go practice now. Report immediately to the vocational department where you will learn to hunt like eagles."

In the vocational department the students applied themselves to learning the job skills necessary to become hunters. Their teacher had a comprehensive step-by-step curriculum. The first lesson was the head tilt. "Watch me. Notice how my neck turns and the direction of my eye gaze. Now you try it." The line of students attempted to copy the teacher. "No no your heads must be turned even more" the teacher growled.

The students practiced this posture using marks on the floor as a guide to help them achieve the correct eye gaze. Once they mastered the head tilt they moved on to the next lesson: advanced flying skills which involved unfurling the wings and flying in an upward spiral.

The teacher was very disappointed at their first attempts. Their wings flailed around unsteadily and they couldn't gain much altitude. One by one the students practiced until they filled the sky in an upward spiral. Over time the students mastered this step as well and the teacher was pleased.

Next was the dive for prey. This involved adopting the head position practiced in the first lesson and then aerodynamically pressing their wings against their bodies to reach maximum speed while diving for a target. Again the students were quite clumsy at first but with practice they managed to master this lesson. Now they were ready for the next lesson: capturing the prey.

After diving, they were to spread their wings wide and open their talons forward grabbing their prey by the shoulders. Then they were to fly away with the prey in their clutches. Using toy rabbits for practice the students attempted this maneuver but their rabbits were too heavy for the students and try as they might to use proper technique they ended up just slinging the rabbits over their shoulders and walking away instead of grabbing them by the shoulders and flying.

The teacher was frustrated but nonetheless encouraged them saying "You're all doing very well."

Each student got a gold star on his forehead.

And then the day came when the teacher announced "You are all now ready to graduate."

All the families attended the ceremony weeping with pride at the line of straight beaked students filing in. One by one the students received their diplomas moving their tassels from one side of their caps to the other as they did so. It was a wonderful and joyous occasion. What everyone did not acknowledge though is that these students were still straight beaked.

Nevertheless they carried on with the festivities greeting the students after the ceremony with warm embraces and lots of picture taking. Then all the students went home with their families.

At home Straight Beak's father unrolled the diploma to read it. "Specialty: Hunter" it declared.

"There it is. It must be true" thought Papa Eagle. Tomorrow morning you shall go hunting with us" he said to Straight Beak.

Straight Beak was so excited he woke up at 4 AM the next day. His family was pleased to see him up and ready. His three brothers, each of whom had turned into tall strapping eagles with perfect beaks, joined the hunting party.

"Let's go" they said and they began to fly away.

Straight Beak was the first to notice a target. In keeping with eagle tradition the first hunter to spot a target was allowed the first shot at it. Straight Beak assumed the head tilt position, just as he had learned, and noticed that the first target was a rabbit. Straight Beak began his downward spiral toward the rabbit. His father and brothers were very impressed with his technique.

Then Straight Beak broke into his dive. The rabbit was oblivious, munching on a carrot, as Straight Beak descended on him. At the last minute Straight Beak spread open his wings, righting himself, and clamped down on the rabbit's shoulders. The rabbit suddenly realized that something was on his back and he turned around to see Straight Beak flapping away, struggling in vain to lift him.

"Excuse me, I need food. Would you like to come with me?"

"Get out of here" cried the rabbit.

"Oh please, please?" pleaded Straight Beak.

The rabbit reluctantly handed his carrot to Straight Beak and then took off running. Straight Beak flew back with the carrot.

Straight Beak presented the carrot to his father. At that moment Papa Eagle came to the sad realization that his son could not live independently. He ordered the family to return home and called a family meeting.

Papa Eagle told Mama Eagle what happened during the hunt.

"He's not independent. He can't even catch a rabbit. A rabbit's weight is too much for him. Do you know what this means? Who will care for him the rest of his life?"

Mama Eagle sadly resigned herself to this. "Who will feed him? Who will take care of him? The two of us are getting too old. Then what will he do? He'll die" she cried.

"My point exactly" said Papa Eagle.

They summoned Straight Beak's brothers into the room.

"Do you three swear that if something happens to your father and me that you will take responsibility for your brother for the rest of his life?"

The brothers all nodded in solemn agreement. And this is how Straight Beak's family decided his fate as he unwittingly sat in the other room watching television.

Then one day Papa Eagle arrived home with an announcement.

"We're moving. I have found us a new home on a mountain far away from here. It's a fine home with lots of animals and plenty of food" he said.

The family packed all their belongings into the large moving van that would meet them at their new home.

With Papa Eagle in the lead the rest of the family set off in formation for the long trip. Straight Beak was struggling to keep up with the others. For every two of their majestic wing strokes Straight Beak had to flap his little wings ten times. He was getting further and further behind. He was so exhausted that he didn't even have the energy to get his family's attention.

"I'm so tired" he gasped. "I have to rest" he thought. "What am I going to do?"

He realized at that moment he was flying directly above the Forbidden Valley, the very place his family and teachers at school had repeatedly warned him about.

"I know I'm not supposed to go there but I have to rest" he thought.

As the rest of the family kept flying toward their new home Straight Beak descended into the Forbidden Valley.

Exhausted, he landed on a tree branch gasping for breath. He noticed a strange sound and realized it was coming from the other side of the very tree he was sitting on. There sat a bird singing in full voice.

"Singing? How disgusting. He's nothing but a low-life bird" he thought.

The bird stopped his singing and looked at Straight Beak.

"What are you looking at?" he asked.

"That was disgusting" replied Straight Beak.

"Well, whatever do you mean?" asked the bird.

"You're nothing but a low-life bird."

"What are you calling me? Where did you learn to talk like that?"

"I learned all about your kind at school. You're just a bird, right?"

"Well, I'm a bird all right, but so are you."

"Excuse me? I am an eagle."

Laughing, the bird says "You, an eagle? No, you're not. You are a bird."

"I am not. I'm an eagle" Straight Beak said angrily flying over to sit next to the bird.

"You can sing too. Did you know that?"

"I certainly cannot. I am an eagle and we do not sing."

"Oh, sure you can. Just watch me." The bird sang a simple note.

"Come on, just try it."

"Oh all right" said Straight Beak and he let out a few tentative notes.

To his surprise he liked it. Then he launched into a long complicated song full of melody and richness. The other bird looked on astonished. Straight Beak suddenly realized what had been locked inside him for all these years. It was all coming out at once. He thanked the bird profusely for helping him and continued singing and singing.

"You're doing great" said the bird.

"I'd like to repay you. I'll hunt down some food for you" said Straight Beak.

"Sure, I'd be happy to accept your gift" replied the bird.

Straight Beak torqued his head intro the head tilt position.

"What in the world?"

"Just watch." He assumed the head tilt position again and spied a squirrel. I'll be right back."

Then he spiraled down to the squirrel grabbing it by the tail. The squirrel easily plucked Straight Beak's claws off its tail.

'What do you want?"

"You for dinner."

"Get out of here" and he kicked Straight Beak away.

"Oh, he got away. I'll look for another one."

The other bird stared at him, "You actually eat squirrels?"

"Sure, don't you?"

"No, I eat berries."

"Berries? But that is so low class."

"Whoever told you that?"

"Never mind. Are they tasty?"

"Sure. Look over there at that berry bush. See those few right on top? Follow me."

They both flew over to the berry bush.

"Now, do what I do" said the bird. He began to pluck the berries off the bush with his beak. Straight Beak copied him plucking a few berries off a branch. To his surprise they went down easy.

"Why, these are delicious" he cried and he began to devour all the berries he could see.

"Slow down there" cried the bird.

But Straight Beak kept on eating berries. He was completely taken by the bird world. He met many different birds and joined them in songs and at meals. He enjoyed being in their company.

He stayed with the birds for a long time until one day someone spotted an eagle in one of the trees.

"Hide, hide" cried one of the birds.

They all scrambled to find a hiding place but Straight Beak just looked up at the eagle and realized it was his mother. Mama Eagle circled in the air coming to rest on the tree.

"Where have you been?"

"I got tired trying to keep up with you all. I fell behind."

"Do you know how long we've been looking for you? We were so worried." And with that she grabbed Straight Beak and flew away.

When they got home he was locked in his room. Meanwhile the family was around the dinner table for their meal. While papa Eagle was eating, however, he was distracted by something.

"What is that noise?"

It was coming from Straight Beak's room. He crept over and opened the door. There was Straight Beak lying on his bed in a trance-like state, singing.

"What are you doing?" shouted his father.

Straight Beak was startled out of his revelry.

"Don't you ever, ever sing. You're an eagle. Do you hear me? An eagle!"

"Yes sir."

"You are an eagle. If I ever hear you sing again you'll live to regret it."

"Yes sir."

His father left, slamming the door behind him.

Straight Beak sat in his room quietly while the family continued their meal.

Over the next few days all he could think about was the friends that he'd made in the Forbidden Valley and the wonderful singing they'd shared.

As time passed, these thoughts began to fade away and Straight Beak found himself assimilating back into the eagle world.

So things were until one day Mama and Papa Eagle arrived with some news. They eagerly called their children together.

We have some great news" they said. It's about Straight Beak.

"What is it?" asked Straight Beak.

"We found a doctor who can perform an operation to make you an eagle" they declared with delight.

"You'll be normal at last."

"Me, normal?" he cried incredulously.

"Yes" they cried.

The whole family jumped for joy. "This is wonderful" they said. "We are so happy for you" and they urged Straight Beak to agree to the procedure.

Straight Beak mulled it over. "Will I truly be normal after the surgery?"

"Of course."

Straight Beak began warming up to the idea. With his family behind him, he said "yes."

When the big day came the hospital was prepped for Straight Beak's surgery. He was put on a gurney and wheeled through the corridors of the hospital. In the operating room a bright light was positioned over his head and he was put under anesthesia. IN no rime he was out cold.

When he woke up he found that his beak was wrapped in bandages. His family was at his bedside. Mama Eagle had tears in her eyes.

"I'm so thrilled" she cried.

Straight Beak looked at her lovingly. The doctor entered the room and removed the bandages. When they were all off, Straight Beak immediately turned to his mother. She was overjoyed.

Then He looked at himself in a mirror. His beak was now curved like a typical eagle beak.

"Now you are normal" mother cried. "You are truly an eagle now."

Straight Beak was filled with pride and confidence. I'm now an eagle" Straight Beak marveled.

The family hosted a huge party to celebrate. Everyone was complimentary and overjoyed at his transformation. Everyone, that is, except the young eagles. They could see that there was something not quite right about Straight Beak's new look.

"He looks like a parrot" the laughed cruelly.

Straight Beak was mortified. "I look like a parrot? Mother, do I really look like a parrot?"

"Oh, they're just children. They don't know what they're talking about."

Straight Beak was confused and suddenly unsure of what he was.

Just then, it was time for the feast. They brought in a huge roast pig on a spit with an apple in its mouth. Straight Beak felt nauseous at the sight of it. Since he had been introduced to berries in the Forbidden Valley he no longer could stomach meat.

"I'm too full to eat now" he said.

"I understand. After all you just had surgery. You need your rest. Run along now."

While Straight Beak rested the feast continued well into the night. The next morning Straight Beak, whose beak was no longer straight, woke up missing his old friends in the Forbidden Valley. Then it dawned on him. He could go visit them.

"Mama, I'm going out for a while. I'll just be flying around the neighborhood. See you later, okay?" he asked.

"Be sure you're back here in time for dinner" she said. He then took off.

Straight Beak headed back to the Forbidden Valley. Spotting a group of birds singing in a tree he flew over to join them. When they saw him they abruptly stopped their singing. "What happened to your beak?" they asked.

Straight Beak was suddenly embarrassed. He didn't want to flaunt his new status as a normal eagle but how could he explain his change of appearance to them? He got an idea.

"Oh I was so clumsy. I was flying around one day and didn't notice that a window was closed. I flew right in to it and bent my beak."

"Oh that sounds painful you poor thing" they sympathized.

Mind if I sing along with you?"

"Oh sure" they said.

The birds were arranged in two rows facing a conductor who raised his baton and cued them to start singing. As the song went along the leader noticed that something was not quite right.

"Stop" he said. "Let's try that again."

Again he detected an awful noise. One by one he had each bird sing a short segment to determine where the distraction was coming from. Then one by one each bird sang its part perfectly until it was Straight Beak's turn.

"It's you" said the conductor. "You have to leave."

"But I want to sing."

"I can't have you ruining our music. When you sing air is supposed to go straight out not down out of your crooked beak. You just don't fit in" explained the conductor.

Straight Beak move doff to the sidelines forlornly watching the other birds sing.

"I want to sing so badly" thought Straight Beak. He began to hum the melody to himself. All day long he sat there humming while the rest of the group sang.

Eventually it was time to eat. All the birds flew together to look for berries. Straight Beak excitedly joined them in the search. Each bird claimed his own branch and began to feast on the luscious ripe red berries.

But Straight Beak's new curved eagle beak was the wrong shape. He couldn't hold on to the berries. Every time he grabbed one it would fall out and roll away. He tried tilting and twisting his head to grab them from below and still they fell out. He looked over at the other birds happily eating away and here he was struggling to grab just one. A profound sadness overcame him.

"I can't eat berries anymore" he said to himself.

He looked over at the valley birds merrily eating berries singing and having a good time. Then he looked toward the mountain where the eagles circled above. After one last look at the valley he finally looked to a solitary place between those two worlds where the sun was lowering in the evening sky. With grim resolve he extended his wings and took flight to the middle place toward the setting sun.

For a Decent Living

WRITTEN BY

SAM SUPALLA AND BEN BAHAN JUINE

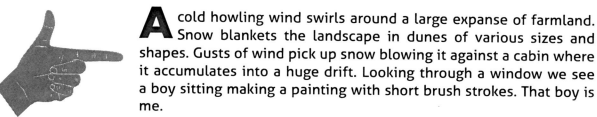 **A** cold howling wind swirls around a large expanse of farmland. Snow blankets the landscape in dunes of various sizes and shapes. Gusts of wind pick up snow blowing it against a cabin where it accumulates into a huge drift. Looking through a window we see a boy sitting making a painting with short brush strokes. That boy is me.

In through the door bursts my father, the booze sloshing around in the bottle he is holding, his breath reeking of alcohol. He staggers over to me mumbling something and gesturing toward the window. I see my father turn toward my mother arguing. Unhappily I put my paintbrush and painting away and walk over to the coat rack one by one finding the clothes I need to bundle up: my parka, my scarf, my hat.

The hair that is exposed from under my hat is now flying in the wind as I walk out of the cabin. A sudden gust of wind nearly topples me. Step by step I approach the barn and I have to grope along the outside wall to find the door handle.

Snow swirls then settles as I close the barn door behind me. The floor in the barn is creaky and uneven and tilts with each step I take. I grab a lantern form a hook on the wall and lifting the glass cylinder I ignite the lamp. Light streams out from the lamp illuminating everything in the vicinity.

I replace the cylinder and see what the lantern reveals. I am standing in sheep shit a foot deep. Now searching for the shovel I aim the light at each wall of the barn. One wall I notice a broken window covered over with one of my paintings that "he" nailed there.

Throwing the light on another wall I see another one of my paintings has been used as a patch.

"Father!" In a burst of anger I run out of the barn through the bleak landscape and toward the city.

The city's buildings loom large in my sight. I see crowds of people milling about on the sidewalks. Releasing my bags I stand and take in the scene. I approach a store window and gaze at the two mannequins clad in shiny jewelry. I approach the next window and the next wandering around town the entire day.

While standing around at the end of the day a hand holding a card comes into my view. I look at the person who's presented the card to me then take the card and read it: the manual alphabet.

Turning it over I read "I have no job. I cannot hear. Please give what you can. God bless you."

I look at the man who gave me the card and say "You're Deaf."

The man grabs the card back from me and runs off into the crowd. I react by running after the man eventually grabbing him by the coattails. The man's body sways back and forth when he's caught.

"Tell me where there are other Deaf people" I ask.

The man quickly blurts out the address in a burst of finger spelling. I reach for m pencil and paper.

"Wait, wait. Repeat that." I look down to write the first part and when I look up again the man is gone.

With the limited information I have I board a trolley car, a wooden box-like vehicle with a metal pole on top that connects with overhead wires. Sprays of sparks intermittently fly out as the trolley makes its way down the street. I bounce back and forth with the movement of the trolley.

When the trolley comes to a stop, the doors swish open and I stick my head out. I step down from the trolley and see the lonely street illuminated by street lights. Stepping into the cone of light un der one of these street lights I compare the street numbers with the address I scribbled down. I have arrived at the Deaf club!

I put the paper with the address back into my pocket and make my way toward the building. In front of me lies a steep set of stairs. After I ascend the stairs I peer through the doorway at the top. I see a long narrow hallway which I walk down slowly. At the end of the hallway there's another door. I try the handle and it opens.

Here is what I see: a "sea" of hands using sign language. Now someone is approaching me, a man with a hump on his back. The hunchback looks me over.

"Are you Deaf" he asks?

"Yes" I reply.

"Where are you from?" asked the hunchback. I tell him.

"I went to the same school. What's your name" cries the hunchback.

I tell him my first and last name.

"I remember you. I was in the class a few years ahead of you" says the hunchback as he lurches forward to embrace me.

I hesitate but return the embrace.

"Well, let me introduce you around" says the hunchback.

He leads me around the room, introducing me to everyone. At each introduction I tell the person my name. Suddenly the hunchback is pushing me toward a table at the end of the room. There is a crowd of people around the table. Seated in the middle of the round table is a large man holding some cards. I look at the hunchback inquisitively.

"That's the president of the club." The hunchback says "I'll introduce you."

"No, don't bother" I start to say. But it's too late.

The president looks up from his hand, folds his card with a snap, and motions for me to sit down. He looks me over. Without a word the other players at the table get up and leave. I look around mystified.

"Come and sit over here" says the president.

"Who me? Sure." I say. I take a seat next to him.

"What brings you here?" asks the president.

"I'm looking for work" I say.

"Oh, sure you are. Well, I'll tell you something. You're lucky" cries the president. "There's a war on son."

I'm startled.

"We're at war with Japan and Germany. All the man have gone off to fight. Our factories are screaming for workers. All Deaf men are finally getting jobs!" explains the president.

"Wow" I say, "what kind of jobs?"

The president gives me a sly smile. He turns to the people standing across the room.

"Someone tap William and tell him to come over here" says the president.

"Someone tap Bob over there too." The two men join us at the table.

I sense that these two men are very important people. The president looks at William.

"Explain to the boy what kind of work you do" he says.

"Well, I'm a printer" says the man.

"A printer" I say.

"Yes and I earn pretty good money." "I'm a member of the union." I look on as the man continues. "I'm a full member."

"I see" I reply.

The president gestures to William to let the other man explain his job.

The other man wipes his chin and says "I work at a saw mill. Lots of Deaf people are working there now. There are plenty of openings."

As the man makes a final gesture I see that the end of his index finger has been cut off. I cringe at the sight.

The president says "Let's talk about other job possibilities. There's the aircraft factor."

"Oh, that's where I'd like to work" I exclaim. "All my life I've been fascinated by aircraft. Is the factory near here?"

"Yes, and it's an enormous facility" says the president, "but Deaf people cannot work there."

"They can't" I asked.

"No Deaf person has ever been hired there" says the president.

I'm crestfallen and continue talking to the other men.

Just then, someone comes walking across the room towards us. I look up and notice that it's the peddler whom I had seen earlier in the day. You remember the peddler, don't you?

At that moment the president stops the conversation he is having with someone else and looks narrowly at the peddler and me. He bangs on the table with his fists, loudly scattering the cards that lay there. I feel the eyes of the president and the other men staring at me accusingly.

"You're a peddler" cries the president.

"On no I'm not" I protest." But it's too late.

"You're lying" interrupts the president. "And all that talk about wanting a job, that was a lie" and he bangs on the table loudly once again.

Everyone in the room notices the commotion and they all start to talk about it. I start to run and bump into the hunchback who whirls me around to face the president.

"Get out" screams the president.

The hunchback and I back away from the table and toward the door. The crowd parts the way for us staring as we leave. The door slams behind us.

The two of us make our way down the stairs. Arriving outside I look back up at the building.

"But I'm not a peddler" I cry to the hunchback.

"I know" says the hunchback.

I continue to plead my innocence.

"Stop now. You can rest at my place. It's nearby. Relax" says the hunchback attempting to silence me. He leads me by the hand down the street.

All night long I have a fitful sleep wondering "What am I going to do with my life?"

By the time morning arrive I have made a decision. I'm going to that aircraft factory and see for myself if there are any openings. I got on the streetcar trolley swaying back and forth as it runs.

The trolley stops to a stop and I get out. In front of me is a large building. I walk toward it and enter. I see a sign near a door and walking toward it I enter the room. A secretary with a large hairdo and reading glasses is seated at a desk typing away. I approach her and attempt to get her attention by waving my hand. The secretary sees my hand out of the corner of her eye and it startles her. Taking off her glasses she begins to speak to me and I don't understand her.

Gesturing toward my ears I take out my pad and pencil from my pocket.

I write down "I want a job" and hand the note to her.

She puts on her glasses, reads the note and looks back at me shaking her head and says something I don't understand. I hand the pencil back to her so she can write down what she's saying.

"We're full" she writes. I look at her and putting away my pencil and pad. I walk out of the office.

The next day I return. Startled the secretary again mumbles something that I can't understand. I return every day until finally one day she hands me a long application form. I stare at all the information there. I look at the top and see that the first line is where I am to write my name. I go ahead and write my first, middle and last name. For the address I write down the hunchback's address. The form then says "sex." Puzzled I write "no." The form then has a long blank space in which I am to write my work experience. I leave it blank and sign it at the bottom and hand the form to the secretary who puts it in a drawer.

I return every day and each time the secretary gestures exasperatedly that there's nothing available until one day she reluctantly gestures for me to wait. She picks up the phone and says something into it. Then a door behind the secretary opens and a man in a white shirt and tie appears. Obviously the boss, I think.

The man looks at me and fingerspells my name. I'm shocked to see that the man knows finger spelling. I use sign language too tell the man my name. The man then takes out of his pocket an ABC card. Shocked I take the card. The man motions for me to follow him.

"I got a job" I'm thinking as I waltz past the secretary who is smirking at me. I close the door behind me.

Entering another doorway I follow the man into an enormous room with aircraft lined up on either side. Seated on the aircraft are men with safety glasses and blowtorches welding the metal on the plane. Sparks fly out in all directions as the men work. Another man operates a drill press machine.

As the man bears down on the lever pieces of metal spin off the center. From each aircraft issues a thunderous noise. The man leads me through this area down to a lower level and across to the corner of a lower room. He gestures that this is where I am to work. It's a cubicle.

The man points out what's on the wall of the cubicle. I look and see that there are rows of nuts on shelves there. The man then puts before me an aircraft part and demonstrates how I am to take the nuts and attach them at the proper places on the part. As each part is finished another part appears and I have to do the same thing again finding the right nuts and attaching them in the right places.

I don't know why I need to do this or what the part is for. It doesn't matter. The man pats me on the back to encourage me. I work away on the assembly line quickly finishing each part as it comes to me. The boss comes over after a while and fingerspells G O O D to me. I work happily away.

After a while I am curious and look into the cubicle next to me. In front of that worker sits a radio blaring away. The worker seems to be moving in time to the music. I then look into the cubicle on the other side. There sit two workers talking and laughing. I feel lonely seeing how the other workers have company and I don't.

The worst part of it is the bell that announces lunchtime. Since I am Deaf I cannot hear the bell. I will be working away and suddenly look up and see that the other workers are gone. Then I look up at the bell and see its ringing. By the time I run to the cafeteria which is down a flight of stairs and at the end of a hallway, I'm the last in line. I stand there panting as the line slowly moves along.

By the time I get served I have to wolf down my food because the bell to return to work starts ringing. The cafeteria is empty when I start to run back to my cubicle to make it in just the nick of time hoping the others won't notice that I am just a little bit late. This happens every day and every day I get indigestion because of it.

One day when I need to go to the bathroom I notice on the way that at the end of the hallway there is a large opening in the floor. I walk up to the edge of it and notice that there's a huge cylinder with gears grinding around in the middle of the opening. As the gears turn a conveyer moves on the upper level. Looking down I can see how on the level below there's an opening to the hallway that leads to the cafeteria.

Just then the bells rings and I can see through the opening the workers going through the different hallways that lead to the cafeteria.

"Great, a short cut!" I think to myself.

I look at the gear turning to make sure I get the timing right and at the right moment I jump through the opening. The gears in the cylinder pass before my eyes as I descend and land on the lower floor.

I can see the line of workers headed toward the cafeteria behind me. I'm the first in line. The server in the food line is shocked to see that I'm first and I have the full lunch period to eat. I don't have to rush.

The plan works so well that I decide to repeat it every day. Now I'm first to finish my lunch instead of the last.

One day when it's time to jump through the opening my timing is off. The grinding gears get hold of my shirt at the shoulder yanking it back and causing all the buttons to pop off the front. My body is being rotated around with the movement of the gears. I cry out alerting the other workers who run to a master switch and turn it off. All the lights go off and the gears come to a halt. Smoke and dust rise up and I am pinned to the side of the cylinder screaming in pain. The doctor's called and a crowd gathers around the site of the accident. Slowly I am pulled out of the hole and lay on the floor.

Someone clears away the people who have come to look and the doctor makes his way through the part in the crowd putting on his headlamp and stethoscope. The doctor listens at different places on my body for a heartbeat. The crowd stares with anticipation. The doctor mumbles something and shakes his head. The crowd reacts in horror backing away.

Then suddenly the boss comes running in breaking through the crowd. He mumbles something then looks at the crowd gathered around.

"Why did this happen?" he screams. "Why?"

They cover my body in a white sheet and send it to the funeral home. I lay on a gurney one of a long line of other gurneys on their way to embalming room.

Suddenly I awake. Blinking my eyes I can see there's a white sheet over my face. I push it off and raise my head. The lights are off but I see the head of a dead person next to me and scream. I sit up and my right leg is throbbing in pain. I manage to jump off the gurney. I realize I am naked and grab a sheet to cover myself. I see a set of doors which small windows and limp over toward them.

Peering through I see a worker preparing a dead body inserting a tube into its mouth to inflate the s kin and applying makeup to the cheeks.

Horrified I throw open the doors. The workers jump back in horror. I want to explain myself to them but I have no pad and pencil. I try to talk but the workers only scream. I run past them out of the funeral home and limp all the way to the hospital. I find an empty gurney and throw myself on top of it my leg sticking up in the air.

Two weeks pass. There is no way for me to contact the boss at the aircraft factory to let him know what has happened. I feel stuck in the hospital. The doctor comes in and tells me that I am being discharged. I am given crutches and handed some forms to sign.

I manage to use the crutches to get on the trolley. At my stop the trolley doors open and I awkwardly get off the trolley with the crutches. I am determined to go back to work. I manage to get through the front door of the factory and down the hall to the secretary's office. She's there typing away as usual.

I run into her office poking my finger at her. She screams when she sees me. I walk my way down the hall until I see some workers standing around talking and the boss is looking through some papers. I wave at them. When they look up and see me they cry out my name and hearing this all the workers come and gather around. I amble over to my boss and he embraces me.

"What happened?" cries my boss.

"I broke my leg" I reply. My boss is so impressed that a Deaf man has such perseverance.

"I want to hire more Deaf employees" he says.

All the workers are shocked to see me again. As I make my way back to my cubicle one of the welders lifts up a mask. It's the president of the Deaf club.

"Hi" I say.

"Hello" says the president respectfully and puts his welding mask back on. I go back to work and work happily ever after.

CREDITS

Gretchen Brown-Waech, "Interaction with Deaf People: A to Z." Copyright © 2014 by Gretchen Brown-Waech. Reprinted with permission.

William Vicars, "Deaf Culture," http://lifeprint.com/asl101/pages-layout/culture1.htm. Copyright © 2006 by William Vicars. Reprinted with permission.

"ASD Archives/History Room," http://www.asd-1817.org/page.cfm?p=10. Copyright © by American School for the Deaf. Reprinted with permission.

"History of Deaf Education in America," http://www.asd-1817.org/page.cfm?p=430. Copyright © by American School for the Deaf. Reprinted with permission.

F. C. Stamps, "Medical and Cultural Views of Deafness," http://tobermorey.com/deaf/views.php. Copyright © by F. C. Stamps. Reprinted with permission.

F. C. Stamps, "ASL & English: ASL/PSE/MCEs," http://tobermorey.com/deaf/asl.php. Copyright © by F. C. Stamps. Reprinted with permission.

F. C. Stamps, "Communication Technologies," http://tobermorey.com/deaf/tty.php. Copyright © by F. C. Stamps. Reprinted with permission.

Annette Leonard, Deb Duren, and John Reiman, Considerations for Mediating with People who are Culturally Deaf. Copyright © 2007 by Consortium for Appropriate Dispute Resolution in Special Education (CADRE). Reprinted with permission.

Michelle Jay, "Deaf Culture: What Is It?" Copyright © 2014 by Michelle Jay. Reprinted with permission.

Barbara A. Dimopoulos, ASL Glossing: American Sign Language 1 & 2. Copyright © 2003 by Barbara A. Dimopoulos. Reprinted with permission.

Michelle Jay, "Notable Deaf Men and Women." Copyright © 2014 by Michelle Jay. Reprinted with permission.

Deborah Chen Pichler, "The Development of Sign Language," Language Development Over the Life Span. Copyright © 2009 by Taylor & Francis Group. Reprinted with permission.

Hearing and Balance, http://www.asha.org/public/hearing/. Copyright © by American Speech-Language-Hearing Association. Reprinted with permission.

Paddy Ladd, "Deafhood: A Concept Stressing Possibilities, Not Deficits," Scandinavian Journal of Public Health, vol. 33, no. 66 (suppl.), pp. 12-17. Copyright © 2005 by SAGE Publications. Reprinted with permission.

Helen R. Thumann and Laurene E. Simms, "Who Decides for Us, Deaf People?" Handbook of Social Justice in Education, ed. William Ayers, Therese Quinn, and David Stovall, pp. 191-208. Copyright © 2009 by Taylor & Francis Group. Reprinted with permission.

Audrei Gesser, "Learning about Hearing People in the Land of the Deaf: An Ethnographic Account," Sign Language Studies, vol. 7, no. 3, pp. 269-283. Copyright © 2007 by Gallaudet University Press. Reprinted with permission. Provided by ProQuest LLC. All rights reserved.

Annelies Küsters and Maartje De Meulder, "Understanding Deafhood: In Search of Its Meanings," American Annals of the Deaf, vol. 157, no. 5, pp. 428-438. Copyright © 2013 by Gallaudet University Press. Reprinted with permission. Provided by ProQuest LLC. All rights reserved.

Harlan Lane, "Construction of Deafness," The Disability Studies Reader, ed. Lennard J. Davis, pp. 153-171. Copyright © 2006 by Taylor & Francis Group. Reprinted with permission.

Jack Gannon, "American Sign Language," Deaf Heritage: A Narrative History of Deaf America, pp. 359-376. Copyright © 2012 by Gallaudet University Press. Reprinted with permission.

Susan Burch, "Deaf Poets' Society: Subverting the Hearing Paradigm," Literature and Medicine, vol. 16, no. 1, pp. 121-134. Copyright © 1997 by Johns Hopkins University Press. Reprinted with permission.

"What is Deaf Art?," http://www.deafart.org/Deaf_Art_/deaf_art_.html. Copyright © by Deafart.org. Reprinted with permission.

Genie Gertz, "Dysconscious Audism: A Theoretical Proposition," Open Your Eyes: Deaf Studies Talking, ed. H-Dirksen L. Bauman, pp. 219-224. Copyright © 2008 by University of Minnesota Press. Reprinted with permission.

Benjamin Bahan, "Upon the Formation of a Visual Variety of the Human Race," Open Your Eyes: Deaf Studies Talking, ed. H-Dirksen L. Bauman, pp. 83-90. Copyright © 2008 by University of Minnesota Press. Reprinted with permission.

Sam Supalla and Ben Bahan, "Bird of a Different Feather Transcript," Bird of a Different Feather and For a Decent Living Teacher Manual. Copyright © 1994 by Dawn Sign Press. Transcription with permission of Dawn Sign Press by Lisa Koch.

Sam Supalla and Ben Bahan, "Bird of a Different Feather Transcript," Bird of a Different Feather and For a Decent Living Teacher Manual. Copyright © 1994 by Dawn Sign Press. Transcription with permission of Dawn Sign Press by Lisa Koch.

CPSIA information can be obtained
at www.ICGtesting.com
Printed in the USA
LVOW09s1943210717
542172LV00001B/1/P

9 781634 876926